WOMEN'S WRITING IN CONTEMP[...]

MANCHESTER
UNIVERSITY PRESS

Edited by GILL RYE and MICHAEL WORTON

Women's writing
in contemporary France

New writers, new literatures in the 1990s

Manchester University Press
Manchester and New York

distributed exclusively in the USA by Palgrave

Published by Manchester University Press
Oxford Road, Manchester M13 9NR, UK
and Room 400, 175 Fifth Avenue, New York, NY 10010, USA
www.manchesteruniversitypress.co.uk

Distributed exclusively in the USA by
Palgrave, 175 Fifth Avenue, New York,
NY 10010, USA

Distributed exclusively in Canada by
UBC Press, University of British Columbia, 2029 West Mall,
Vancouver, BC, Canada v6T 1z2

British Library Cataloguing-in-Publication Data
A catalogue record for this book is available from the British Library

Library of Congress Cataloging-in-Publication Data applied for

ISBN 0 7190 6226 8 *hardback*
ISBN 0 7190 6227 6 *paperback*

First published 2002

10 09 08 07 06 05 04 03 02   10 9 8 7 6 5 4 3 2 1

Typeset in 10.5/13pt Bulmer
by Servis Filmsetting Ltd, Manchester
Printed in Great Britain
by Biddles Ltd, Guildford and King's Lynn

CONTENTS

I   Rewriting the past

II   Writing the dynamics of identity

CONTRIBUTORS

SARAH ALYN STACEY is Lecturer in French at Trinity College, Dublin. Her main research and publishing area is French Renaissance literature. She is author of the forthcoming *Marc-Claude de Buttet: étude historique* (Slatkine) and editor of Marc-Claude de Buttet's *Amalthée (1575)* (Slatkine) and *Heroism in Sport: Ireland and France* (Mellen) both forthcoming in 2003.

MARIE-CLAIRE BARNET is Lecturer in French at the University of Durham. Her research interests are in surrealism, autobiography, visual arts, feminist theory and psychoanalysis. Author of *La Femme cent sexes ou les genres communicants* (Peter Lang, 1998), she has published articles on Derrida, Cixous, Duras and Sarraute, Leiris and Ponge, Desnos, surrealist reviews and book illustrations. She is currrently working on contemporary French fiction and the representation of parents and childhood memory in texts and visual arts.

VICTORIA BEST is Lecturer in French at St John's College, Cambridge. She is a specialist in modern French literature with a particular interest in the links between identity and narrative, and has published widely on Colette, Duras and Julia Kristeva. Her latest publication is *An Introduction to Twentieth-Century French Literature* (Duckworth, 2002).

ELIZABETH FALLAIZE is Professor of French at Oxford University where she also teaches women's studies. Her recent publications include *French Women's Writing: Recent Fiction* (Macmillan, 1993), *Simone de Beauvoir: A Critical Reader* (Routledge, 1998), and, with Colin Davis, *French Fiction in the Mitterrand Years* (Oxford University Press, 2000).

JOHNNIE GRATTON is Professor of French at Trinity College, Dublin. He is the author of *Expressivism: The Vicissitudes of a Theory in the Writing of Proust and Barthes* (Legenda, 2000), and co-editor of *Modern French Short Fiction* (Manchester University Press, 1994), *La Nouvelle hier et aujourd'hui* (L'Harmattan, 1997) and *Subject Matters: Subject and Self in French Literature from Descartes to the Present* (Rodopi, 2000). His articles include studies of Barthes, Breton, Colette, Foucault, Proust, Sarraute and Jean-Loup Trassard.

MARGARET-ANNE HUTTON, Senior Lecturer in the French Department at Nottingham University, is the author of *Countering the Culture: The Novels of Christiane Rochefort* (University of Exeter Press, 1998), *Michel Tournier's Vendredi ou les limbes du Pacifique* (Glasgow University French and German Publications, 1992) and editor of *Text(e)/Image* (Durham Modern Languages Series, 1999). She is currently working on a monograph on French female deportees' testimonial accounts of their deportation to, and incarceration in, Nazi concentration camps, and has edited a volume of *Nottingham French Studies* entitled 'French Fiction in the 1990s' (spring 2002).

SHIRLEY JORDAN is Senior Lecturer in French at Oxford Brookes University. She publishes on Francis Ponge, on French women's writing and on ethnography. Her recent projects have focused on Marie Darrieussecq, Virginie Despentes and Amélie Nothomb and she is currently writing a monograph on six contemporary French women writers.

MARGARET A. MAJUMDAR has taught at the Universities of Westminster and, most recently, as Professor of French and francophone studies at the University of Glamorgan. She has published in the area of French political philosophy (including *Althusser and the End of Leninism?* (Pluto Press, 1995)), Franco-Maghrebian relations and Maghrebian thought and literature, including the work of Leïla Sebbar. She was a founding editor of the *Bulletin of Francophone Africa* and is currently editing *Francophone Studies: The Essential Glossary*.

SIOBHAN MCILVANNEY is Lecturer in French at King's College London. Her teaching and research interests lie in *beur* women's writing and contemporary French women's writing generally. She has recently published a book on Annie Ernaux, entitled *Annie Ernaux: The Return to Origins* (Liverpool University Press, 2001).

KATHRYN ROBSON has recently submitted her doctoral thesis on contemporary French women's writing at St Catharine's College, Cambridge, and is now Lecturer in French at the University of Newcastle. She is co-editor, with Emily Butterworth, of *Shifting Borders: Theory and Identity in French Literature* (Peter Lang, 2001).

GILL RYE is Lecturer in French at the Institute of Romance Studies, University of London. She publishes widely on contemporary French women's writing; co-editor (with Julia Dobson) of a special issue of *Paragraph* on Cixous (2000), she is author of *Reading for Change: Interactions between Text and Identity in Contemporary French Women's Writing (Baroche, Cixous, Constant)* (Peter Lang, 2001).

MARION SADOUX teaches French language at UCL Language Centre. She has published articles on epistolary writing and on Marie Darrieussecq.

AINE SMITH completed a Ph.D. on identity in the works of Annie Ernaux and Marie Redonnet in 2000. She has taught at the Universities of Lancaster, Durham, Lille III and Rennes II.

MICHAEL WORTON is Vice-Provost and Fielden Professor of French Language and Literature at UCL. He has written extensively on modern French literature and on issues in critical theory and gender theory. His publications include *Textuality and Sexuality: Reading Theories and Practices*, co-edited with Judith Still (Manchester University Press, 1993), *Michel Tournier*

(Longman, 1995) and *Typical Men* (Djanogly Art Gallery, 2001; catalogue of the exhibition 'Typical Men: Recent Photography of the Male Body by Men', co-curated with Judith Still; venues: Nottingham, Colchester and Glasgow, 3 March 2001–27 January 2002).

ACKNOWLEDGEMENTS

We would like to thank Nicola Cotton for the background research she did for this volume, for her important contribution to the copy-editing of the essays and for the compilation of the Index.

GILL RYE AND MICHAEL WORTON

Introduction

The 1990s proved to be an exciting period for women's writing in France. It was a decade in which publishers and the media celebrated a 'new generation' of writers, and writing produced by women assumed its place at the forefront of what is new – and sometimes controversial – on the French literary scene. Paperback publishers J'ai lu and Pocket both launched new series (*Nouvelle génération* and *Nouvelles voix* respectively) devoted to new names, among them many new women authors. Thus, a wide-ranging readership was introduced to the work of writers such as Christine Angot, Virginie Despentes, Linda Lê and Lorette Nobécourt at the very same time that these authors were still in the process of establishing their names.[1] On the cusp of a new century and, of course, a new millennium, it is both time and timely to publish this collection of critical essays on writing by women in contemporary France. The writers discussed include a number of important names, such as Angot, Marie Darrieussecq, Régine Detambel and Agnès Desarthe, whose work was first published in the 1990s, as well as providing the first sustained critical evaluations of lesser-known writers like Clotilde Escalle and Louise L. Lambrichs. The volume also includes essays on writers whose work began to gather interest in the preceding decade but who, in the 1990s, were still in the process of becoming firmly established, like Paule Constant, Sylvie Germain, Marie Redonnet and Leïla Sebbar.

In her influential book on 1970s and 1980s French women's writing, one of Elizabeth Fallaize's stated aims is to make the texts she translates in her volume available to anglophone readers and 'recognised as forming part of the pool of texts from which reading-lists are constructed and bookshop shelves filled'.[2] Similarly, part of our own project in this volume is to

introduce to English-speaking readers, through critical readings, some of
the most interesting writing published by women in France in the 1990s.
This volume is none the less more than a celebration or commemoration
of contemporary women's writing. On the one hand, we and our contributors foreground and explore some of the key themes and issues that we
have identified in this particularly dynamic moment for contemporary
French women's writing. On the other hand, we are looking forward into
the twenty-first century, to the next decades, as we chart the ways in which
contemporary women writers are themselves in the process of shaping
wider literary debates. In all these ways and in its specific focus on writing
by women in 1990s metropolitan France, *Women's Writing in
Contemporary France* marks out its difference from existing volumes on
French women's writing.[3]

Historical context

The second half of the twentieth century was a period of substantial change
and experimentation in literary writing in France, notably with regard to
the novel. The publication in 1948 of Sartre's *Qu'est-ce que la littérature?*
marked a major turning point in the development and the willed and perceived stature of the novel, since it led many writers and theorists to re-
evaluate the relationship between literature and society and the part that
could be played by fiction in modifying social attitudes and, ultimately,
even societal structures. The influence of writers of *littérature engagée* or
'committed literature' dominated post-war literary culture, with Jean-Paul
Sartre, Albert Camus and Simone de Beauvoir continuing up to – and
beyond – the death of Sartre in 1980 and of Beauvoir in 1986. Indeed, in
1981, a survey conducted by the literary magazine, *Lire*, demonstrated that
Beauvoir was considered one of the ten most important intellectuals in
France, the other writers being the (traditional) novelists Michel Tournier
and Marguerite Yourcenar and the poet and artist, Henri Michaux.
Furthermore, in many millennium polls conducted in France, the UK and
the USA, Camus's *L'Etranger* (*The Outsider*) (1942) was voted one of the
most important books of the twentieth century. While the political influence of these writers was undeniable, they focused more on content
than on form, seeing their novels as vehicles for messages and politico-
philosophical debates and thereby maintaining patriarchy's structures
through their use of the genre and through their own discourses at the very
time that they were questioning post-war society. Beauvoir is still revered

as the mother of feminism, yet her own espousal of, or sharing in, the Sartrean model of writing has caused some second-wave feminists to accuse her of behaving socio-culturally and of writing like a man.[4]

The most radical experiments in novel-writing were undertaken in the 1950s and 1960s by the writers, grouped together under the label of *le nouveau roman*. The group comprised, essentially, Michel Butor, Jean Ricardou, Alain Robbe-Grillet, Nathalie Sarraute, Claude Simon, with Marguerite Duras and Samuel Beckett as novelists often included in the list of key figures. What characterised all of their work was a rebellion against the traditional 'Balzacian' novel, with its commitment to and dependence on character, plot, and the distinction between form and content. For them, form *was* content, as well as determining it. Consequently, their novels explicitly examine and foreground their own signifying processes, especially the ways in which language can – and must – be used to programme the reader and his or her modes of receiving and processing the text. While their works may today seem outdated and overly self-conscious to some, their experimental audacity undoubtedly continues to exercise an influence on writers and to suggest new ways of engaging simultaneously with the constraints and the possibilities of language and with the function of the reader. In many ways, the *nouveau roman* 'group' was nothing more than a publishing ploy orchestrated by Jérôme Lindon, literary director of Editions de Minuit, and Alain Robbe-Grillet, literary adviser to Minuit and himself both an experimental novelist and a theorist, much as some contemporary women writers are branded and packaged as the 'New Barbarians'. However, the fact that, at one and the same time, several writers were turning their backs on realist literary techniques and assumptions and confronting the need to find new modes of saying and telling has been important in the construction of new ways of writing and reading.

After the seismic events of 1968, the focus of much political, psychological, social and cultural thought became the issue of otherness and difference. Many writers turned their gaze away from the 'failures' of France and Europe towards other cultures which offered alternatives to what they saw as the cultural impasse in which Western Europe was trapped. On the one hand, this involved travelling to the East to explore political and economic alternatives to the American and Soviet models and reconsidering European culture and practices in the light of these discoveries, as with Kristeva's *Des chinoises* (*Of Chinese Women*) (1974), or Roland Barthes's *L'Empire des signes* (*The Empire of Signs*) (1970), in which he presents a highly subjective and partial construct of Japan. This new Orientalism became more and more bound up with questions of individual and collective identity and enabled such recent fictional expressions as Christiane Baroche's *Le Collier* (1992), which, modelling itself on the Arabic traditions of storytelling and calligraphy shows how two cultures are often almost invisibly embedded and implicated in each other and how moral and social codes can never be fixed but must always remain fluid and open to modification.[5] Interestingly, Baroche chose for her Oriental tale not the conventional novel or short story, but, rather, an album with paintings and calligraphies by Frédéric Clément which counterpoint the written text and present different signifying systems to the reader. *Le Collier* is a hybrid text, one in which language is not privileged but presented as only one of a series of possible expressive media. In this way, the work challenges the reader to reconsider his or her presuppositions about language (and about fiction). Experiments with hybridity are increasingly to be found in the work of today's women writers, with particularly interesting examples being Detambel's exploitation of *implicit* iconicity in her play with the Renaissance genre of the *blason anatomique* and Sophie Calle's phototextual works which address the nature of the creating subject and its self-implication in the artwork through what can in some ways be seen as illustrated diaries. Significantly, in much recent women's work of this type, the concern with the other and otherness weaves in and out of a concern with the self as creator, created and yet-to-be created.

When the full extent of China's totalitarian oppression was revealed, some French intellectuals turned their gaze in the opposite direction, towards another place of 'exotic' otherness – the USA, which, despite its rampant capitalism and cultural imperialism, was now read as the site of possible cultural transformation and transcendence because of its 'melting pot' nature and the vast variety of its social, ethnic, cultural and sexual groups. While the global dominance of American English continues to be a major source of anxiety for France and the French, its capacity to assimilate and integrate not only the concepts but also the discourses of seemingly endless stream of groups from 'elsewhere' fascinates cultural theorists. It is worth noting, however, that the interest in the USA is expressed mainly in works by male thinkers, the most celebrated recent example being Jean Baudrillard's *America* (1986). While Beauvoir was, for personal as well as intellectual reasons, seduced by North America and while writers such as Paule Constant embed in their works references to America and terms coming from American English, Americanism/Americanisation has hitherto proved much less attractive to women writers than Orientalism.[6] As globalisation moves on apace and as the new technologies, ineluctably associated with the USA and the Gates–Microsoft empire, enter our lives ever more permanently, not only with their insidious promotion of American English but also, more positively, with the new possibilities they offer in terms of democratisation, identity formation, self-modification and self-replication, it will be interesting to see whether more French women writers turn their attention to the otherness that is (in) the USA.

In the 1970s, feminist literary criticism drew attention to the stark lack of horizons for women writers in France because of the overarching male dominance of the literary canon. Female authors who came to prominence in the 1990s are the first to benefit from a visibly rich female literary heritage. They write in the wake of the explosion in published writing by women that was an outcome both of feminist movements of the 1970s and of feminist archaeological work which has revealed a heterogeneous female literary tradition that had hitherto been lost from view. In the climate of radical feminist activism of 1970s France, women's writing was heavily politicised. Cixous's *écriture féminine*, which, it must be remembered, was a term that she applied to male-authored texts of the past as much as to women's writing of the future, was a political project. It was conceived in the tradition of the avant-garde as writing which would transgress and subvert literary conventions both through and for the expression of feminine difference or otherness.[7] *Ecriture féminine* itself proved to be impossible to pin down; although part of Cixous's point, this fuelled much controversy and even outright rejection as having little to do with the situation of real women.[8] None the less, writing by women more generally in France in the 1970s did gain a high profile, making the personal political, bringing into the public domain – into culture – what had previously been considered personal and private and unworthy of literary concern: women's bodies, women's voices, women's experiences and relationships – all from women's perspectives, as diverse as these have proved to be.

The political (feminist) thrust of 1970s French women's writing – in particular the work of Marie Cardinal, Annie Ernaux, Benoîte Groult, Annie Leclerc and, of course, Cixous herself – fuelled much discussion on the aesthetic categorisation of both 'women's writing' and *écriture féminine*. The debate occupied anglophone feminist critics of French literature for some time, muddied and muddled by arguments about essentialism and the pros and cons of asserting the (potentially unitary) identity 'women' over and above the diversity of individual women and different groups of women. The rather controversial search, which was characteristic of

French 'difference' feminism, for a language and aesthetics of writing to express women's own perspectives must be taken in the context of the intellectual climate of that time. In the 1970s, Lacanian psychoanalysis was highly influential, and its focus on language and the Symbolic precluded the expression of what Lacan deemed was inexpressible, especially, that is, women's sexuality. Predictably perhaps, such an unequivocal decree as Lacan's worked more to provoke, rather than to prevent, women's literary experimentation, and, as Fallaize charts, what was at stake in much 1970s writing by women was precisely women's bodies (Fallaize, pp. 9–14). The essays in this volume on Darrieussecq, Detambel, Escalle and Sebbar show how this theme reverberates in the 1990s even as it has developed in very different ways. The commercial hype and media activity in 2001 surrounding Catherine Millet's *La Vie sexuelle de Catherine M.*, an account of the narrator's voluntary, indeed actively desired, participation in sexual orgies and 'gang-bangs' confirms that, in the new millennium, women who write about their bodies continue to be both provocative and controversial.[9]

From their visible, albeit still marginal, position in relation to the mainstream of French literature in the 1970s, women gradually began to accede to a more central place in the 1980s. Two very different writers, Marguerite Duras and Annie Ernaux, became established as commercial and, to a significant degree, literary successes.[10] A number of female authors won both literary recognition and commercial momentum along with literary prizes and appearances on prime-time television shows, and these cautious successes continued into the 1990s with a growing profile.[11] As Marion Sadoux's essay endorses here, Christine Angot's controversial appearance – or rather performance – on 'Bouillon de culture' in the Autumn of 1999, when she attacked a fellow guest, confirmed her status as *le phénomène Angot* and *l'enfant terrible* of the French literary scene.

Reading and writing subjects

If the events of 1968 contributed enormously to the move towards a focusing on otherness and difference as the defining issues for social and personal understanding and development, they also catalysed the dramatic loss of authority that would lead both to Barthes's seminal essay, 'La mort de l'auteur' (1968), which ends with the proclamation that 'la naissance du lecteur doit se payer de la mort de l'Auteur' ('the birth of the reader must be at the cost of the death of the Author'),[12] and to Michel Foucault's response in his 1969 lecture, 'Qu'est-ce qu'un auteur?' ('What is an author?'), which examined the institutional mechanisms employed by a society to give authority to a discourse and thereby itself to 'author' it.[13] The writer had previously occupied a privileged position as a respected and legitimate commentator, even if he or she was regarded as contestatory or subversive, as with Sartre and Beauvoir. However, after 1968, the writer began to be seen as marginal. The irony of Barthes's theorising having itself an authoritative force cannot be denied in the context of the new women writers who were coming to the fore in the 1970s even as they remained marginal to the mainstream literary canon. While some still lament the demise of the writer's oracular status, many seized on this apparent diminution in their social power in order to experiment not only with form but also with subject matter and to push back the frontiers of what was perceived as political. By exposing – and themselves accepting – the fact that every text necessarily articulates an ideology (of which the writer may or may not be explicitly aware), writers have positioned the reader differently and included him or her in their conception of how their texts operate and signify. In this movement, women theorists have played a crucial role, notably through their questionings of gender positions and identities and through their quests for new modes of writing that will *say* rather than *talk about* what it is to be a woman, a sexual and sexualised being, a friend, a mother, a child, etc.[14]

In 1980, the poet and theorist, Adrienne Rich, famously wrote of the *compulsory* heterosexuality that lies at the heart of the determining structures of modern society, affirming that at the heart of this compulsory heterosexuality, like a Russian doll, lies a firm and unquestioned belief in sexual difference as a system that operates functionally like a binary opposition – and this belief is often tantamount to considering that sexual difference is indeed itself a binary system.[15] More recently, in a key text, *Masculin/Féminin: la pensée de la différence*, the French social anthropologist Françoise Héritier has considered the ways in which sexual difference, as a determining social structure and mechanism, organises human thought by its imposition of a largely binary model. Reminding us that one cannot conceive of the individual in isolation, since s/he exists only in a relational way, in his or her interactions with others, Héritier analyses the social, which, she argues, is to be understood as a construct of individuals united under a set of somewhat arbitrarily established rules, in which social filiation cannot be reduced to pure biology or anatomy as destiny.[16]

Luce Irigaray has convincingly argued that, in ethical terms as much as in political terms, sexual difference is one of the most – if not *the* most –

essential issues to address in the modern world,[17] and this belief, shared by other theorists cited in this volume, underpins much of the thinking articulated by the contributors in their evaluations of individual writers. As we recognise ever more that identity is performative rather than fixed and stable (and, furthermore, that in patriarchy it is usually reactive in its performativity), we rightly become more and more aware of the dangers of essentialist conceptions of what it is to be a woman or a man. However, while it is important to remember that masculinity and femininity are above all culturally specific ideologies and contextually determined practices, it should not be forgotten that the biological body has a more than symbolic role in their formation. Consequently, both individual and collective awareness of the body's physicality and its performance and performativity must be taken into account when seeking to assess femininity or womanness. After all, as Diana Fuss persuasively argues, 'essentialism underwrites theories of constructionism and . . . constructionism operates as a more sophisticated form of essentialism'.[18] The role of the body will be discussed more fully later, but for the moment it is appropriate to highlight recent shifts in our understandings of the subject and the role played in these shifts by the theoretical and creative writings of women.

Julia Kristeva has always had an ambivalent relationship to feminism, and in a 1990 interview on the avant-garde, she argues that, instead of trying to establish 'women's writing' as a homogenous, albeit political, category, women should, rather, value the singularity and diversity that is evident in writing by women, in order to allow for the full expression of individual voices.[19] If, in the 1970s, the experiential was understood as bordering on the essential and fired the search for new forms and new aesthetics of writing, women's writing today has developed into a chorus of diverse, even occasionally discordant, voices. Importantly, women as writers (and artists and filmmakers) are now firmly part of French culture as *subjects* of writing rather than simply as objects of representation (of male desire, fantasy or fear). This is a major achievement, particularly in the intellectual climate of the late twentieth century and early twenty-first century, in which the very notion of the subject has been radically called into question. What characteristics enable woman writers to assert their authorial voice in the shadow of the dominant literary conceit of the 1970s, the Barthesian dissolution of the authority of the writing subject over the interpretation of the texts she or he writes? Furthermore, what is the nature of these new female (and/or feminine) writing subjects in the 1990s as they continue to operate in the tension between the postmodern deconstruction of the subject and a feminist, queer or post-colonial interest in identity politics? On both counts – the postmodern fragmentation of the subject and the demise of authorial power – female/feminine subjects were threatened even as they at last began to come to the fore in French culture.

Kristeva's term, *le sujet en procès* (subject in process and on trial), is rarely used to describe the late twentieth-century subject of women's writing in France, but, in practice, the notion is apposite. Far from privileging a nostalgic pre-Oedipal plenitude, or even a schizophrenic negativity, *le sujet en procès* is a speaking subject which is characterised by its mobility. It allows productively for the disrupting influence of what has been repressed (the semiotic) on the social order (the symbolic) as well as for the slippage of a dynamic subject between what may otherwise be considered opposing terms: for example, between the individual and the collective in concepts of subjectivity and identity; between the autobiographical and the fictional in texts. Indeed, what is most striking about contemporary women's writing is precisely the slippage between these latter two terms, between these two types of writing subject.

The use of the first person in writing by women is extensive, but conventional definitions of genre no longer retain their hold in the 1990s. Third-person narration is, of course, traditionally associated with narrative authority, whereby the writer (or his or her narrator) is vested with omniscience, knowledge and insight. First-person narration, on the other hand, is usually received as being perhaps sincere, but necessarily to be read with a certain scepticism, since it is personal and subjective – autobiographical, and therefore prone to the partiality of memory and the foibles of prejudice. The privileging of 'objectivity' over 'subjectivity' goes back to the Enlightenment's elevation of, and dependence on, reason and rationality. However, in fictional texts, both the first person and the third person are equally artificial. Why then believe one rather than the other? Why choose objectivity – or 'sincere' subjectivity, for that matter – rather than its apparent opposite? As can be seen in many of the works discussed in this volume, the distinction between first-person and third-person narration is dissolved by several writers. Building on the experiments with point of view and narrative voice carried out by Nathalie Sarraute and especially Marguerite Duras, today's writers see fiction not as the vehicle for dissemination of information and ideas or even the locus of the construction of meaning but rather as the site of an exploration both of the self as other and of the self as a discernible and familiar identity.

Indeed, much contemporary women's writing does not sit comfortably with a distinction between autobiography and the novel, even allowing for the fact that all autobiography has its fictional aspects, and fiction, to a greater or lesser degree, emanates from the life or concerns of the author – as, in this volume, Margaret-Anne Hutton analyses the extent to which Sylvie Germain's Christianity is in tension with her literary aesthetics. The misfit does not, however, warrant the creation of a subcategory, 'the autobiographical novel', or even a blurring of the category 'novel' towards a less specific idea of 'fiction', or of 'non-fiction' towards *récit* (narrative); and it is certainly not a question of imposing biographical criticism on creative works of art. Already in the 1970s and 1980s, writers like Cixous and Ernaux (and their publishers) eschewed generic classification on the covers and title pages of their books, the very ambiguity of genre being part of the point. In the 1990s, Christine Angot was one of the writers at the forefront of this trend, in which new relations between autobiography and fiction were actually in the process of being forged. The hybrid term *auto-fiction* is certainly useful here (as Marion Sadoux reasons in her essay on Angot in this volume). However, as recent post-colonial theorising has shown, the hybrid, for all its liberating potential, also risks homogenising anew. The existence of a 'third term' does not necessarily allow for greater flexibility or nuancing than the binary system of identification that fixes meaning – and people – as either 'one' or the 'other(s)'.[20] Rather, in the tradition of earlier avant-garde movements, we are seeing the strategic use of play between previously understood generic categories upon which a more monolithic notion of the literary canon (or 'Literature' with a capital 'L') rests. On the one hand, this play may be (or at least claim to be) a politically subversive move in itself. On the other, however, it points to the inability of old criteria of classification to accommodate the writing of a new generation of writers who need not only to mark out their own stylistic originality but also to introduce 'new objects of thought' into their writing.[21] What is required is that 'autobiography' and 'fiction' are rethought as a literary continuum rather than as separate, albeit themselves hybrid, categories.[22]

This development is not, it has to be said, restricted to writing by women; for example, Angot's interstitial work builds on, even as it marks out its space as difference from, what has gone before. Rejecting the novel as a satisfactory form of writing, even within the very texts which were categorised *roman* (novel), Angot's work has affiliations with that produced by male writers such as Hervé Guibert and Serge Doubrovsky as well as with female precursors from outside the French tradition, like Gertrude Stein.[23] However, in Angot's case, the impetus for the change in writing style, both for the writer within the texts and for the author who writes the texts we read, each of whom is Christine Angot, is motherhood. This is not to say that becoming a mother has changed Angot's own style of writing – although the possibility remains – but rather to say that she renders it so within the text. In her 'novel', *Léonore, toujours*, the narrator/writing subject is forced into ever more mobility as she negotiates the tensions between being a mother, being a woman with a particular psycho-social history, and being a writer.

In pushing at the limits of genre, in working at the very boundaries between reality and text – boundaries she both contests and reaffirms – in exploring (the sometimes unacceptable nature of) fantasy as integral to reality rather than in opposition to it, Angot engages with contemporary literary debate as, by means of her writing, she moves it on. The always uncertain relationship between Angot's first-person narrator (Christine Angot), the real-life woman (Christine Angot) and the Foucauldian author-figure (Christine Angot) presents a challenge to the reader, who is moreover confronted with, and may even be implicated in, statements which may offend and shock, such as: 'Si on me donne le choix entre violée et lesbienne [pour Léonore], je prends le viol' (*Léonore, toujours*, p. 46) (If I had to choose [for Léonore] between being raped and being a lesbian, I'd choose rape); or 'Comme tous les mongoliens, la fille de Maurice Compaing est laide' (*Normalement*, p. 58) (Like all Down's Syndrome children, Maurice Compaing's daughter is ugly). In turn, however, Angot's stage-managed confusion means she does not – and cannot – completely dissociate herself from her textual narrator and thus, as author, does not let herself off the hook. Christine Angot, in whatever way we choose to understand that persona, is implicated – and implicates herself – in her readers' interpretations of her writing. The uncertain status of a narrating 'I', as performative as Angot's, at once announces and undermines the writing subject, producing a slippery *sujet en procès* which provokes and resists at the same time, and setting up a politics of reading which tempts (re-)containment and (re-)appropriation of the writing subject even as it works against it. The writer/narrator Angot's subsequent counter-statements and claims, within her texts, to be misinterpreted are an intrinsic part of what has been seen as a narcissistic monologue, but which, by its provocative nature, is rather an ongoing *dialogue* that she and her texts are enacting with her readers. As Johnnie Gratton suggests in his discussion of Sophie Calle's phototextual projects in this volume, the tension between experiment and experience and the self-implication that is involved is a risky business for contemporary (women) writers and artists.

In *French Fiction in the Mitterand Years*, in the wake of the dominance of the *nouveau roman* in French literature during the 1950s and 1960s, and in the context of debates about the future of 'the novel', Elizabeth Fallaize and Colin Davis identify three 'returns': 'the return to history, the return of the subject and the return of storytelling' (p. 13). In the texts discussed in this volume, the subjects who have 'returned' range from strong subjects to subjects in deep crisis, all asserting their gendered experiences – as mothers, as lovers, as abused daughters, as perpetrators of violence, as *voyeuses*, as writers. Here, the female subject is sometimes traumatised (Angot, Chawaf, Constant, Darrieussecq, Lambrichs), misunderstood (Desarthe), or on a quest for identity (Redonnet), yet elsewhere in this volume, more positive formulations are to be found. In Margaret Majumdar's analysis of Sebbar's work, the female subject subverts the subordinating gaze. In Gill Rye's reading of Baroche's novels, narrative uncertainty is an enabling factor leading to transformative possibilities in the gendered subject. In Michael Worton's discussion of Escalle, the female subject is not so much a victim of sexual violence as an agent of transgression.

In all these works, there is a concern not only to tell stories, but also to tell women's stories, all of which are, in one way or another, variations of Woman's story. And they want to tell, to *say*, rather than to describe or embellish, hence the sparseness of the discourse of writers such as, say, Angot or Escalle. We should remember, also, that narrative structures are inherently conservative and that to change them requires considerable conviction – and creative energy. Narratives enable us to navigate and to order our emotions, to understand and evaluate the work of our senses, and thereby to engage with – and, ultimately, to shape – the world. Narratives also bind us socially to others. Without shared narratives and without a shared grasp of how narrative functions (even if this functioning is not always successful), we are isolated and it becomes impossible to establish any identity: without the other's presence in our actions as much as in our minds, we cannot develop or separate ourselves from the prison-house of solipsism.

While femininity/womanness continues to be a social and political phenomenon, it needs to be increasingly recognised as a personal narrative or representation. Writers share their concerns with their readers in uncertainty and often with hesitation, rather than handing them down from an

Olympian height or from some oracular cave. They turn inward toward themselves, not (only) because that is what they know best but because that is where they can best explore what it is to be in the world, to have a sense of *Dasein*.

Writing the body

In his part-autobiographical study, part-theoretical treatise, *Roland Barthes by Roland Barthes*, the theorist affirms that 'the body is irreducible difference, and it is also at the same time the principle of all structuration'.[24] It is undeniable that each of our bodies is absolutely unique, yet it is equally true that the body is what we have in common with everyone else and also that it is what structures all social relations, being both the site of desire and the outward image of inner changes. Furthermore, and crucially, the body is invisible: it is what we are, yet we cannot ever see it in its totality. The gaze of the other sees us and our bodies 'better' than we can ever see ourselves, and for this reason our relationship with our individual bodies is necessarily not only mediated by but also facilitated by the other who stands outside us yet is borne inside us. Furthermore, the body is simultaneously both the self-centring site of desire, and therefore intensely personal, and also the locus of manifestations of inner changes, and therefore ineluctably public. And, crucially, the individual body must remain invisible to the person who inhabits it and is defined by it: it is what we can never *see* properly, even if we can *feel* it totally. The communication of the feelings aroused by this knowledge is one of the great challenges of contemporary fiction: there is the need to write the body – to bring it into view and into existence – yet the more one focuses on one's own body and personalises the definitions and descriptions of it, the more one potentially risks losing one's reader. However, in the work of today's women writers, the personalising of the body is no privatisation or appropriation or manipulation of power through secrecy and overcoded referentiality. It is a staging of difference, a play of and with representation that entails a repositioning of the question(s) of gender outside the traditional binary oppositions of male–female and heterosexual–homosexual.

The body is the site and the living proof of mortality, as it sags, sickens and ages; it is also the site and the (submissive) medium of social control, as its activities and its very shape are determined by institutional(ised) rules and norms. To write the body is therefore to engage in a political act as much as in a personal one. And to write the body is different from writing about the body or even on the body. It is to say and thereby bring into presence in the imagination of the reader something which is in essence radically other and absent.

We cannot see our bodies totally. However, we should not as a result fall into the trap of hoping to find some impossible, unified body, as can occur during the mirror stage of psychic development discussed by Lacan.[25] None the less, the body is often represented societally and consequently even internally as a protective dwelling place, the locus of whatever certainty we can have, our one true home. This is, of course, a fiction, but it has force, and so any narratives that present the fragmentation or fragility of the body are threatening and induce anxiety.

The dislocation, exploitation and dismemberment of the body operated and represented in much of the recent fiction under consideration here should be seen in the context of the controlling mechanisms of patriarchy which the writers wish to transgress. As women take possession of their bodies and of what may or may not be done with them, they may choose to engage in sexual practices that not only express their liberation from oppressive norms but also challenge social conventions and defy established taboos. This enterprise is, it must be noted, not solely one of sexual exploration or of the quest for (new) pleasure; rather, it is a search for agency and autonomy. In these circumstances, the use of narrative is appropriate, for interdictions, taboos and transgression are, as Georges Bataille, has shown, bound together in a powerful narrative structure: 'Transgression belongs to humanity given shape by the business of work. Transgression itself is organised. Eroticism as a whole is an organised activity, and this is why it changes over the years'.[26] According to Bataille, taboos are fundamentally irrational in absolute human terms, although they are certainly necessary for society to function and control; for this reason, Bataille goes so far as to make the controversial statement: 'The taboo is there in order to be violated' (p. 64). Today's women writers understand the power of the taboo, but they question its validity and challenge its authority. To take one example: Bataille notes the way in which we 'fence off certain areas to be kept free of sexual activity'; these areas 'protected' from eroticism include the doctor's surgery where 'the most intimate kind of nakedness is not obscene' (p. 216). In Escalle's *Où est-il cet amour*, the novelist precisely confronts this taboo, making of the consulting room not only a trysting place for illicit sexual encounters between the gynaecologist and his patients (whom he will later abort) but also the site of necrophiliac desires and enactments. The effect is to shock, but it also engages the reader in (anxious but ultimately healthy) speculation on the role of taboos and the nature of both direct and vicarious transgression.

The focus on women's bodies and women's desires has led to accusations that some of the new writing is little more than pornography. One can see that works such as Millet's *La Vie sexuelle de Catherine M.* lend themselves to being considered pornography passing themselves off as literature in order to gain cultural legitimacy – as well as millions of euros in royalties! However, in the past decade, attitudes towards pornographic writing have changed. In her introduction to *Making Violence Sexy* (which mainly considers male heterosexual pornography), Diana E. H. Russell differentiates between the pornographic and the erotic according to one key moral criterion: respect for the other, whoever or whatever that other may be. For her, pornography is material that combines exposure of the genitals with abuse and degradation, and she insists that it is not the acts depicted or described that are pornographic but the position of the pornographer.[27] In other words, there is nothing inherently immoral or pornographic about engaging in or representing 'perverse' sexual acts as long as respect is maintained. This position seems clear and useful. However, it does pose the question of whether we do really know what 'respect for the other' is.

If women are to exist autonomously in society, they need to explore their own relationship with sexuality, eroticism and even violence. As Linda LeMoncheck puts it: 'Without the ability to create a woman-identified model of the relation between sex and power, feminists have no way of loosening the patriarchal stranglehold on defining sexual power as the power of victimization'.[28] A woman-identified model does not mean that only women can understand or work with it; rather, it is a model which calls into question the ways in which (male-determined) society operates its regulatory and monitoring procedures. The 1990 *Operation Spanner* case is a different but useful example of how society deals with sexual activity that deviates radically from its norms. The police came into possession of videotapes of a group of gay men who engaged in sadomasochistic sex. This involved hitting the penis with a ruler, caning and dripping hot wax on the genitals, all of which are activities not normally associated with gay sex. However, crucially, all were consenting adults. Fifteen of the men were given criminal convictions, five of these being prison sentences. They appealed to the European Court of Human Rights, which, in 1997, upheld the convictions on the grounds that assault cannot be consented to. The implications of this case are grave, for it is evident that the state (in this case, both the individual sovereign state of the UK and the federated state of the

European Union) has usurped and diminished personal rights and, more importantly perhaps, has removed responsibility for one's actions from anyone engaging in 'perverse' activities – which are not actually forbidden by legislation but which contravene the social code of what is permitted. Musing on this case in *A Defence of Masochism*, Anita Phillips concludes that 'this backlash against sexual freedom is the same kind that first brought masochism into disrepute over a century ago. From being an illness, it is now definable as a crime'.[29]

Transgression is therefore not merely a question of contravening moral codes; it risks bringing the perpetrator into conflict with the aptly named forces of law and order. Within this context of increasing state interventionism into private lives (despite legislation such as the Human Rights Act 2000), the act of writing transgressively becomes both more daring and more necessary as there is an ever greater need to fuse the personal and the political, the fictional and the lived, the subject and the object, the victim and the oppressor.

Trauma

A significant number of the chapters in this volume are concerned with pain, loss or death and throw into relief a darker side to women's writing in the 1990s. This trend – and its prevalence allows it to be identified as such – points to a trauma at the heart of the writing subject and indicates that much women's writing is produced in response to the experience of loss or pain. This is not the same loss or lack or absence that has been theorised (in psychoanalysis, in philosophy) as being at the heart of women's identity,[30] though some examples may be particularly connected with women's experiences in a still male-dominated society – vis-à-vis the trauma that, Shoshana Felman argues, women's lives implicitly contain.[31] In particular, as Siobhán McIlvanney's chapter on *beur* writers argues, the texts of first-generation French-born Algerian writers involve the negotiations for identity between French culture and education and Algerian culture and repressive family relationships. As we have seen above, the 1970s saw a search, in writing, to express the inexpressible – a reparative impulse, in which the subject – women as subjects – came into being in and through writing. Over the past decades, the diversity of writing by women shows they have both created the cultural loci and found countless different voices in which to become, precisely, subjects of writing.

Traumatic experience is of course not gender specific but rather part of the human condition. The twentieth century saw the publication of a significant number of 'witnessing' texts, by both men and women, bringing into the literary domain, for example, the accounts of Holocaust survivors and AIDS victims.[32] 'Traumatic experience' can be understood more widely, however, to include the loss – the death – of loved ones, abuse (physical, mental or sexual), terminal illness, exile and experience of collective tragedies: wars, terrorist attacks, major accidents, natural disasters.[33] Indeed, the currency of the term has led Hal Foster to identify a general tendency in contemporary culture 'to redefine experience, individual and historical, in terms of trauma', linked to the theoretical and cultural return of the subject we have discussed above. In trauma discourse, trauma entails a loss of self, but is at the same time an event that guarantees the subject – the traumatised subject – as 'witness, testifier, survivor'.[34]

Trauma is, by definition, what cannot be narrated, but, as Victoria Best shows in her analysis of dreams in Louise L. Lambrichs's work in the opening chapter of this volume, narrative can be identified as fundamental to the process of healing or, at least, to the validation of the traumatic experience. Analysts of life writing, like Suzette Henke in *Shattered Subjects*, value above all the act of writing itself as therapy.[35] Still other theorists point to the importance of the reader. In *Testimony*, Shoshana Felman and Dori Laub address Holocaust witnessing principally, but their sensitive discussion of the problematics of listening to – and reading – testimonial accounts can inform more widely.[36] The point of bearing witness is to communicate the experience or event, and thus the listener has to take responsibility as 'the enabler of the testimony' (p. 58). In the healing process, the listener/reader is likewise crucial to this process as 'an *addressable other* . . . who can hear the anguish of one's memories and thus affirm and recognize their realness' (p. 68).

Felman and Laub do not deny, however, that reading harrowing accounts of traumatic loss is risky – to the reader and to the writer. Not only does the witness, therapeutically, need the listener or reader to enable the testimony and to validate the account, but also the interpretation of the reader is needed, textually, to make the text meaningful. Indeed, if trauma is literally unspeakable – if it cannot be narrated – then the reader must locate it in the gaps, in the ellipses, in the metaphors and images, rather than in the story that is being told. In this volume, Kathryn Robson shows how the figure of the female vampire in Chantal Chawaf's *Vers la lumière* gives voice to the unspeakable loss of the narrator's mother as, elsewhere, she reads the trauma of childhood sexual abuse in the fragmentary aesthetics of

Béatrice de Jurquet's writing.[37] Literary testimonies can challenge the limits of our practices of reading. How should we – and, indeed, can we – ethically negotiate the tension between reading as listening to a testimony and reading as interpretation of a text? It is precisely this challenge that, in Chapter 5, Elizabeth Fallaize's analysis of Jacques Lacan's daughter Sibylle's *Un père: puzzle* makes explicit. Fallaize tackles the power of the intellectual legacy of Lacan-*père* on readings of the daughter's autobiographical text (about her father), and, creatively, suggests alternative theoretical frameworks through which to read it.

One particular framework that lends itself to reading narratives where traumatic experience is evident is psychoanalyst Melanie Klein's work on mourning, employed in Chapter 4 in Gill Rye's reading of Paule Constant's little girl characters. Klein's account, as set out in her essay 'Mourning and its relation to manic-depressive states' (1940), differs from Freud's more well-known 'Mourning and melancholia' in several ways.[38] In particular, Klein conceives of the mourning of lost loved ones throughout life as reworking the psychical processes of early infancy which enable the child to deal with the loss of, or separation from, the primary love object (for Klein, the mother) and to become an independent individual. This involves both destructive and reparative impulses, the conflicts of which are worked through over a period of time, resulting, on the one hand, in the internalisation of a realistic (rather than idealised) lost love object, and on the other, in the rebuilding of the self that has been damaged by the loss. The psychical work involved in reparation renders Kleinian mourning a creative process, and Klein herself indeed valued the creativity of art and literature as an important part of the process of dealing with loss. The number of texts by women that deal directly or indirectly with experiences of loss point to the reparative nature of writing even as they attest to women's survival and creativity in the face of loss of all kinds, from the everyday to the apocalyptic.

Identity

According to Klein's work, negotiations with loss are defining moments of the self, from the perspectives both of originary loss and, in mourning, throughout life. For Klein, the self is psychically determined: the inner and outer worlds interact, but it is the work done in and by the psyche that makes us what we are. Moreover, the ways in which infantile conflicts are dealt with, psychically, determine our relations with others throughout life.

Psychoanalysis continues to be an influential discourse of the self into the twenty-first century, and is the motor for both Victoria Best's perceptive teasing out of the complexities of Lambrichs's *Journal d'Hannah* and Robson's analysis of the image of the vampire in Chawaf's work, as well as Rye's placing of Constant's *Confidence pour confidence* at the heart of this writer's œuvre. Psychoanalysis is not, however, the only way of thinking about our/selves and our identities. Sociologists, such as Liz Stanley, eschew the unconscious and consider that identity is, above all, forged socially in and by relations with others.[39] For her part, Carolyn Steedman looks to the way memories and desires are transmitted across generations in a case study of her own family, in order to supplement the shortcomings of sociological, economic, historical and psychoanalytical accounts in explaining how the individual consciousness of social class becomes an aspect of identity.[40] In this volume, Aine Smith examines the role of memory in relation to writing and the photograph and its place in the constitution of identity in the work of Marie Redonnnet.

The self had become a complex phenomenon in late twentieth-century discourse, and terms like 'the subject', 'the self', and 'identity' are understood differently depending on whether they are being used in psychoanalytical, sociological, political, philosophical or textual contexts or within perspectives such as ethnicity, sexuality or gender. 'Identity' is, on the one hand, a positive political category of perception and locus from which to speak in identity politics. On the other hand, from a more philosophico-literary standpoint, identity is linked with representation, and thus may be considered to be dangerously retrospective – always already at risk of being fixed and frozen into stereotypes.[41] The main problematic of identity relates to the gaps between the two positions of self-perception and the perceptions of others. We have already noted above the mobility of the writing subject in much contemporary literature. If the subject is, here, 'a position of enunciation' and thus structural, identity, according to Margaret Whitford in her discussion of Irigaray's work, is 'imaginary' and 'pours itself into the available structures to form representations'.[42] Representations 'flesh out' the subject, but, in order to avoid rigidity, identity also needs to be thought as dynamic.[43] Chapter 8 shows how Baroche's use of uncertainty avoids the fixing of identities and self–other relations in a none the less realist mode of writing.

The chapters in Part II, 'Writing the dynamics of identity', are most centrally concerned with this issue. Between them, they plot, temporally as well as spatially, the vagaries of identity, the intersections between the individual and the group, the interconnections between self and other, as in Siobhán McIlvanney's discussion of *beur* identity. Nonetheless, identity, in all its heterogeneity, is actually a unifying factor in this book, since all the essays relate to it, in one form or another, from Elizabeth Fallaize's weaving of the photo of Sibylle Lacan on the cover of her book into that author's search for understanding of her paternal legacy to Marie-Claire Barnet's discussion of Régine Detambel's inscription and dissection of the writer in the aesthetics of her writing.

As society changes rapidly, the place of literature in it naturally becomes modified, the role and the function of readers change, and writers assume a different position both within and in relation to social structures. One of the most welcome features of recent years has been the turn towards ethical criticism and a greater understanding of the fact that the stories we tell and hear or read are not merely reflections of the society in which they are produced but are reflections *on* it. More even than this, they play an important role in determining how we respond to experience and what we are, both as individuals and as members of a community. Furthermore, they contribute significantly to the shaping of the values that underpin society and permit the bonding that is essential if that society is to cohere and survive. As Colin McGinn puts it in *Ethics, Evil, and Fiction*:

> Stories can sharpen and clarify moral questions, encouraging a dialectic between the reader's own experience and the trials of the characters he or she is reading about. A tremendous amount of moral thinking and feeling is done when reading novels (or watching plays and films, or reading poetry and short stories). In fact, it is not an exaggeration to say that for most people this is the primary way in which they acquire ethical attitudes, especially in contemporary culture. Our ethical knowledge is aesthetically mediated.[44]

McGinn is right to stress that we feel as well as think when reading fiction – and he is also right to equate them syntactically, since the feeling is of the same order of creative seriousness as the thinking. However, one might go further than McGinn and suggest that our ethical knowledge is not only aesthetically mediated but is actually to a great extent determined by the stories that we read – and by the stories that can be told (and published). In the Introduction to *Love's Knowledge*, Martha Nussbaum argues that literary works are concerned among other things with extreme emotions such as those of grief, pain and loss. These texts are sometimes difficult to read, but they are crucial testaments in the modern world, since they are 'subversive of morality narrowly construed'.[45] As we have suggested above and as several of the chapters in this volume discuss, suffering and pain are real and so must be said and told. Yet the saying is more than narrowly, personally therapeutic: it is reparative, recounting the past survival of women, demonstrating and proclaiming survival and creation in the present of the writing and the reading, and promising future survival to those who have yet to encounter loss and trauma.

As we move decisively into the third millennium, the world is undergoing massive transformations, not only technologically, politically, legally, economically, demographically but also in personal relations and in how we perceive ourselves and others. The essays in this book throw light on these changes, and affirm that contemporary French women's writing functions at once as a reflection of the changing times and as a space for innovation. The women who write are exploring and experimenting with form, genre, aesthetics and representation, as they cross boundaries and as they push at the old limits and freedoms of textuality.

Notes

1 See Emilie Grangeray, 'Nouvelle génération', *Le Monde* (8 October 1999), www.lemonde.fr.

2 Elizabeth Fallaize, *French Women's Writing: Recent Fiction* (Basingstoke: Macmillan, 1993), p. 2.

3 Other volumes can be divided into four main categories: (a) Anthologies: see, for example, Mary Ann Caws *et al.* (eds), *Ecritures de femmes: nouvelles cartographies* (New Haven and London: Yale University Press, 1996), a wide-ranging anthology of texts selected from across the twentieth century and across a broad sweep of French and francophone cultures, arranged thematically with short introductions; Madeleine Cottenet-Hage and Jean-Philippe Imbert (eds), *Parallèles* (Quebec: L'Instant même, 1996), a critical anthology of short stories by women in French; Fallaize's *French Women's Writing: Recent Fiction*, which, together with a substantial and informative introduction, presents introductions to and English translations of selected 1970s and 1980s texts; Martin Sorrell (ed.), *Elles: A Bilingual Anthology of Modern Poetry by Women* (Exeter: University of Exeter Press, 1995), poetry in both French and English with a bio-bibliographical introduction by each author whose work is included; (b) Collections based on conference papers: see, for example, Ginette Adamson and Eunice Myers (eds), *Continental, Latin-American and Francophone Women Writers* (Lanham and New York: University Press of America, 1987 (vols. I and II); 1997 (vols III and IV)), drawn from a series of conferences in the 1980s; Michael Bishop (ed.), *Thirty Voices in the Feminine* (Amsterdam and Atlanta: Rodopi, 1996), a collection of short papers from a 1994 Canadian conference on contemporary French and Canadian women's writing; (c) Collections of critical essays: for example, Margaret Atack and Phil Powrie (eds), *Contemporary French Fiction by Women:*

Feminist Perspectives (Manchester and New York: Manchester University Press, 1990), a volume of essays focusing on narrative and gender identity in a wide range of authors; Alex Hughes and Kate Ince (eds), *French Erotic Fiction: Women's Desiring Writing 1880–1990* (Oxford: Berg, 1996), essays on erotic fiction by women over the last century; Sonya Stephens (ed.), *A History of Women's Writing in France* (Cambridge: Cambridge University Press, 2000), a collection of essays which treat historical periods from the Middle Ages to the late twentieth century, the latter period including separate essays on women's fiction, autobiography, theatre, poetry and feminist literary theory; (d) Monographs: for example, Michele Bacholle, *Un passé contraignant: double bind et transculturation* (Amsterdam and Atlanta: Rodopi, 2000), on Farida Belghoul, Annie Ernaux and Agota Kristof; Colin Davis and Elizabeth Fallaize, *French Fiction in the Mitterand Years: Memory, Narrative, Desire* (Oxford: Oxford University Press, 2000), an analysis linking selected fiction texts by both male and female writers to socio-political and cultural issues; Jeannette Gaudet, *Writing Otherwise: Atlan, Duras, Giraudon, Redonnet, and Wittig* (Amsterdam and Atlanta: Rodopi, 1999), a discussion of one text by each of the named authors; Diana Holmes, *French Women's Writing 1848–1994* (London: Athlone, 1996), a survey of the last 150 years; Warren Motte, *Small Worlds: Minimalism in Contemporary French Literature* (Lincoln: University of Nebraska Press, 1999), which brings together under the theme of minimalism analyses of ten diverse texts, including three by women (Bernheim, Ernaux and Redonnet); Susan Sellers, *Language and Sexual Difference: Feminist Writing in France* (Basingstoke: Macmillan, 1991), selected fiction of the 1970s and 1980s read in tandem with French feminist theory.

In addition, an increasing number of studies are being published dedicated to the rich and culturally diverse body of francophone writing, among them many specialising on female authors. See, for example, Laurence Huughe, *Ecrits sous le voile: romancières algériennes francophones, écriture et identité* (Paris: Publisud, 2001); Yvette Bénayoun-Szmidt and Najib Redouane, *Parcours féminin dans la littérature marocaine d'expression française* (Toronto: La Source, 2000); Nicki Hitchcott, *Women Writers in Francophone Africa* (Oxford: Berg, 2000).

4   See Toril Moi's discussion of the reception of Beauvoir in her chapter, 'Politics and the intellectual woman: clichés and commonplaces in the reception of Simone de Beauvoir', in Toril Moi, *Simone de Beauvoir: The Making of an Intellectual Woman* (Oxford and Cambridge, MA: Blackwell, 1994), pp. 73–92.

5   Christiane Baroche, *Le Collier*, illustrations by Frédéric Clément (Paris: Ipomée-Albin Michel, 1992).

6   Constant's Goncourt-winning novel *Confidence pour confidence* (Paris: Gallimard, 1998), discussed in Chapter 4 is actually set in the USA, the academic setting of which is similarly taken up – and criticised – by Catherine Cusset's *Le Problème avec Jane* (Paris: Gallimard, 1999). Cusset lives and works in the USA, like other French women writers before her, not least Marguerite Yourcenar and Monique Wittig. Africa is a more frequent other than the Orient in French women's writing, albeit in a different way. Like Duras's Indo-China or Linda Lê's Vietnam, this is an other within in the writing of the generation of writers who grew up under French colonialism, and is evident in, for example, Constant's Africa novels and the work of Marie Cardinal and Hélène Cixous. A recent

example of fascination with the Orient is Luce Irigaray's *Entre Orient et Occident* (Paris: Grasset, 1999).

7 See for example, Morag Shiach, *Hélène Cixous: A Politics of Writing* (London: Routledge, 1991); Susan Rubin Suleiman, *Subversive Intent: Gender, Politics, and the Avant-Garde* (Cambridge, MA and London: Harvard University Press, 1990); Susan Sellers, *Hélène Cixous: Authorship, Autobiography and Love* (Cambridge: Polity Press, 1996).

8 For an example of this type of criticism, see Toril Moi, *Sexual/Textual Politics: Feminist Literary Theory* (London and New York: Routledge, 1991).

9 Catherine Millet, *La Vie sexuelle de Catherine M.* (Paris: Seuil, 2001). See also the Dossier, 'Quand les femmes disent tout', *Le Nouvel Observateur*, 1907 (24–30 May 2001), pp. 4–12.

10 At the age of 70, Duras was awarded the Prix Goncourt in 1984 for *L'Amant*; in the same year, Ernaux won the Prix Renaudot for *La Place*. Ernaux's work is not only popular with French and Anglo-American readers but it has also generated substantial academic interest. However, some of her writing is still criticised as not being much to do with 'literature' (see Lynn Thomas, *Annie Ernaux: An Introduction to the Writer and her Audience* (Oxford: Berg, 1999), p. 147) and indeed Ernaux has an ambivalent relationship with the term, the writer-narrator of *Une femme* professing that she wants to write 'au-dessous de la littérature' ('a cut below literature'), whatever that might be taken to mean (Annie Ernaux, *Une femme* (Paris: Gallimard, 1987), p. 23; *A Woman's Story*, trans. Tanya Leslie (London and New York: Quartet Books, 1990), p. 13).

11 Major literary prizes went, in the 1980s and 1990s, to a number of French and francophone female authors. Following Duras's 1984 Goncourt success, the prize was won by women in 1996 (Pascalle Roze) and 1998 (Paule Constant). The Prix Renaudot went to several women authors in the 1980s and 1990s: Danièle Sallenave (1980), Ernaux (1984), Raphaëlle Billetdoux (1985), Dominique Bona (1998) and Martine Le Coz (2001). The Prix Médicis, which Hélène Cixous had won in 1969 for *Dedans*, was awarded in the 1980s to Christiane Rochefort (1988) and, in the 1990s, Emmanuelle Bernheim (1993) and Jacqueline Harpman (1996). The Prix du roman de l'Académie Française was dominated by male authors in the 1970s, but in the 1980s was won by Liliane Gignabodet (1983), Frédérique Hebrard (1987), Geneviève Dormann (1989) and in the 1990s by Paule Constant for *White spirit* in 1990, Calixthe Beyala (1996), Anne Wiazemsky (1998) and Amélie Nothomb (1999) for *Stupeur et tremblements*. The Prix Fémina, awarded historically to more women writers than other prizes, was won by Sylvie Germain in 1989 for *Jour de colère* and in the 1990s by Geneviève Brisac (1996), Maryline Desbiolles (1999), Camille Laurens (2000) and Marie NDiaye (2001). In the 1990s, women authors were well represented among the winners of the Prix du Livre Inter, including Agnès Desarthe (1996) for *Un secret sans importance*. Bernard Pivot's 'Apostrophes' (1975–90) and 'Bouillon de culture' (1991–2001) were important and democratising forums for writers and provided a valuable impetus to book sales.

12 Roland Barthes, 'La mort de l'auteur', in *Essais critiques IV: le bruissement de la langue* (Paris: Seuil, 1973), pp. 61–7 (p. 67); 'The death of the author', in Roland

Barthes, *Image, Music, Text*, ed. and trans. Stephen Heath (London: Fontana, 1984), pp. 142–8 (p. 148).

13 Michel Foucault, 'Qu'est-ce qu'un auteur?', in *Dits et écrits, vol. 1, 1954–1988* (Paris: Gallimard, 1994), pp. 789–821; 'What is an author?', in James D. Faubion (ed.) *Aesthetics, Method and Epistemology: Michel Foucault*, vol. 2, trans. Robert Hurley and others (London: Allen Lane, 1998), pp. 205–22.

14 In this respect, see especially Luce Irigaray, *Ce sexe qui n'en est pas un* (Paris: Minuit, 1977), pp. 122 and 133; *This Sex Which is Not One*, trans. Catherine Porter with Carolyn Burke (Ithaca, NY: Cornell University Press, 1985); *Je, tu, nous: pour une culture de la différence* (Paris: Grasset, 1990); *Je, tu, nous: Toward a Culture of Difference*, trans. Alison Martin (New York and London: Routledge, 1993); and more recently 'Au-delà de tout jugement, tu es', *Sémiotiques*, 10 (June 1996); 'Beyond all judgement, you are', trans. Michael Worton, *Journal of the Institute of Romance Studies*, 7 (1999), 1–10.

15 See Adrienne Rich, 'Compulsory heterosexuality and lesbian existence', *Signs: Journal of Women in Culture and Society*, 5(4) (1980), 631–60.

16 See Françoise Héritier, *Masculin/Féminin: la pensée de la différence* (Paris: Odile Jacob, 1996), p. 288.

17 Luce Irigaray, *Ethique de la différence sexuelle* (Paris: Minuit, 1984), p. 13; *An Ethics of Sexual Difference*, trans. Carolyn Burke and Gillian C. Gill (London: Athlone Press, 1993), p. 5.

18 Diana Fuss, *Essentially Speaking* (London: Routledge, 1989), p. 119.

19 Julia Kristeva, 'Entretien avec Julia Kristeva: l'avant-garde aujourd'hui', *Avant Garde*, 4 (1990), 158–75. In this interview, Kristeva does, none the less, acknowledge the short-term value of collective groups and categories. It is notable that her recent work focuses on twentieth-century women writers: Hannah Arendt, Melanie Klein, Colette (Julia Kristeva, *Le Génie féminin: la vie, la folie, les mots, I Hannah Arendt* (Paris: Fayard, 1999), *II Melanie Klein* (Paris: Fayard, 2000) and *III Colette* (Paris: Fayard, 2002)).

20 This is not to say that *autofiction* itself is straightforward as a category. Indeed, Alex Hughes describes how celebrated practitioners of the genre Hervé Guibert and Serge Doubrovsky 'practice *autofiction* in different ways': Guibert privileging uncertainty; Doubrovsky, in psychoanalytical mode, reworking his past self (Alex Hughes, *Heterographies: Sexual Difference in French Autobiography* (Oxford and New York: Berg, 1999), n. 42, p. 162). Rather, we are concerned here with the *structuring* of processes of categorisation and the power systems in which they are implicated.

21 For this expression, see Ross Mitchell Guberman (ed.), *Julia Kristeva Interviews* (New York: Columbia University Press, 1996), p. 124; the interview in question was originally published in 1993 and refers to the importance of content in writing by women instead, simply, of the aesthetic or political categorisation of 'women's writing'.

22 See Michael Sheringham, *French Autobiography: Devices and Desires, Rousseau to Perec* (Oxford: Clarendon Press, 1993). Sheringham describes the heterogeneous 'hybrid form' (p. 13) of autobiography as involving: (a) interaction with other

confessional modes of writing; (b) the borders of fact and fiction; (c) a function of the writer's materials (types of memories, stories heard and invented, past writings, archives and records); (d) 'the "missing chapter" of the unconscious' (p. 14); (e) the diversity of the contexts of its writing; (f) a 'highly intertextual character' via citations and references to reading (pp. 15–17). Autobiography is 'a patchwork assembled out of this disparateness' (p. 14), a genre characterised by 'indefinition' (p. 17). Elsewhere, Sheringham glosses: 'autobiography is no longer considered to be a generic straightjacket but a multi-faceted and essentially hybrid set of practices having in common a basis in the referential (whilst not excluding the fictive)' (Michael Sheringham, 'Women writers and the rise of autobiography', in Sonya Stephens (ed.), *A History of Women's Writing in France*, pp. 185–203). Notwithstanding the already-recognised hybrid nature of autobiography, our own point here, as in note 11, concerns the structuring principles of categorisation.

23 Until the publication of *L'Inceste*, Angot's texts were categorised as *roman* (novel). See Alex Hughes, ' "Moi qui ai connu l'inceste, je m'appelle Christine" [I have had an incestuous relationship and my name is Christine]: writing and subjectivity in Christine Angot's incest narratives', *Journal of Romance Studies*, 2(1) (spring 2002), 65–77, which comments on the connections between Angot's work and Guibert, Doubrovsky and Stein.

24 *Roland Barthes by Roland Barthes*, trans. Richard Howard (London: Macmillan, 1977), p. 175.

25 See Jacques Lacan, 'The mirror stage as formative of the function of the I', in *Ecrits: A Selection*, trans. Alan Sheridan (London: Tavistock, 1977), pp. 1–7.

26 Georges Bataille, *Eroticism*, trans. Mary Dalwood (London and New York: Marion Boyars, 1987), p. 108.

27 Diana E. H. Russell (ed.) *Making Violence Sexy: Feminist Views on Pornography* (Buckingham: Open University Press, 1993), pp. 2–3.

28 Linda LeMoncheck, *Loose Women, Lecherous Men: A Feminist Philosophy of Sex* (New York and Oxford: Oxford University Press, 1997) p. 98.

29 Anita Phillips, *A Defence of Masochism* (London: Faber & Faber, 1998), p. 122.

30 For feminist critiques of psychoanalytical and philosophical positions, see Kate Millett, *Sexual Politics* (London: Hart-Davis, 1971); Simone de Beauvoir, *Le Deuxième Sexe* 2 vols (Paris: Gallimard, 1949; repr. 1976); *The Second Sex*, trans. and ed. H. M. Parshley (London: Picador, [1953] 1988); Hélène Cixous and Catherine Clément, *La Jeune Née* (Paris: 10/18 UGE, 1975); *The Newly Born Woman*, trans. Betsy Wing (Manchester: Manchester University Press, 1986); Hélène Cixous, 'Le Sexe ou la tête?', *Les Cahiers du GRIF*, 13 (October 1976), 5–15; 'Castration or decapitation?', trans. Annette Kuhn, *Signs*, 7(1) (autumn 1981), 41–55; Shoshana Felman, *What Does a Woman Want? Reading and Sexual Difference* (Baltimore and London: The Johns Hopkins University Press, 1993); Elisabeth Bronfen, *Over Her Dead Body: Death, Femininity and the Aesthetic* (Manchester: Manchester University Press, 1992).

31 Felman, *What Does a Woman Want?*, p. 16.

32 See, for example, the work of Charlotte Delbo, Jorge Semprun, and Hervé Guibert.

33 This is a wider and more common-place use of the term than that clinically iden-
    tified in the context of 'post-traumatic stress disorder', which is restricted to expo-
    sure to events outside the range of normal human experience rather than to the
    more common experiences of bereavement, financial difficulties, marriage break-
    down, etc. See Luís Quintais, 'How to speak, how to remember: post-traumatic
    stress disorder and the Portuguese colonial wars (1961–74)', *Journal of Romance
    Studies*, 1(3) (winter 2001), 85–101.

34 Hal Foster, *The Return of the Real: The Avant-Garde at the End of the Century*
    (Cambridge, MA: MIT, 1996), p. 168.

35 Suzette A. Henke, *Shattered Subjects: Trauma and Testimony in Women's Life-
    Writing* (Basingstoke: Macmillan, 1998).

36 Shoshana Felman and Dori Laub, *Testimony: Crises of Witnessing in Literature,
    Psychoanalysis, and History* (New York and London: Routledge, 1992).

37 Kathryn Robson, 'Falling into an abyss: remembering and writing sexual abuse in
    Béatrice de Jurquet's *La Traversée des lignes*', *Journal of Romance Studies*, 2(1)
    (spring 2002), 79–90. Another example of this type of reading is Colin Davis's
    chapter on Jorge Semprun in *French Fiction in the Mitterand Years*, pp. 61–82.

38 Melanie Klein, 'Mourning and its relation to manic-depressive states' (1940), in
    Love, Guilt and Reparation and Other works 1921–1945 (London: The Hogarth
    Press and the Institute of Psycho-Analysis, 1981), pp. 344–69; Sigmund Freud,
    'Mourning and melancholia' (1917 [1915]), in *On Metapsychology: The Theory of
    Psychoanalysis*, Pelican Freud Library vol. 11 (Harmondsworth: Penguin, 1984),
    pp. 245–68.

39 Liz Stanley, *The Auto/biographical I: The Theory and Practice of Feminist
    Auto/biography* (Manchester: Manchester University Press, 1992).

40 Carolyn Steedman, *Landscape for a Good Woman* (London: Virago, 1986).

41 See Rosi Braidotti, *Nomadic Subjects: Embodiment and Sexual Difference in
    Contemporary Feminist Theory* (New York: Columbia University Press, 1994), p.
    14.

42 Margaret Whitford, *Luce Irigaray: Philosophy in the Feminine* (London:
    Routledge, 1991), p. 91.

43 See, for example, Christine Battersby, *The Phenomenal Woman: Feminist
    Metaphysics and the Patterns of Identity* (Cambridge: Polity Press, 1998), for a
    philosophical approach that accommodates the relationship between feminist
    identity politics and the diversity between individual women; Morwenna
    Griffiths, *Feminisms and the Self: The Web of Identity* (London and New York:
    Routledge, 1995), for a philosophical rethinking of identity using the metaphor of
    a web.

44 Colin McGinn, *Ethics, Evil, and Fiction* (Oxford: Oxford University Press, 1997),
    pp. 174–5.

45 Martha Nussbaum, *Love's Knowledge: Essays on Philosophy and Literature* (New
    York and Oxford: Oxford University Press, 1990), p. 22.

I

Rewriting the past

Louise L. Lambrichs: trauma, dream and narrative

The novels of Louise Lambrichs are brilliant but troubling psychological dramas focusing on the traumas that inhabit the family romance: incest, sterility, the death of those we love and the terrible legacy of mourning. Bringing together themes of loss and recompense, Lambrichs's novels trace with infinite delicacy the reactions of those who suffer and seek obsessively for comfort and understanding. But equally they perform a subtle and often chilling evocation of the secrets, lies and crimes that bind a family together and create a pattern of behaviour that can motivate or cripple subsequent generations. Louise Lambrichs's œuvre comprises five novels but also a number of factual or biographical works on medical issues such as cancer, dyslexia and sterility. These concerns are reflected in her novels which often deal with the pain of having, losing and desiring children, and indeed the two novels I shall be discussing here, *Journal d'Hannah* and *A ton image*, conform to this pattern.[1] *Journal d'Hannah* concerns a woman forced to abort a much-wanted second child and subsequently rendered sterile, while *A ton image* deals with the issues of cloning and incest. However, the fascination of Lambrichs's novels lies less with the medical issues than in the psychological perspective she adopts. Her work persistently explores the creative possibilities inherent in our psychic resources – the way that unconscious mental life conjures up both convoluted resolutions and swift, brutally annihilating breakdowns in the aftermath of traumatic experience. Memory and dream dominate Lambrichs's work as she explores the mind's ability to reorder and retell damaging experience.

The telling of stories is always central to her novels and for Lambrichs, when narrative fails or proves insufficient, dreams provide powerful and significant stories too. The links between narrative and the dream will provide the focus of my analysis on Lambrichs's work, in which I will suggest that dreams function as densely signifying microcosmic narratives. Dreams are related to memory, and to traumatic memory in particular, in the way that they offer a form of symbolic expression to events that would otherwise remain beyond the power of narrative to represent. In retrospect, the protagonist's first-person narrative in Lambrichs's texts often turns out to have performed a slow and exacting elaboration of the intense but confusing message which the dream conveys. My aim, then, in this analysis, is to consider the interplay between dream and narrative in the long process of rehabilitation and expiation performed by the narrators of Lambrichs's novels in their endeavour to survive trauma.

The most striking exploration of dreams to be found in Lambrichs's texts comes in *Journal d'Hannah*, which recounts in diary form the story of a Jewish woman forced to abort her much-wanted second child by her husband who is fighting in the Resistance. The operation leaves her sterile and traumatised, but the child she has lost lives on in an intense and vivid dream life. These dreams develop into a kind of parallel existence for Hannah, a phantasy life in which her aborted child grows and ages in real time. It is a life which denies loss and mourning, for in these dreams not only Louise, the baby she lost, but also her family, deported during the war, are restored to her. This is then, quite literally, a haunting novel that unites the personal tragedy of a lost child with the historical tragedy of genocide. In both private and public cases of trauma the problem of memory is paramount. In her diary Hannah asks 'Comment faire pour ne pas oublier sans vivre hanté par le souvenir?' (p. 201) (How to manage not to forget without living on haunted by memory?), and this enquiry provides a hidden guiding principle to the text, a principle that is rarely articulated, but is blatantly manifest in the workings of her dream life. Hannah embarks on a series of dreams a couple of months after her abortion that will continue for some twenty years. She gives birth to a baby girl, Louise, who will develop in perfect conjunction with temporal reality: 'je m'apercevais que mon rêve la représentait à l'âge exact qu'elle aurait eu, si elle avait vécu' (p. 60) (I realised that my dream showed her at the precise age she would have been, if she had lived). But more than this the dreams themselves have a narrative quality to them that is astonishing. Hannah writes: 'les images que je vois sont si vraies, si logiquement assemblées, si conformes à la représentation habituelle du monde réel, que j'ai l'impression d'assister à un spectacle où un autre que moi, qui simplement porte le même nom, Hannah, s'occupe d'élever une petite fille, Louise' (p. 61) (the images are so real, so logically put together, so true to the usual picture of real life, that I have the impression of watching a drama where someone other than me, who simply shares my name, Hannah, is busy bringing up a little girl, Louise). These are dreams, then, because they take place at night, while she is asleep, but not dreams in the usual understanding of the term.

Dreams are not narratives in the conventional sense; they do not generally tell coherent stories or generate readily understandable significance. Instead they tend to play havoc with our notions of cause and effect, rework and reformulate relations of space and time, and push back the boundaries of representation in their excessive use of symbolism and metaphor. Dreams are to reality what particularly obscure modern poetry is to the novel; they are playful improvisation with a dash of karaoke, instead of the sober method acting of everyday life. Dreams are performative in the Butlerian sense of the word; they bring something into being, enact something, and this process is taken to its logical excess in *Journal d'Hannah*. Freud suggested that dreams were the dramatisation of an idea: 'But this feature of dream-life can only be fully understood if we further recognise that in dreams . . . we appear not to *think* but to *experience*'.[2] And the ideas that we experience in our dreams are essentially derived from the translation of reality as a whole into a field of emotive forces. The longing, the wishing, the fearing, underlying our everyday behaviour becomes the stuff of our dreams, but recontextualised in odd and unsettling ways. The emotional punch of *Journal d'Hannah* lies in the unspoken recognition that Hannah's loss is too unbearable to accept and is instead transformed into the hallucinatory experience of her dream life with Louise.

Freud's essential premise in *The Interpretation of Dreams* was that dreams are exercises in wish-fulfilment, but that wishes are disguised and distorted so that the dreamer's sleep should remain untroubled. While *The Interpretation of Dreams* was written almost before the birth of psychoanalysis proper,[3] dream analysis has subsequently become intrinsic to clinical practice. The hope remains that unravelling the complex web of associations and symbols will lead back to the unconscious wishes lying behind a patient's neurosis. Melanie Klein understood dreams as being made from the stuff of unconscious phantasy.[4] To borrow Hanna Segal's definition: 'a phantasy is an unconscious wish, worked on by logical thought so as to give rise to a disguised expression and imaginary fulfilment of the original wish'.[5] Klein watched young children at play and noted the extent to which phantasies dominated the child's game and guided his or her perception. She came to believe that phantasy is with us from the earliest moments of subjectivity (in opposition to Freud who believed that fantasies came much later in life and then only intermittently), and that there can be no desire without an imaginary picturing of its fulfilment, and no form of hunger that is not experienced mentally as torture or persecution. Wishes are insistent, demanding but ambivalent creatures, urging us on to the joys of their satisfaction, but reminding us always of the terror underlying absence or loss. Wish-fulfilment phantasies defend us against the unpalatable thought of not having while continually reminding us that our fragile mental balance requires such excessive defence.

This ambivalence is openly apparent in the Lambrichs text. To begin with, pleasure and comfort characterise Hannah's dreams, along with their curious lifelike quality. But as the journal progresses her struggle to regain control over her life reflects her investment in the dream existence. Periods of profound stress are also periods of intense dreams, and the desire to stop dreaming about Louise always accompanies the desire to 'return' to her family. Hannah's ambivalent response to her dreams goes beyond the ambivalence of wish-fulfilment to reflect a more profound schism in the structure of her life. Hannah's dream life marks the start of a period of extreme instability, fraught with psychic traumas, near breakdowns, persecutions and paranoia, and recounted with odd breaks and lacunae. In comparison her dreams are impossibly coherent, linear and representational. It would seem that, in this text, dream and reality have changed places, dreams providing a compensatory narrative to combat the nightmare of Hannah's existence. But the pleasure of these dreams is nevertheless transgressive and forbidden. They are too real, transcending the rules of dreamwork and becoming alarming in their own right. And while they represent a recompense for an unbearable loss, that recompense cannot be reconciled with reality. The recompense takes place, precisely, in another life, an alternative, not a complement to the one she inhabits.

One reason why this dream life is so complex in its motivation involves the excessive mourning that surrounds Hannah's lost fertility. As a covert accompaniment to the narrative of her aborted child, Hannah mourns the loss of her Jewish identity and the death of her family members. In the dream landscape she creates, her father, mother and sister share her life with Louise. The guilt of the survivor inhibits her mourning work, translated into other forms of implied, understated, but crippling guilt: guilt at having denied her Jewishness in order to avoid deportation, and guilt at having 'murdered' her baby as she puts it, in order to avoid detection. This private atrocity renders her, in her own eyes, complicit with those who murdered her family. Occasionally the relationship between war trauma and abortion trauma is made painfully explicit: 'Moi je ne peux pas. Ni faire des enfants. Ni oublier la guerre. Peut-être en effet, cela va-t-il de pair' (p. 107) (As for me, I can't. Have children. Or forget the war. Perhaps in effect the two go hand in hand). 'Moi je ne peux pas', she states, and it is the 'cannot-ness' here that is so striking and so unconquerable. The convoluted interrelation of loss, guilt, anger and anxiety proves impossible to overcome or assimilate in any meaningful way. In order to continue at all in the face of such loss, Hannah needs a neurotic solution in the form of a symbol, created to carry the weight of her trauma; that symbol is Louise.

I will return to this concept of symbol formation in more detail below, but the function of a psychic symbol is beautifully illustrated within the text itself. Hannah recounts a nightmare in which she is bouncing a ball against a wall with her friend Elizabeth, who has just betrayed her in real life. She knows that if she drops the ball she will be deported to the concentration camp by Elizabeth, but she has just sustained an injury to her hand and will bleed to death unless she can attend to it. 'J'ai le choix entre deux morts' (I have the choice between two deaths) Hannah recounts, and at this precise moment Louise arrives and takes her place in the game. This scenario offers a neat figurative representation of her psychic life, caught between two deaths: the death of her Jewish identity represented by the fear of the concentration camp, and the death of her maternal identity, represented by the cut that will cause her to bleed to death. The fact that what she most fears has already happened – she is sterile and a Gentile – is psychically irrelevant. Her unconscious mind is unable to accept the finality of her loss and she is simply caught between these deaths, facing the prospect of radical breakdown represented in the dream by her inability to play the game any more. Into this stalemate situation comes Louise who will play on for her. Her investment in Louise does not solve the problem of these two deaths, but it provides a viable alternative to breakdown in the face of trauma which cannot be assimilated.

So, although Hannah's dreams may appear superficially to be paradise dreams, their motivation stems from extreme anxiety. Implicitly, the story of this curious dream life is really the story of a psychic breakdown, the processes of which I will now attempt to uncover. The psychoanalysts van der Kolk and van der Hart make a distinction between traumatic memory and narrative memory.[6] Narrative memory functions like a kind of personal soap opera, in that every little scene we experience is assigned a meaning because we recognise it as part of an ongoing plot. The mind is continually sifting experience to fit into existing categories, as well as seeking new ways of putting things together. This kind of memory is wholly flexible, but also perhaps, unreliable, somewhat distant from the events that inspired it. Traumatic memory, by contrast, concerns horrific, terrifying events that cannot be tamed into general narratives. Under these circumstances the memory enters psychic space as an insistent image that cannot be possessed because it cannot be mentally digested, broken down into understandable parts and assimilated. The memory therefore loses none of its lived reality and returns to consciousness as if it were happening all over again. At this point there is, I believe, an important link to be made between the memory of trauma and the dream life that Hannah experiences in the novel. This link involves the process of symbolisation.

Symbolisation is the basic process in the creation of phantasies, which are, as I discussed earlier, the means by which the mind copes with desires and fears. There is a necessary distinction between what we can hold in our minds and what we experience in reality, just as the contents of our stomachs are not identical to the food that we eat; in both cases transformation takes place and symbolisation is the main way that mental digestion occurs. In *Dream, Phantasy and Art*, the psychoanalyst Hanna Segal makes an opposition between two forms of symbolisation, one healthy and one neurotic, that echoes the distinction between memory categories by van der Kolk and van der Hart. Segal opposes the healthy *symbolic representation*, where the symbol represents the object but is not experienced as the same thing, to the neurotic *symbolic equation* where a mental symbol is so identified with the object symbolised that the two are equated. Segal argues that symbolisation is essential in the work of mourning, where the mind deals with loss by creating a symbol in place of the object, which can then be mentally internalised. Symbols do not deny loss, but rather actively work to overcome it by offering a valid psychic recompense for the lost object. Segal argues that: 'It is only if the dead person can be felt as symbolically introjected and the internal object is symbolic of the lost person that internal reparation, necessary to overcome mourning, can be achieved' (*Dream, Phantasy and Art*, pp. 37–8). However, when symbol formation goes wrong, that symbol is experienced concretely, that is to say, not as a representation of the lost object, but as the object itself. I think that Lambrichs's text offers a possible perspective on this kind of pathological mourning. It can be understood as a kind of mental indigestion whereby the introjected symbol resists the mind's attempt to break it down and remains instead autonomous, separate, solid. Hannah introjects her lost baby in her process of mourning, but the nature of the baby's loss, bound up as it is with the loss of her family and her personal guilt, make this such an overdetermined symbol that a hitch occurs in the mourning. Louise and her family live on inside Hannah, that is the symbolic recompense, but they live an autonomous existence, a life experienced as 'real', which is the neurotic solution.

That this neurotic solution should be accomplished through dreams is interesting for a number of reasons. Freud's premise that all dreaming was covert wish-fulfilment ran aground when it hit the anxiety or trauma dream: he could find no satisfactory explanation for it.[7] As I argued earlier, Hannah's dreams, although fulfilling wishes to some degree, are actually closer to anxiety dreams in structure and motivation. Trevor Pateman argues that: 'An anxiety dream is a failed dream – a dream which fails to symbolize the anxiety-creating wishes which it represents in such a way that the dreamer can sleep on without waking'.[8] Hannah's dreams reflect this argument to a certain degree, but any failure of symbolic achievement in Hannah's dreams is offset by their persistence. The twenty-year span of her dream life would imply that some kind of mental work was neverthe-less underway. In his essay 'The psychological function of dreams' James L. Fosshage presents a useful summary of current theory, arguing that instead of wish-fulfilment: 'new models of dream formation . . . have emphasized the function of integration, synthesis and mastery'.[9] In other words, dreams have a significant role to play in maintaining, and also repairing, the healthy psychic structures of the mind. We can understand the dream as a space in which the mind's creativity comes into juxtaposi-tion with both trivial details of the day and the excessively significant emotive forces of the unconscious. In this crucible, symbolisation takes place, promoting the process of healthy mental digestion, albeit in a hap-hazard if ingenious fashion. While the dreams represented in Lambrichs's texts certainly seem to aim for this reparative function, the texts themselves show this process to be long, imperfect and perhaps endless without the help of narrative. I stated at the beginning of this analysis that I would argue that the dreams in Lambrichs's texts constitute condensed stories that need a narrative reworking and interpretation in order to perform success-fully their restorative function. This point is clearly illustrated by reference to the dream that stands at the heart of Lambrichs's later novel, *A ton image*.

A ton image tells the chilling tale of Jean Letertre, an obstetrician des-perate to escape the incestuous crimes of his childhood. Seduced by his retarded younger sister the night before he leaves for medical studies in

Paris, he discovers that she has been repeatedly abused by his father. Like Oedipus before him, he attempts to leave these sins as far behind him as possible, little knowing that he is unwittingly moving towards a dramatic confrontation with them in the future. In Paris he meets an older woman who has lost her husband and sons in a car crash. They marry and, when Françoise turns out to be sterile, he secretly arranges for her to clone a child. Jean adores his daughter, France, but her existence fills him with fear; fear for her future well-being, fear that Françoise will find out she is a clone (she does eventually and commits suicide), and an unknown, primal fear that stems from his own childhood. Their story ends in tragedy when France, developing unusually fast for her age, seduces him (she is after all fulfilling her destiny as a replica of Françoise, she is not his biological daughter) and full of anger, shame and guilt, Jean kills her. This complex and mesmerising novel is a long disquisition on love, desire and the vulnerability of parents. It is an exploration of traumatic memory and the ambivalence of sin, a sophisticated enquiry into issues of cloning, genetic inheritance and repetition, but most significantly here it is a hymn to the power of the dream. 'J'avais aimé, rêvé et tout perdu, j'avais à la fois réalisé et tué mon rêve' (p. 365) (I had loved, dreamed, and lost everything; I had both brought my dream to life and killed it) Jean declares at the end, and the dream refers to the way France troubled the borderline between fantasy and reality, as well as the dream of a happy childhood unscarred by incest which Jean had dreamed for himself, as well as for France. Actual dreams are a recurrent feature of the text, and one dream which stands at its centre provides a key prophetic moment. In this dream Jean enters a hall full of mirrors and people where a clown guides them through a series of games. Jean cheats by using a pack of cards he has in his pocket, but pleasure at winning is offset by fear of being found out. In the final game the clown displays letters on an overhead projector, but rather than spelling out 'clown', as they should, the word 'clone' appears. Jean fears the worst but the clown blames the machine, the people leave and Jean is injected with truth serum.

Many details in this scenario offer transformed representations of key elements in the text; the hall of mirrors signifies the reflection and reproduction of cloning, 'using his own cards' signifies the insider knowledge he took advantage of to create France, and the fact that he has to build a house of cards in one game points to the fragility of his domestic situation. The figure of the clown mirrors Jean's position, emphasising disguise and illusion and the masking of his identity ('Ce que j'étais vraiment, ce que je suis, je ne l'ai partagé avec personne' (p. 366) (The truth of who I was, who I am,

I have never shared with anybody)). Although it is necessary for him to create a new, successful persona, he longs to take off the mask to reveal and understand himself. Above all the dream's emotive field is one of deceit. Transgression and guilt colour the dream and motivate its twists and turns, but equally they capture the mood of Jean's narrative as a whole. Jean is writing the narrative retrospectively as he waits in prison for his trial (although the reader does not know his crime until the end), but what his narrative resists above all is hindsight:

> lire l'histoire à rebours, l'interpréter à la lumière de la fin, désormais connue, est-il légitime? Si la lecture qui en résulte est cohérente et ainsi plus satisfaisante pour l'esprit, elle trahit à mes yeux ce qui fait le prix de l'existence, cette part d'inconnu et de hasard, cette incroyable succession de croisées de chemin où, chaque fois, on a cru librement choisir sa direction. (p. 47)

> (Is it permissible to read the story backwards, to interpret it in the light of the conclusion, now that it is known? If the reading that results is coherent and therefore more intellectually satisfying, it fails to represent what I see as the price of existence: the part played by chance and the unknown, that unbelievable series of crossroads where, every time, we thought we chose our way freely.)

The importance of the borderline between chance and predetermination is represented in the dream by the series of games Jean plays and his cheating. But the meaning attached to chance is bound up covertly, significantly with France; as a clone her biological future, her health and mental well-being are entirely unpredictable, and the narrative continually hints that she is at risk in this respect. The bitter irony resides in her perfect predictability as the exact replica of her mother. She will come to desire Jean and bring about their downfall.

This too is inscribed in the dream but, appropriately and tellingly, in a tiny detail; the tapestries on the walls depict a hunting scene where the hunters are men and the prey women. But all is not as it seems: 'je me rendis compte que le danger venait moins des hommes, qui tenaient leurs fusils comme des stylos, que des femmes qui, toutes, dissimulaient dans une main la lame brillante et aiguisée d'un poignard de poche' (p. 217) (I realised that the danger came less from the men, who held their guns like pens, but from the women, whose hands contained hidden the brilliant, sharpened blades of pocket knives). Although Jean is ostensibly the criminal, he has been a victim of the overwhelming desires of the women he has loved; his sister's desire for him, France's desire for him and Françoise's desire for a child. Jean's real crime has been an inability to oppose their wills – this craven lassitude stems from his childhood: 'avec une implacable constance j'avais dans cette maison choisi la soumission comme une solution de facilité' (p. 39) (with unshakeable consistency I had chosen submission as the easiest option in that household). But what I suggest is most interesting about the scene on the tapestries is precisely the sudden switch that accompanies its interpretation. The picture is not what it seems; women are the aggressors, just as Jean's crime is not what it seems; he is not France's father but her creator. The abrupt volte-face of interpretation becomes a guiding principle of the narrative overall; where we expect harm to come to France from an external source, it is Jean who loves her who is her murderer; where we are afraid Jean will be caught out for conducting the experiment, the court of justice dismisses the claims that France is cloned as ridiculous. The impossibility of anticipation orders this narrative as it orders any dream narrative, but equally the consequences of Jean's actions are perfectly logical with hindsight, or at least with a second glance, a look that sees differently, that assembles the elements of his narrative from a different perspective. And of course dream interpretation behaves in exactly this way, seeking a latent content from a manifest one. Shoshana Felman in her work *What Does a Woman Want?* tells how she 'learned how dreams are indeed, concretely and materially, the royal road to the unconscious, how they were susceptible of telling us *about our own autobiography another story* than the one we knew or had believed to be our own'.[10]

Dreams, then, offer a way to experience our difference within, our internal and hidden otherness that nevertheless has a profound impact on our lives. Dreams act out the conflictual motivations that both dominate and cripple our psyches, but of course, the dream as an experience is confusing and complex. It requires recounting and interpreting if it is to be of psychic value, and Jean's dream exemplifies this. It gains its significance from the narrative context in which it is situated and plays its part in the psychoanalytic scenario that the text enacts. Jean writes his narrative for his defence lawyer: 'Comme si le seul fait d'avoir un lecteur autre que moi-même donnait enfin du sens à mon entreprise' (p. 29) (As if the mere fact of having a reader other than myself gave some sense to my venture). Jean's dream dramatises the cleavage he feels between his role as instigator of criminal actions, transgressing the rules of chance, and his sense of being an impotent spectator in his existence, prey to fear of disclosure precisely because he has tried to control and deny fate. What he finally comes to terms with is the inescapable repetition and circularity of the family romance. Like Oedipus before him, he has tried and failed to evade his family destiny, and like Oedipus, he has been punished for attempting to play God.

If telling his narrative does not manage to elucidate and reduce the mysterious power of the family romance, Jean does at least end his tale both reconciled to it and making a final attempt to exert his will. He bequeaths some of his DNA to his defence lawyer in the hope that she will mother his clone. This is a narrative cure of sorts, but a more striking cure is effected in *Journal d'Hannah*. Hannah's dream life continues for many years until, suddenly, Louise falls ill. Hannah is afraid not only of losing her phantasised daughter but of being unable to survive the loss. At this moment she makes the link to narrative, realising that she has been writing her journal in order to trace the contours of her subjectivity, in order to be in communication with herself. As she writes this she is unconfident in narrative's ability to rescue her, arguing that: 'L'écriture n'est pas une béquille. Elle aussi n'existe qu'à condition d'être une vie en plus. Comme Louise' (p. 226) (Writing is not a crutch. It also exists on condition of being an extra life. Like Louise). This is a fascinating equation, investing autonomy in the text that is emotionally equivalent to Louise's autonomy, that is to say, excessive, alarming, luxurious, compensatory. And indeed what happens next is that narrative does rescue her. Visiting a doctor she has never seen before she tells him the story of Louise, a story she has never told before (just as Jean has never before told the 'truth' of his tale), and this simple, if painful, expedient ends her dream life. I suggest that the dream life has fulfilled its purpose at this point, hence the weakness of Louise. It has provided a neurotic solution to carry Hannah over an impossibly difficult period of mourning, but now Hannah is finally ready to move on. The account of the narrative is described as: 'une espèce de vomissement entrecoupé de larmes, comme si tout mon corps participait à l'expulsion de ce rêve impossible' (p. 239) (a kind of vomiting, interspersed with tears, as if my whole body were involved in expelling this impossible dream). The terrible and wonderful secret is finally given up as a kind of vomiting, a symbolic expulsion of that mental indigestion, but equally a symbolic transformation from a concrete internalised sign to the more fluid and flexible representations of narrative. After all, Hannah has made the equation herself: narrative, like Louise is 'une vie de plus'. Louise and her lost family can live on, but elsewhere.

In the final analysis, these two texts highlight the paradoxes that structure the workings of the psyche, the way that the mind creates complex and clever solutions in times of impossible conflict, and also the way that those solutions are often partial, neurotic and fraught. The dream exemplifies this contradiction perfectly, being at once a creative and masterful dramatisation of psychic disorder, and a troubling, haunting revelation of irreconcilable difference within. Dreams can provide powerful recompense in the face of loss and clever encapsulations of psychic dilemmas. However, they are incomplete without their interpretation in narrative. This is possibly why dreams fascinate so: they demand explanation as their essential counterpart. Both narratives point to the limits of the mind's creative power in the face of trauma. The events of the Holocaust, for instance, continue to prove resistant to any form of symbolisation. Yet, in the final analysis, creativity holds our best hope of mental health, not just in the mind's spectacular resources, nor in the infinite possibilities of narrative, but in the process of transformation between the two. Lambrichs's work urges us to consider the alchemy of metamorphosis that takes place between inner and outer worlds, between experience and its internalisation, and between differing forms of symbolic representation, to discover to what extent we can truly possess our many lives.

Notes

1 Louise L. Lambrichs, *Journal d'Hannah* (Paris: La Différence, 1993); *A ton image* (Paris: Olivier/Seuil, 1998). All subsequent page references are given in brackets in the text.

2 Sigmund Freud, *The Interpretation of Dreams* (1900), Penguin Freud Library, vol. 4 (London: Penguin, 1976), pp. 114–15.

3 On this point see Melvin R. Lansky, 'The legacy of *The Interpretation of Dreams*', in Melvin Lansky (ed.), *Essential Papers on Dreams* (New York: New York University Press, 1992), pp. 3–31 (p. 4).

4 My reading of Klein is taken here from Melanie Klein, 'The rôle of the school in the libidinal development of the child' (1923), in *Love, Guilt and Reparation and Other Works 1921–45* (London: Hogarth Press, 1975), pp. 59–76.

5 Hanna Segal, *Dream, Phantasy and Art* (London and New York: Routledge, 1991), p. 16.

6 See Bessel van der Kolk and Onno van der Hart, 'The intrusive past: the flexibility of memory and the engraving of trauma', in Cathy Caruth (ed.), *Trauma: Explorations in Memory* (Baltimore and London: Johns Hopkins University Press, 1995), pp. 158–82.

7 Freud believed that traumatic dreams were a retrospective wish to master unpleasant stimulus by developing the anxiety which caused the neurosis. This led to his deduction of the repetition compulsion. For a more detailed reading of this, see

Joseph Weiss, 'Dreams and their various purposes', in *Essential Papers on Dreams*, pp. 213–35.

8 Trevor Pateman, 'How to do things in dreams', in Laura Marcus (ed.), *Sigmund Freud's The Interpretation of Dreams: New Interdisciplinary Essays* (Manchester: Manchester University Press, 1999), pp. 66–82 (p. 78).

9 James L. Fosshage, 'The psychological function of dreams', in *Essential Papers on Dreams*, pp. 249–71 (p. 261).

10 Shoshana Felman, *What Does a Woman Want? Reading and Sexual Difference* (Baltimore: Johns Hopkins University Press, 1993), pp. 122–3.

Evermore or nevermore? Memory and identity in Marie Redonnet's fiction of the 1990s

The body of writing produced by Marie Redonnet between 1985 and 2000 is an unusually coherent one. Settings and characters drawn up in one text are echoed in later works; certain stories and motifs figure again and again; the style of writing rarely changes from one text to the next. This is not to suggest, however, that the work does not evolve over the period. Indeed, while there is a large degree of overlap between the works published in the 1980s and more recent texts, there are also significant differences, of which the most obvious is increased realism in characterisation and setting. Thus, whereas the characters in the early texts lack physical attributes and psychological depth, are endowed with nonsensical, nursery-rhyme-like names, and exist in the most indeterminate of landscapes, characters in the texts produced in the 1990s are more fully realised, have more realistic names, and figure in places such as Paris and Brooklyn. This shift towards the construction in the later texts of a more realistic if not also more contemporary fictional world is reinforced by a number of sporadic references to the attributes of modern life. Thus, in *Candy story*, the central character Mia drives a Golf GTI, while the Internet plays a role in promoting the islanders' struggle against a despotic dictator in *Villa Rosa*. Moreover, the essentially age-old and fairy-tale quality of the stories evoked in texts like *Doublures* and *Rose Mélie Rose* is superseded in the later texts by sinister tales of Mafiaesque corruption, murder, greed and prostitution.[1] And what can be described as the increasingly Americanised flavour of Redonnet's later fiction is compounded by the incorporation into the texts of elements of the classic detective novel.

But if certain elements of the œuvre have changed, others have proved to be more abiding. Still very much to the fore in the later texts is what one

critic has termed the 'disarming simplicity' of the writing.[2] Equally enduring has been the thematic interest in the notion of identity. Indeed, identity,
and more specifically the quest for identity, remains at the very core of
Redonnet's work. It is even possible to argue that the texts of the 1990s are
merely updated or modernised versions of the story played out in the earlier
texts, with the following proviso: if the quest for identity taking place in the
texts of the 1980s is a predominantly female one, that quest has been broad-
ened out in the more recent texts to include a number of central male characters whose sense of identity is as fragile as that of their female predecessors.

Identity is a particularly elusive commodity in Redonnet's textual universe. From the eponymous *doublures* (doubles) of the 1986 text who
strive, however erroneously, to compensate for their radically depleted
sense of self via the assimilation, even plagiarism, of the attributes and
characteristics of others, right through to the 1996 text *Villa Rosa* whose
protagonist – an artist called Henri Matisse – must divest himself of his
name and forge a new identity if he is to be able to produce paintings which
are more than mere copies of the works of his illustrious namesake, the
struggle to elaborate a more coherent and enduring sense of self than that
which originally exists is the main issue at stake in Redonnet's work. There
are, of course, a number of factors which can be used to account for the
enfeebled – and ultimately enfeebling – nature of the identity with which
characters are afflicted. The majority of Redonnet's characters exist in a
largely hostile landscape, one which threatens not only some abstract
notion of identity but their very material existence. A recurrent feature of
the œuvre is the threat and/or eventual experience of death through *en-
gloutissement* (being swallowed up) by the landscape. Much more significant, however, than the threat to identity posed by the landscape are the
implications for identity of the complete absence of characters' immediate
forebears. The absence or erasure of the protagonists' biological parents is
virtually *de rigueur* in Redonnet's œuvre, with the result that they never
know or have only the scantiest of information about their origins. One
consequence of this deletion of the protagonists' antecedents is that they
are effectively denied access to the past: there are no forebears to act as
repository of the past, to foster and/or pass on memory and identity.
Hence, when Mélie in *Rose Mélie Rose* remarks, 'Quand Rose m'a trouvée
dans la grotte, j'étais sans rien' (p. 10) ('When Rose found me in the grotto,
I had nothing' (p. 3)), one may read her words not merely as a statement of
physical destitution. One may also infer from them a much more profound
and debilitating kind of impoverishment; that is, the absence or loss of the

psychological inheritance which memory, knowledge and understanding of the past constitute.

For many of Redonnet's characters, then, the past is a blank and their memories are either full of holes or completely non-existent. In *Splendid Hôtel*, Adel is described as having gaps in her memory (p. 20), while Ada suffers from amnesia.[3] In *Rose Mélie Rose*, Mélie starts out upon her quest for identity with just one memory or *souvenir*,[4] while in *Nevermore*, Cassy Mac Key can empathise with Willy Bost because both of them lack memory (p. 158).[5] Although it is never made explicit, the consequences of this deficient memory – or consummate lack of memory – for characters thus afflicted are that their quest for identity will be a frustrated and empty one, if it is not premised first upon a quest for memory. To put it quite simply, the ramifications of lacking memory include the inability to forge a lasting identity. The fundamental role played by memory in the formation of identity is pointed up by Milan Kundera in the novel *Identity*:

> Remembering our past, carrying it with us always, may be the necessary requirement for maintaining, as they say, the wholeness of the self. To ensure that the self doesn't shrink, to see that it holds on to its volume, memories have to be watered like potted flowers, and the watering calls for regular contact with the witnesses of the past.[6]

Similarly, for Luce Irigaray, memory is 'the place where identity is formed, the place where each person builds his or her ground or territory'.[7] If memory *is* the place where identity is formed, if 'wholeness of the self' is indeed contingent upon one's ability to remember the past, then little wonder that so many of Redonnet's characters, devoid of a past or with a severely truncated knowledge of it, are destined to remain identity-less. For those who do go on to develop a more fully-fledged sense of self, at least part of their success is, as we are about to see, due to their capacity to make memory for and of themselves, to *create* a past.

The artistic endeavour is a recurrent feature of Redonnet's texts. From *Doublures*, with its cast of costume-makers, toy-makers, acrobats and performers, right through to *Villa Rosa*, whose eponymous villa is a haven for painters, dancers and musicians, the desire to invent and create is one which impels a vast array of characters. In many cases a veritable compulsion, the creative act is seen by Redonnet's characters as a means of generating identity, or, at the very least, of elaborating a fuller, more cohesive and enduring sense of self than that which originally exists. This, as will be seen, is because of its ability to preserve, and even to produce memory.

The range and diversity of creative acts carried out by the characters is, at times, bewildering, but certain forms crop up again and again. In *Candy story* and *Villa Rosa*, (self-)portraiture is a common pursuit, whilst photography, and its correlative of film-making, feature in the texts *Rose Mélie Rose, Candy story, Le Cirque Pandor* and *Fort Gambo*.[8] The importance of the photograph is illustrated in many of Redonnet's texts. In *Candy story*, Ma's photograph album is a cherished possession, the only thing retained by the narrator, Mia, when Ma dies, while in *Seaside*, the grandmother's tenacious grip on her album is relinquished only as a result of her death.[9] In each of these cases, the photograph and/or photograph album is perceived and treated as a kind of lifeblood, a potent symbol of the past and a means of retaining some kind of grip on, or control over it.

At its most basic level, a photograph is evidence, a visual sign or signifier of the existence now or in the past of an individual or thing. As Susan Sontag puts it in *On Photography*: 'Photographs furnish evidence. Something we hear about, but doubt, seems proven when we're shown a photograph of it . . . A photograph passes for incontrovertible proof that a given thing happened'.[10] The evidential capacities of the photograph are what render it so important in Redonnet's œuvre. In the quest for, and construction of, identity taking place in her works, photographs play a vital role because they offer visual – and thus seemingly irrefutable – proof of the subject's existence. But what Sontag neglects to make explicit here is that the photograph is also a means of gaining purchase upon the past. The real significance of the photograph as far as Redonnet's work is concerned resides in the fact that it not only offers an *entrée* into the past, but can also actually create a past for those characters whose history is a blank, as well as acting as an incitement to, or trigger of, memory. Annette Kuhn contends that the photograph is 'a prop, a prompt, a pre-text: it sets the scene for recollection'.[11] This contention is clearly borne out in the following excerpt from *Candy story*:

> J'ai seulement emmené une photo . . . C'est la plus belle photo de Ma que je connais. On ne voit qu'elle sur la photo. Elle sourit d'un sourire que je ne lui connais pas. C'est de ce sourire-là que j'ai envie de me souvenir. (p. 65)

> (All I took away was a photo . . . It's the most beautiful photo of Ma I know. All you can see is her. She is smiling a smile I don't recognise. It's this smile I want to remember.)

What is most interesting about the above is the way in which the narrator Mia construes the photograph not merely as a prompt to memory, but, more significantly, as a means of filling in the gaps in her own memory, as a means, therefore, of *manufacturing memory*: as she makes clear, Mia has never actually seen Ma smile as she does in the photograph. This capacity of the photograph to witness the past and thereby to create or make memory is particularly important in Redonnet's textual universe, made up as it is of characters starved of memory, and explains also the avidity with which they take and hold onto photographs.[12] In Redonnet's œuvre, there seems to be a consensus among the characters that, as Sontag puts it, 'photographs are not so much an instrument of memory as an invention of it or a replacement' (p. 165).

In *Family Secrets*, Kuhn includes the photograph in the genre of what she terms the 'memory text' (p. 4). This is a category into which many of the artefacts resulting from the creative exploits of Redonnet's characters fall. In addition to photographs, there is a variety of other types of 'memory text' in the process of being constructed, some of them solely visual in nature, some made up of writing, some a mixture of both. *Villa Rosa*, for example, closes with an evocation of the abandoned Villa Rosa, upon whose walls the traces of the paintings of monsieur Jean still remain:

> Entre les plantes et les fleurs . . . un visiteur curieux aurait pu découvrir . . . des morceaux de fresques et de tableaux, aux couleurs toujours vives . . . Il aurait pu alors rêver à la Villa Rosa telle qu'elle avait dû être avant de tomber en ruines, et en réinventer l'histoire pour en sauver la mémoire. (p. 81)
>
> (Among the plants and flowers . . . the curious visitor could have found . . . remnants of frescoes and paintings, their colours still bright . . . He could then have dreamed of the Villa Rosa as it must have been before it fell into ruin, and have reinvented its history in order to preserve its memory.)

When all else has faded and fallen into ruin, a veritable treasure trove of images, their bright colours undimmed, has resisted the passage of time. The capacity of the painting to act – in much the same way as the photograph – as a witness to the past is made clear, and its capacity for endurance pointed up. More importantly, the role imputed here to the visitor of the future is that of the (re)creation or (re)invention of the past and thus the memory of Villa Rosa. That this invention may well be pure fabrication based on the visitor's imagination or dreams is of little significance; what is important is the need to preserve memory, fictional or otherwise, and the paintings will constitute the raw materials of, or cata-lyst to, the process of memory production. In *Villa Rosa*, it is also worth noting that what becomes the artist's haven of Villa Rosa was used for-merly as a refuge for members of the island's resistance movement. An analogy between the act of (political) resistance and the artistic act is thereby implied, and the artistic endeavour does indeed become a form of resistance in Redonnet's œuvre; that is, resistance against amnesia. Thus, for Willy Bost in *Nevermore*, the production of a written text is a means both of resisting a dearth of memory as well as restoring lost memory, irrespective of whether the memory thus created is a fictional or imagined one:

> Willy Bost a beau chercher dans sa mémoire, il ne se rappelle rien de ses parents ... Ce qui rend son livre si difficile à écrire, c'est d'être un livre de mémoire qui s'écrit d'une absence de mémoire. Cette mémoire s'invente au fur et à mesure qu'il écrit. (pp. 142-3)
>
> (Willy Bost searches his memory in vain, for he remembers nothing of his parents ... What makes his book so difficult to write is that it's a book of memories founded on an absence of memory. As he writes, memory is being invented.)

Incidentally, the memory that Willy Bost is inventing here takes on a particularly sinister configuration, for, as the text progresses, it becomes clear that his parents died in a death camp which has now been erased. His text, and by extension, Redonnet's œuvre, may thus be read as an allegory of the necessity for the creative act, and especially writing, as a means of resisting memory loss or collective amnesia. And *Nevermore* in particular – seeking to resist the deletion of the memory of the horrors of the past – might even be read as a contemporary commemoration of the victims of the Holocaust.

Willy Bost is far from being alone among Redonnet's characters in ascribing to writing the role of making and saving memory. Indeed, writing is one of the most common forms of artistic endeavour in her work, and books or written documents tend to be perceived by many char-acters as preferable to those 'memory texts' constituted purely of visual images. Evident in Redonnet's *L'Accord de paix*, for example, is a subtle vilification of the contemporary cult of the visual image, symbolised by the flashy and futuristic Palais de l'Image (Palace of the Image), and an under-lying sense of regret at the way in which books are being increasingly side-lined by the creation of more sophisticated – but perhaps also more

ephemeral – technologies.[13] Similarly, in *Rose Mélie Rose*, a sneaking dis-
trust of the effectiveness on its own of the photographic 'memory text' is
implied by Mélie's assiduous formulation of a written inscription to
accompany each image: '*Au dos de la photo, j'ai écrit: Mélie à douze ans,
photographiée par le photographe de Oat au 1 rue des Cigognes*' (p. 47) ('On
the back of the photo, I wrote: *Mellie aged twelve, photographed by the
photographer of Oât at 1 Storks Street*' (p. 33)). Whereas Roland Barthes
argues that writing, because it is made out of language, can never be as
trustworthy as the photographic image (for him the ultimate means of
authentication),[14] Redonnet's Mélie has limited faith in the capacity of the
photograph alone to capture the past. She sees the need for words as well
as for images, and her inscriptions are intended to flesh out, but also to
anchor the image, to fix its meaning. That there is much need for this kind
of anchorage is implied by Sontag when she writes: 'A photograph is only
a fragment, and with the passing of time its moorings come unstuck. It
drifts away into a soft abstract pastness, open to any kind of reading' (p.
71). Given the particularly wayward quality, *even at the moment of their
conception*, of the photographs in Redonnet's œuvre (in *Rose Mélie Rose*
alone, they are imprecise and blurred, even empty of their intended subjects),[15] the supplementation of a written inscription is utterly essential if
they are to act as meaningful and lasting 'memory texts'.

Of all of Redonnet's texts, it is, however, in *Candy story* that the role of
the writer as a witness to the past and that of the written text as a repository
of memory and potential identity are most fully explored, since a bewildering number of characters (Witz, Curtz, Rotz, Dilo, Stev, Will, Lou, Erma,
Bobby Wick, to cite but a few) engage in the act of writing. Thus, the narrator Mia is a writer, whose first book is significantly entitled 'Sise
Memories', Sise being the name of a place in the text. It is my contention
that the English homonym contained in the title of Mia's text acts as
Redonnet's imperative to her characters to grasp onto or *seize* memory, in
much the same way that the book itself is a means of seizing, containing and
preserving the memories of the place named Sise.[16] Further examples of
the text's multifaceted capacity to seize and preserve memory are demonstrated when Mia recounts the story of loss and obliteration underpinning
Sise's past, and also when she claims to have signed 'Sise Memories' not
with her own name but with that of Ma. This desire to safeguard *via the
text* both memory and identity is contrasted starkly with the story of the
ship's captain who, in spite of an illustrious past, dies unknown and largely
forgotten:

Ma m'a toujours dit que les habitants de Sise ne ressemblaient à personne ... C'étaient les rescapés d'un grand naufrage. Dans leur barque de sauvetage, ils étaient arrivés à Sise ... Ma me racontait que le commandant, qui avait disparu avec son bateau, était le premier à avoir découvert l'Amérique. Mais il avait emporté sa découverte dans la mort et son nom était resté inconnu. Son fils, qui commandait la barque de sauvetage, était l'ancêtre de son grand-père, le gardien du phare de Sise, qui portait son nom. C'est pour continuer de porter ce nom que Ma ne s'est jamais mariée, et c'est pour que ce nom ne se perde pas que j'ai signé *Sise Memories* du nom de Ma. (pp. 49–50)

(Ma always told me that the inhabitants of Sise were like no one else ... They were the survivors of a great shipwreck. They arrived in Sise in a lifeboat ... Ma told me that the captain, who went down with his ship, was the first person to discover America. But he took his discovery with him to his death and his name remained unknown. His son, who took charge of the lifeboat, was the ancestor of [Ma's] grandfather, who was lighthouse-keeper in Sise and who had the same surname. It was in order to preserve this name that Ma never married, and it was to prevent this name from dying out that I signed *Sise Memories* with Ma's name.)

This perception of the written text as a means of preservation is illustrated again and again in *Candy story*. Thus, another more contemporary captain attempts to capture his own memories by writing his memoirs. When his text is discovered after his death, it turns out to be nothing more than a notebook containing lists of numbers and calculations, its cover stained in blood (p. 76). And yet, one might well argue that this captain does indeed succeed in leaving behind a text replete with memory and identity, for what more effective and tangible means of (self-)inscription can there be than a notebook imprinted with one's own blood?[17] Other characters who attempt to produce what are quite literally 'memory texts' include Witz, the celebrated spy-novelist, who is engaged in writing his memoir (p. 24), and Lou who throughout her life has kept a diary or journal (p. 55). That 'Candy story', the text Mia purportedly sets out to write at the end of the text, is also a kind of memoir, even an autobiography, seems plausible, given that the book is, as its title suggests, the story of Candy, Mia's alias.

This effort on the part of the characters above to render memory into text, to render *themselves* in text is contrasted with those characters in Redonnet's œuvre who are not inscribed in or via text. Thus, in *Silsie*, the memory of the engineer will eventually be occulted, for, without some form of inscription, that memory will not endure: 'Personne à Dolms ne se souvient de l'ingénieur, sauf Souie et moi. Pour Souie, c'est un souvenir sans paroles' (No one in Dolms remembers the engineer apart from Souie and me. For Souie, the memory is one without words).[18] An identical fate awaits the mine in which the engineer spent so much of his time. Not mentioned in the town's archives, it is destined to fall into oblivion: 'La mine appartient au passé de Dolms . . . et c'est un passé sans archives' (p. 125) (The mine belongs to Dolms's past . . . and there is no archive of this past). It is the wordless memory or the archiveless past which the memory-makers in Redonnet's œuvre are so desperate to avoid, for their own place in that past will be fixed and confirmed, perhaps even immortalised, if only they can succeed in rendering that past into text.

Of course, not all Redonnet's memory-makers do succeed, and immortality is far from being guaranteed. In *Candy story* alone, Witz will drown, taking with him his memoir (p. 70), and the captain's bloodstained notebook will be burnt by Mia (p. 78), who also gives away Ma's self-portrait to a random security guard, himself engaged in the deletion of memory (p. 78). Thus, while many of Redonnet's characters are the guardians of memory, others (and sometimes even those characters who simultaneously attempt to preserve it) engage in its wilful destruction. In an article on memory in Redonnet's work, Marie Darrieussecq claims that there is no real consensus in Redonnet's œuvre about the benefits of remembering versus the dangers of forgetting, and that it is, in fact, quite difficult to decide which is the more threatening – forgetting or remembering.[19] While I agree with Marie Darrieussecq's contention that a kind of ethics of memory is established in Redonnet's work, I would argue that, as far as identity is concerned, and in keeping with Kundera's and Irigaray's contentions about the role of memory in the construction of identity, a lack or loss of memory is far more dangerous than the act of remembrance. Moreover, it is more often than not the 'good' characters – Rose and Mélie in *Rose Mélie Rose*, Mia and Ma in *Candy story* – who succeed in making and preserving memory and inscribing identity. And it is the memorial made out of writing which is perceived as the surest way of preserving oneself as well as others, for, in the uncertain and treacherous spaces of Redonnet's texts, it is the written sign or text which lasts longer than anything else. Thus, in *Candy story* and in other of Redonnet's texts, the 'nevermore' (the constant threat of death and obliteration) is resisted or, at the very least, tempered by the 'evermore' of the characters' inscriptions. The past (and its inhabitants) may indeed be gone forever, but as Redonnet's work intimates:

that does not mean it is lost to us. The past is like the scene of a crime: if
the deed itself is irrecoverable, its traces may still remain. From these
traces, markers that point towards a past presence, to something that has
happened in this place, a (re)construction, if not a simulacrum . . . can be
pieced together. (Kuhn, p. 4)

In an article on the contemporary novel in France, Christian Michel
claims that, in the work of novelists such as Marie Darrieussecq and Marie
NDiaye, it is possible to identify an interrogation of the function of literature and, more specifically, of writing as a means of safeguarding the past
and transmitting memory.[20] In the same article, Michel characterises
writing (interestingly, in contrast to the photograph) as '[le] dernier, voire
unique, média à avoir la mémoire longue' (p. 66) ([the] last, indeed the
only, medium with a long memory). Although he makes no mention of
Redonnet's fiction, the pertinence of his remarks for her work is striking.
For, in Redonnet's work, the act of writing is perceived as a palliative – to
lapsed, lost or obliterated memory as well as to the fragile or fragmented
identity which is a consequence of it. More than that, writing offers some
kind of protection against the ephemeral nature of life, the vagaries of
memory and the omnipresence of death. Protected, even immunised
against obliteration by their (self-)inscriptions, characters like Mélie can
expire in peace. And that this urgent compulsion to write impels Redonnet
herself is revealed in 'Réponses pour une question brouillée', in which the
writer notes the text's power to save: 'Je n'écris pas pour la postérité, mais
pour sauver ma vie en faisant une œuvre' (italics mine) (I am writing, not
for posterity, but in order to save my life by making of it an œuvre).[21] For
Redonnet, therefore, as well as for the characters who people her texts, the
creative endeavour – and the act of writing in particular – is no mere
pastime or trivial pursuit, but lifeblood and lifeline, a thread which may
save.

Notes

1 Marie Redonnet, *Candy story* (Paris: POL, 1992); *Villa Rosa* (Charenton: Flohic,
   1996); *Doublures* (Paris: POL, 1986); *Rose Mélie Rose* (Paris: Minuit, 1987); *Rose
   Mellie Rose*, trans. Jordan Stump (Lincoln: University of Nebraska Press, 1994).
   All translations, apart from those taken from Stump's translation of *Rose Mellie
   Rose*, are my own.

2 See Raymond Bellour's review of *L'Accord de paix*, *Magazine Littéraire*, 390
   (2000), 86.

3 *Splendid Hôtel* (Paris: Minuit, 1986).

4 Note that the French for memory is *souvenir*, so when Mélie takes down the sign over the door of the Hermitage claiming that this is her only *souvenir* (*Rose Mélie Rose*, p. 15), her words can be read on two levels – the sign will act as a souvenir of her life in the Hermitage and as her only memory.

5 Marie Redonnet, *Nevermore* (Paris: POL, 1994).

6 Milan Kundera, *Identity* (London: Faber & Faber, 1999), p. 43.

7 Luce Irigaray, 'Flesh colours', in *Sexes and Genealogies*, trans. Gillian C. Gill (New York: Columbia University Press, 1993), pp. 153–65 (p. 161).

8 Marie Redonnet, *Le Cirque Pandor* followed by *Fort Gambo* (Paris: POL, 1994).

9 Marie Redonnet, *Seaside* (Paris: Minuit, 1992).

10 Susan Sontag, *On Photography* (New York: Farrar, Straus and Giroux, 1973), p. 5.

11 Annette Kuhn, *Family Secrets: Acts of Memory and Imagination* (London: Verso, 1995), p. 12.

12 Mélie in *Rose Mélie Rose* is the best illustration of this as she takes twelve photographs throughout the course of the text.

13 Marie Redonnet, *L'Accord de paix* (Paris: Grasset, 2000).

14 See Roland Barthes, *La Chambre claire: note sur la photographie* (Paris: Seuil, 1980), p. 123, where Barthes contends that 'dans la Photographie, la présence de la chose . . . n'est jamais métaphorique' (in the Photograph, the presence of the object . . . is never metaphorical).

15 See, for example, the photograph taken of Yem and Mélie by Cob, p. 112, in which Yem and Mélie do not appear.

16 It should be pointed out, however, that my reading of the title 'Sise Memories' is in direct opposition to that suggested by Fieke Schoots in *Passer en douce à la douane: l'écriture minimaliste de Minuit: Deville, Echenoz, Redonnet et Toussaint* (Amsterdam and Atlanta GA: Rodopi, 1997). Schoots reads 'Sise Memories' as 'cease memories', claiming that the title calls for an end to memory (p. 95).

17 In other of Redonnet's texts such as *Rose Mélie Rose* and *Seaside*, bloodstains constitute 'memory texts'.

18 Marie Redonnet, *Silsie* (Paris: Gallimard, 1990), p. 125.

19 See Marie Darrieussecq, 'Marie Redonnet et l'écriture de la mémoire', in Dominique Viart (ed.), *Ecritures contemporaines 1: mémoires du récit* (Paris and Caen: Lettres Modernes Minard, 1998), pp. 177–94.

20 Christian Michel, 'Le réel dort aussi: un panorama du jeune roman français', *Esprit*, 225 (1996), 43–67.

21 Marie Redonnet, 'Réponses pour une question brouillée', *Quai Voltaire*, 2 (1991), 45–8 (47–8).

The female vampire: Chantal Chawaf's melancholic *autofiction*

Julia Kristeva opens her text, *Soleil noir: dépression et mélancolie*, with the claim that 'Ecrire sur la mélancolie n'aurait de sens, pour ceux que la mélancolie ravage, que si l'écrit même venait de la mélancolie' ('For those who are racked by melancholia, writing about it would have meaning only if writing sprang out of that very melancholia').[1] This chapter explores the possibility of writing 'de la mélancolie' through focusing on the work of Chantal Chawaf, whose writing may be described as 'melancholic *autofiction*', melancholic autobiographical fiction. We know from interviews and publicity notices accompanying Chawaf's texts that she was born during a bomb explosion in Paris in 1943 in which her parents were killed and she was extracted from her dying mother's womb by Caesarian section.[2] Since Chawaf's first novel *Retable/La Rêverie* (1974), which features a melancholic orphan whose parents were killed in a bomb explosion in the Second World War, her novels have repeatedly returned to fictionalised scenes of parental death.[3] This chapter deals with Chawaf's 1993 novel, *Vers la lumière*, which is narrated by a woman, France, who witnessed the brutal murder of her parents as a very young child – or, perhaps, while in the womb – in the family home, Meininguel. France is melancholically unable to articulate and come to terms with her traumatic loss and remains haunted by the vampiric figure of her dead mother until she commits suicide by drowning at the end of the text. This text foregrounds the question of how to speak, or write, melancholia. In the first pages of *Soleil noir*, Kristeva assumes the subject position of a melancholic: 'La blessure que *je* viens de subir' (p. 13; my italics) ('The wound *I* have just suffered' (p. 3)). In speaking as a melancholic, rather than as an analyst, she seems to suggest that melancholia demands a first-person subject position.

Yet psychoanalytic theories of melancholia following from Freud repeatedly emphasise that melancholia precisely cannot be spoken in the first
person. In this chapter, I focus on the figure of the female vampire in *Vers
la lumière* in order to explore what it means to 'write melancholia' in the
first person.

Chawaf's stated aim is 'écrire, pour que l'indicible puisse se dire' (to
write, so that the unspeakable can be spoken): Chawaf claims to write in
order to give voice to the unspeakable in and beyond her own experience.[4]
She associates the 'unspeakable' with the body, with bodily sensations and
symptoms that are excluded from language: 'Ecrire un roman, pour moi,
aujourd'hui, c'est chercher à accueillir dans le langage ce qui était relégué
hors du langage et restait bloqué à l'état de pulsions, confusion, symp-
tômes' ('Donner aux émotions', p. 10) (Writing a novel, for me, now, means
trying to bring into language what was relegated outside language and
remained blocked, on the level of drives, confusion, symptoms). If the
'unspeakable' is repeatedly linked to the body in Chawaf's writing, it is also
related to the mother's traumatic death that recurs throughout her texts
and yet can never be articulated as such, to the loss that cannot be
mourned. In *Vers la lumière*, this unspeakable loss is given voice through
the figure of the female vampire: this text draws on a longstanding tradition
of dead mothers returning to their daughters as vampires and explores a
specifically feminine melancholia. Yet the figure of the female vampire also
offers a suggestive means of reading Chawaf's writing as autobiographical
fiction. A recurring figure of a bleeding female vampire in *Vers la lumière*
shows up the ways in which melancholia stains and contaminates autobiographical writing, reconfiguring the relation between text and writing
subject and even, perhaps, allowing unspeakable loss to be spoken.

Melancholia and vampirism: Freud and Kristeva

In his 1915 essay, 'Mourning and melancholia', Freud posits mourning and
melancholia as different responses to the loss of a love object. Where the
mourner gradually withdraws libido from its attachments to the lost object,
the melancholic, unable to avow the loss, desires to incorporate the lost
object into the self.[5] This incorporation is oral: Freud writes that 'The ego
wants to incorporate this object into itself and [. . .] it wants to do so by
devouring it', so that the melancholic ego feeds vampirically off the lost
object.[6] Where the mourner must symbolically 'kill off' the love object, the
melancholic directs the murderous impulses inwards and thus tends

towards suicidal fantasies. Melancholia, imaged as 'a painful wound' (p. 268), figuratively drains the subject of his/her lifeblood: it is like 'an open wound [. . .] emptying the ego until it is totally impoverished' (p. 262). Kristeva develops this vampiric imagery in *Soleil noir*, describing the melancholic as one of the living dead. Assuming the subject position of a melancholic, she claims that 'Je vis une mort vivante, chair coupée, saignante, cadavérisée' (p. 14) ('I live a living death, my flesh is wounded, bleeding, cadaverized' (p. 4)). In Kristeva's formulation, the melancholic cannot bear to lose the object and thus vampirically tears open its flesh and devours it: in her words, 'plutôt morcelé, déchiqueté, coupé, avalé, digéré. . . que perdu' (p. 21) ('Better fragmented, torn, cut up, swallowed, digested. . . than lost' (p. 12)).

In *Soleil noir*, melancholia is associated particularly with the loss of the mother, with what Kristeva calls the '*deuil impossible de l'objet maternel*' (p. 19) ('*impossible mourning for the maternal object*' (p. 9)). In Kristeva's model, the melancholic subject, unable to mourn and thus exiled from language and symbolisation, remains attached to the mother. To move into the Symbolic order, Kristeva insists, means symbolically killing and mourning the mother, gaining access to a language and symbolisation that compensate for the mother's loss. Yet this process is gendered: matricide – in her words, 'notre nécessité vitale' (p. 38) ('our vital necessity' (p. 27)) – is particularly difficult for a daughter, who sees her own image reflected in her mother and thus cannot symbolically kill an image of herself. Assuming the subject position of a melancholic daughter, Kristeva writes:

> Comment peut-Elle être cette Erinyes assoiffée de sang, puisque je suis Elle . . . Elle est moi? En conséquence, la haine que je lui porte ne s'exerce pas vers le dehors, mais s'enferme en moi . . . une humeur implosive qui s'emmure et me tue en cachette. (p. 39)

> (How can she be that Bloodthirsty Fury, since I am She . . . She is I ? Consequently, the hatred I bear her is not oriented towards the outside but is locked up within myself . . . an implosive mood that walls itself in and kills me secretly. (*Black Sun*, p. 29)

The melancholic daughter in *Soleil noir* locks her death-bearing hatred inside her own body, and is thus symbolically inhabited by death, a 'crypte habité par un cadavre vivant' (p. 241) ('crypt inhabited by a living corpse' (p. 233)).

Vers la lumière extends this imagery of female melancholia as an eternal yet unspeakable living death, yet it is describing a different scenario

from that presented in *Soleil noir*. For Kristeva, the loss of the mother refers
not to her literal death but to the separation from the mother concomitant
with the subject's entry into the Symbolic order; Kristeva does not consider how traumatic bereavement may be experienced differently from
physical separation. *Vers la lumière* seems to present us with an extreme
loss: not the separation from the mother that every child goes through as
s/he grows up, but loss engendered by a traumatic death, loss that is
'unspeakable' for different reasons. My aim here is not, however, to analyse
different experiences of loss, but to focus on how the loss of the mother is
articulated in *Vers la lumière* through the figure of the female vampire.

The female vampire

Since Dracula, most vampire stories have featured a bloodthirsty male
vampire feeding off and seducing female victims, a plot used by Chawaf in
her 1986 novel, *L'Intérieur des heures* and her 1989 novel, *Rédemption*.[7]
There is, however, also a long-standing female vampire tradition in which
vampires are commonly associated with deceased mothers: in Paul
Barber's words, 'although vampires are far more often male than female, the
exception to this rule is commonly women who have died in childbirth'.[8]
Where the male vampire story tends to involve violent seduction, the
female vampire tradition is rooted in an intimacy and identification
between women that is often associated with the relationship between
mother and daughter; the female vampire is often portrayed as a melancholic mother figure. This is exemplified in a founding text of female vampirism, Sheridan Le Fanu's nineteenth-century novella, *Carmilla*, in which
the vampiric Carmilla is likened to the dead mother of the narrator, Laura.[9]
Although it is Laura's mother who is dead, it is Carmilla who seems melancholic; gradually, however, Laura seems to be contaminated by
Carmilla's melancholia. Carmilla declares to Laura, 'I live in your warm life
and you shall die – die, sweetly die – into mine' (p. 21). The two women
seem to merge into one another and share in a common melancholia
figured as a shared living death (p. 35).

Although *Vers la lumière* bears little resemblance to contemporary
vampire fiction or to modern versions of *Carmilla*, Chawaf's text implicitly
refers back to Carmilla through the character of Carmilla, the woman who
employs France to ghost-write her dead husband's memoirs and to whom
France refers as a 'mère vampire' (p. 167) (mother vampire). The most striking vampire in the text is, however, associated with France's dead mother:

France claims that: 'Moi, dans mon cœur inhabité, je sentais que j'étais la fille de la vampire' (p. 89) (Me, in my inhabited heart, I felt that I was the daughter of the vampire). This vampiric figure embodies France's melancholic fantasy that her mother's death does not mark her loss, but rather the beginning of an eternal life in death. The presence of the vampire (even in fantasy) allows France to deny her loss: to rephrase Kristeva, better dead than lost. Yet, according to popular Eastern European folklore, vampires cannot be easily killed off, and abide eternally in a living death. In imaging the lost love object as a vampire, *Vers la lumière* highlights the near impossibility of symbolically killing it off and thus emphasises the extreme difficulty of overcoming melancholia.

The vampiric mother figure in *Vers la lumière* evokes and recalls the vampiric Carmilla but, where Carmilla moves between life with Laura and her father and death in her tomb, the vampire in Chawaf's text exists in a perpetual state of living death. Like Carmilla, the vampire in *Vers la lumière*, named Vampyra Mélancholia, is, as her name suggests, a melancholic, haunting France throughout the text and calling for her to join her in death (p. 156). Vampyra appears to embody France's own sorrow, performing the extreme grief that France cannot articulate directly, so that France projects her own melancholic refusal of loss onto the fantasised figure of the vampiric mother.

This projection of grief and reversal of roles is emphasised by France's narrative deployment of the Greek myth of Demeter and Persephone, a myth described by Anne Juranville as 'un mythe de la mélancolie originaire propre à la femme' (a founding myth of female melancholia).[10] France repeatedly alludes to herself as Persephone, 'en langue infernale: la traduction de mon nom' (p. 156) (in infernal language, the translation of my name), casting her husband Dagan as Hades and her mother as Demeter. In Homer's *Hymn to Demeter*, Persephone is kidnapped by Hades and taken to the Underworld, whereupon Demeter grieves her daughter excessively.[11] In *Vers la lumière*, France assumes the role of Persephone, abducted by Dagan, 'le dieu des morts' (p. 17) (the god of the dead), and taken to his underground home. The vampiric mother figure, like Demeter, searches obsessively for her daughter. Yet where in the myth, Persephone is symbolically 'killed' (by being abducted to Hades, the world of the dead) and Demeter grieves, in this novel it is the Demeter figure who is killed. In the myth, the living mother grieves for the dead child, whereas in the novel the dead mother grieves for her living child. This reversal highlights France's projection of her unspeakable grief onto a fantasy of her dead mother as a melancholic vampire. France's first-person narrative of loss appears compelled to voice melancholia through the (fantasised) wounds of the other, the grieving mother.

Although this fantasised projection of grief does not figure in Freudian or Kristevan accounts of melancholia, it plays an integral role in the account of melancholia given by Maria Torok and Nicolas Abraham in *L'Ecorce et le noyau* (*The Shell and the Kernel*). According to Torok and Abraham, the melancholic constructs what they call an intrapsychic crypt inside the subject, in which secretly to preserve the lost object. The object, however, succeeds in escaping from the crypt to be, in their words, 'réincarn[é] dans la personne même du sujet' ('reincarnated in the person of the subject'), like a vampire sustained through feeding off human blood.[12] For Freud, this process marks the ego's identification with the lost object, as the ego comes to imitate the object it cannot bear to lose ('Mourning and melancholia', pp. 259–61). Torok and Abraham take this further in proposing that, in the ego's fantasy, the object also imitates the ego. In melancholic fantasy, the object embodies and acts out the subject's grief, so that subject and object are united in sadness, a shared living death. This fantasy of a shared living death, Torok and Abraham suggest, may be used as a basis for successful mourning. In their model, as in Freud's, melancholia marks a fantasy, a denial of so-called 'reality' (in Freud's words: 'a hallucinatory wishful psychosis' (p. 253)) while mourning constitutes a gradual process of acknowledging the 'reality' of loss. Unlike Freud, however, they claim that it is through fantasy that loss can be realised. The melancholic is invited to 'pousser à bout son fantasme de deuil: "Si celui qui m'aime doit me perdre pour de bon, il ne survivra pas à cette perte"' (*L'Ecorce*, p. 275) ('push his fantasy of mourning to its ultimate conclusion: "If my beloved is to lose me forever, he will not survive this loss"' (*The Shell*, p. 138)). This melancholic fantasy that the lost object is so overcome with grief that she or he will commit suicide enables the melancholic to come to terms with the object's death, not as a betrayal but as a sign of grief. Moving from melancholia to mourning, for Torok and Abraham, means using fantasy to accept the 'reality' of loss.

'Cure' and contamination

In *Vers la lumière*, the fantasy of mourning traced by Torok and Abraham is figured as a shared living death in which France and the vampiric mother figure are unable to identify themselves either as living or as dead. In this text, melancholic subject and lost love object merge and bleed into one another. Feminist analyses of the mythology surrounding Demeter and Persephone have emphasised how these myths rewrite the psychoanalytic insistence on matricide and construct a more positive model of relationships between women based on love and sharing rather than on separation and symbolic murder.[13] In *Vers la lumière*, however, this fusion between self and other, far from enabling a liberating interchange between mother and daughter, suspends both in a form of living death. France remains attached to the traumatic loss of her parents by an umbilical cord, a 'cordon . . . rouge' (p. 9) (red cord). This umbilical cord that cannot be cut, even after birth, does not transmit life-giving nourishment from mother to child, but a destructive and contaminating death. France, 'allaitée par une habitante des ruines sinistres' (p. 88) (suckled by one who lives in the deathly ruins), sucks blood rather than milk from the mother's breast.[14] She feeds parasitically off her parents' bloody deaths, not a foetus nourished by the mother, but a blood-sucking vampire. She is haunted by an insatiable vampiric thirst, 'cette soif qui hante' (p. 114) (this haunting thirst).

This contamination impedes a normative process of mourning: Vampyra blocks France's ability to mourn and to move on to substitute love objects, leaving her symbiotically attached to her traumatic loss. Conventional rites of inheritance are impossible: France cannot claim her ancestral home, because the spectre of her mother will not bequeath it to her ('Ma mère, la revenante, ne m'ouvrirait jamais la porte' (p. 154)) (My mother, the ghost, would never open the door for me)).[15] France's mother teaches her how to 'mourir' (p. 90) (die) instead of how to live. *Vers la lumière* traces an unending process of contamination, as France, increasingly obsessed by her mother's death, in turn contaminates her daughter Jasmine, whose anguished voice blurs into France's own.

This process of endless contamination culminates only in France's suicide by drowning at the end of the text, when a third-person narratorial voice reports that 'Le soir . . . on retrouva France Meininguel noyée' (p. 190) (In the evening . . . France Meininguel was found drowned). In dying, however, France remains trapped in her own melancholic fantasy. She describes her death as a rebirth: 'Je pousse le cri que lance le nouveau-né quand il est expulsé du ventre de sa mère à sa naissance' (p. 189) (I let out the cry of a newborn baby ejected from the mother's stomach at the moment of birth). It is as though she is dying only to be reborn as a vampire; death, far from ending her melancholic fantasies, seems bound up in the melancholic fantasies that have structured and shaped her narrative throughout. There is no possibility of mourning, no escape from melancholic fantasy, which, like the vampire it conjures up, pervades and contaminates the narrative on every level. The text is drawn into and infected by France's fantasy, as even the third-person narrative voice remains unable to offer an external viewpoint on France's narrative. The movement in the text between first- and third-person narrative almost passes unnoticed, as the third-person narrative voice adopts France's imagery and perspective, as we see in the following quotation:

> Terreurs et extases dont on retient un tempo assourdi qui continue de palper dans les artères, dans les vaisseaux, et nous congestionne, et pourrait nous pousser à mourir plus vite pour ne plus entendre cette musique obsédante du sang. (p. 60)

> (Terrors and ecstasies leaving us with a muffled sound that keeps palpating in the arteries, in the vessels, and makes us flushed, and could push us into dying faster in order to hear this obsessive music of blood no longer.)

The bodily images of anguish – blood, arteries, death – echo France's own descriptions of her state of mind cited above, while the long sentence, with its piled-up clauses, imitates France's sentence construction. Moreover, the use of 'on' and 'nous' in relation to France suggests an affinity between the narrator and France, so that the third-person narrative voice becomes indistinguishable from France's own voice. This blurring of the distinctions between subject positions or narrative voices is highlighted further through France's job, ghost-writing a dead actor's memoirs, which impels her to merge her narrative with his. The text foregrounds the difficulty, even impossibility, of narrating one's own story and maintaining a stable subject position. The different narrative voices contaminate each other like France and the vampiric mother figure, blurring the distinctions between fantasy and so-called 'reality'. It remains unclear whether the vampire is merely a product of France's fantasy, or whether it is seen to exist outside that fantasy.

Whereas Torok and Abraham situate their psychoanalytic 'cure' in the distinction between melancholic fantasy and the 'reality' of loss, in *Vers la lumière* there is no analyst to draw such distinctions. The reader, like the third-person narrator, is unable to demarcate the boundaries between fantasy and 'reality' in this text and thus prevented from occupying the position of analyst in relation to the text. *Vers la lumière* does not offer a 'case study' of a melancholic, but, in exploring the relation between melancholia, fantasy and narrative, shows up the impossibility of describing melancholia from one fixed and stable subject position. The merging of first- and third-person narrative voices highlights how in this text melancholia is always spoken from shifting subject positions that blur into each other. This also offers an alternative reading of Kristeva's self-positioning in *Soleil noir* and of her claim that writing on melancholia must come 'de la mélancolie' (from melancholia). Although Kristeva initially assumes the subject position of a melancholic, she goes on to occupy the position of a psychoanalytic linguist (chapter 2), an analyst (chapter 3), an art critic and a literary critic without considering the differences in these positions. To write 'de la mélancolie' is perhaps not, as I suggested in the opening page of this essay, to write in the first person as a melancholic, but to speak from different subject positions without being able to fix one's own position in relation to melancholia. If we read *Soleil noir* alongside *Vers la lumière*, it appears that melancholia, in refusing either an entirely external perspective or an 'inside' position implied in the use of the first-person narrative voice, destabilises subject positions. This is, of course, a crucial point to bear in mind in relation to writing described as *autofiction* such as Chawaf's. In the last part of this chapter, I will address the question of Chawaf's subject position in her own melancholic *autofiction*, not through reading *Vers la lumière* as a case study of Chawaf herself, but through the figure of the vampire that the text deploys to inscribe melancholic loss.

Melancholic *autofiction*

As we have seen, France gives voice to melancholia through a fantasy of staging her own loss in the vampire's performance of death: she can express her loss only through the wounded body of the other. This is highly suggestive in relation to Chawaf's writing, *autofiction* that foregrounds the fraught issue of the relation between writer and text and implicitly invites questions about the subject position of the writer in relation to the narrator. Literary critics working on autobiographical fiction and therapists who advocate a 'writing cure' have suggested that writing in the third person offers more space for self-revelation than writing in the first person. In her study of scriptotherapy, Louise DeSalvo insists that 'Writing creative narratives about pain and loss can heal', adding that this is more effective if the writing subject can project grief onto a fictional alter ego, a 'semi-fictional stand-in'.[16] Suzette Henke reinforces this: 'What cannot be uttered might at least be written – cloaked in the mask of fiction'.[17] For these critics, *autofiction* in particular enables the writing subject to affirm a loss that would be unnarratable in the first person through projecting it onto a fictional double: the narrator is seen as a thinly veiled alter ego of the author.

In *Vers la lumière*, however, the narrating subject, France, cannot project her loss onto a fantasised double: the vampire figures France's melancholic loss without enabling her to mourn. This melancholic vampire should not be seen as France's fantasised alter ego, who embodies her melancholic refusal of loss. Like all vampires, Vampyra cannot survive in isolation: she exists only in and through her contaminated relationship with France. The vampire problematises any fixed, stable relation between subject and object through collapsing the boundaries between self and other: France's narrative voice is contaminated by the vampire it inscribes. The shifting, contaminating relation between France and the vampire may, in my reading, be seen to figure the relation between Chawaf as implied author and her text. Where critics like Henke and DeSalvo working on scriptotherapy posit a direct relation between writer and text, *Vers la lumière* points only indirectly to Chawaf's own loss. Chawaf's parents died during the Occupation, while she was in the womb, whereas France's parents are murdered in their ancestral home before her very eyes. If Chawaf's writing indirectly suggests her own traumatic loss, it can never incorporate that loss as such.

Chawaf's text seems to suggest, then, that the writer cannot simply project her own loss onto her fictional characters; moreover, her own voice, bleeding into other blurred textual voices, cannot easily be distinguished in her text. The figure of the melancholic vampire recurs throughout Chawaf's texts, which blur into each other, as do each of the melancholic heroines: as Valerie Hannagan points out, 'There is a single wounded, merged identity running through the whole corpus'.[18] An indistinguishable figure of a melancholic female orphan recurs throughout Chawaf's texts, from her earliest novel *Retable/La Rêverie* to *Issa*, published in 1999, with no significant development or alteration.[19] Hannagan emphasises that Chawaf's female characters are largely indistinguishable: 'Despite the fact they are given different names, *they are the same woman*' (p. 185). The vampire highlights a fusion and contamination between texts, characters and writer, emphasising the impossibility of individuation in Chawaf's writing. The vampire also, however, as we have seen, points to the impossibility of mourning, showing how Chawaf's texts cannot reach curative closure but remain suspended in a melancholic disavowal.

The figure of the melancholic vampire in Chawaf's writing does not, then, denote a liberating fusion or interchange between self and other, writing subject and text, text and reader, that is so often associated with contemporary French women's writing.[20] *Vers la lumière*, which has hitherto been read almost exclusively in relation to Cixous's work, may thus offer a different understanding of the fusion between self and other in contemporary women's writing. In *Vers la lumière*, self and other merge in a crippling, inescapable living death, that offers none of the possibilities of self-reinvention and renewal implied by Cixous in 'Le rire de la Méduse' or *Photos de racines*.[21] Yet Chawaf's writing should not only be read as a point of comparison with Cixous's writing or as a way to rethink what we mean by *écriture féminine*. *Vers la lumière* also, as we have seen, explores the possibilities of inscribing traumatic loss and melancholia in narrative. The melancholic vampire who haunts the text marks an incurable traumatic loss that is constantly reiterated throughout Chawaf's writing. In Chawaf's *autofiction*, text and writing subject constantly traverse each other's boundaries painfully, bleeding into and contaminating each other without resolution. Each text reinscribes the orphaned, melancholic female writer unable to come to terms with her loss. This traumatic loss, repeated throughout Chawaf's textual corpus, marks the unspeakable, invisible link between 'auto' and 'fiction' in her writing, embodied in the recurring, bleeding figure of the melancholic vampire.

Notes

1 Julia Kristeva, *Soleil noir: dépression et mélancolie* (Paris: Gallimard/Folio, 1987), p. 13; *Black Sun: Depression and Melancholia*, trans. Leon S. Roudiez (New York: Columbia University Press, 1989), p. 3.

2 See in particular the publicity notice that accompanies *L'Intérieur des heures* (Paris: Des femmes, 1986), in which Chawaf states that her mother died before she was born.

3 *Retable/La Rêverie* (Paris: Des femmes, 1974). See also *Elwina, le roman fée* (Paris: Flammarion, 1985) and *Le Manteau noir* (Paris: Flammarion, 1998).

4 Chantal Chawaf, 'Donner aux émotions leur écriture', *La Quinzaine Littéraire*, 532 (1989), 10. My translation.

5 Later, in 'The ego and the id', Freud will see melancholic incorporation as a basis for the process of mourning and even as a universal stage in the development of the ego (see Sigmund Freud, 'The ego and the id' (1923), in *On Metapsychology: The Theory of Psychoanalysis*, Pelican Freud Library, vol. 11, trans. James Strachey, ed. Angela Richards (Harmondsworth: Penguin, 1984), pp. 339-407). In 'Mourning and melancholia', however, melancholic incorporation remains pathological and to be distinguished from mourning.

6 Sigmund Freud, 'Mourning and melancholia' (1917 [1915]), *On Metapsychology*, pp. 245–68 (p. 258).

7 Chantal Chawaf, *L'Intérieur des heures* (Paris: Des femmes, 1986); *Rédemption* (Paris: Flammarion, 1989).

8 Paul Barber, *Vampires. Burial and Death: Folklore and Fantasy* (New Haven and London: Yale University Press, 1988), p. 36.

9 Sheridan Le Fanu, *Carmilla* (Mountain Ash: Sarob Press, 1998).

10 Anne Juranville, *La Femme et la mélancolie* (Paris: PUF, 1993), p. 161.

11 See, for example, Helene P. Foley (ed.), *The Homeric Hymn to Demeter: Translation, Commentary, and Interpretive Essays* (Princeton, NJ: Princeton University Press, 1994).

12 Nicolas Abraham and Maria Torok, *L'Ecorce et le noyau* (Paris: Flammarion, 1987), p. 298 ; *The Shell and the Kernel: Renewals of Psychoanalysis*, 1, trans. Nicholas T. Rand (Chicago: University of Chicago Press, 1994), p. 141.

13 See Elizabeth T. Hayes, 'The Persephone myth in Western literature', in Elizabeth T. Hayes (ed.), *Images of Persephone: Feminist Readings in Western Literature* (Florida: Florida University Press, 1994), pp. 1–19 (p. 10).

14 Joan Copjec has written a fascinating (Lacanian) article on the relation between vampirism and breast-feeding: 'Vampires, breast-feeding and anxiety', *October*, 58 (autumn 1991), 25–43.

15 This contamination of inheritance may also be seen in *Carmilla*, as the vampire Carmilla is also called 'Millarca' and 'Mircalla' (*Carmilla*, pp. 73 and 78).

16 Louise DeSalvo, *Writing as a Way of Healing: How Telling Our Stories Transforms our Lives* (London: The Women's Press, 1999), pp. 55 and 166.

17 Suzette Henke, *Shattered Subjects: Trauma and Testimony in Women's Life-Writing* (New York: St Martin's Press, 1998), p. xix.

18 Valerie Hannagan, 'Reading as a daughter: Chantal Chawaf revisited', in Margaret Atack and Phil Powrie (eds), *Contemporary French Fiction by Women: Feminist Perspectives* (Manchester: Manchester University Press, 1990), p. 185.

19 *Issa* (Paris: Flammarion, 1999). See also notably *Elwina, le roman fée* and *L'Intérieur des heures*.

20 See, for example, Susan Sellars, 'Learning to read the feminine', in Helen Wilcox, Keith McWatters *et al.* (eds), *The Body and the Text: Hélène Cixous, Reading and Teaching* (London: Harvester Wheatsheaf, 1990), pp. 190–5.

21 Hélène Cixous, 'Le rire de la Méduse', *L'Arc*, 61 (1975), 39–54; Hélène Cixous and Mireille Calle-Gruber, *Photos de racines* (Paris: Des femmes, 1994).

Lost and found: mother–daughter relations in Paule Constant's fiction

In 1998 Paule Constant won the Prix Goncourt for her seventh novel *Confidence pour confidence* to much controversy. Her novels had been shortlisted for the Goncourt several times before, and she had gained many other literary prizes. However, press coverage was generally of the opinion that, although the most prestigious French literary prize was long overdue to her, *Confidence pour confidence* itself was not especially deserving of that glory. The controversial reception afforded this novel relates primarily to its subject matter: set in contemporary Kansas, USA, it portrays a group of middle-aged women the morning after a feminist conference. Described variously as banal (because it is about women?) and anti-feminist (because of the bitter and rivalrous women-to-women relations it describes), on first impressions this text seems quite different from Constant's earlier novels, four of which are set in Africa, one in Cayenne and the other in eighteenth-century France. Although each novel stands on its own, shared characters, motifs and themes connect them into a coherent body of work. None the less, *Confidence pour confidence* not only actually does have thematic links with other Constant novels but it even alludes to them within the text itself. Most particularly, the problematic relations between women in *Confidence pour confidence* echo difficult female relationships throughout Constant's work, notably between mothers and daughters. This chapter places *Confidence pour confidence* within Constant's œuvre as a whole, and argues for a more positive reading of the novel – a reading that also throws light on the trajectory of mother–daughter relations in her fiction.

   In Constant's work, the mother–daughter relationship is most often represented as negative, even destructive, and many of her little-girl characters suffer from maternal deprivation to the extent of losing all sense of self. Moreover, the deeply ambivalent mother–daughter relationship, which is most evident in Constant's first novel *Ouregano* and again in *La Fille du Gobernator*, is echoed in maternal configurations beyond the biological relationship, such as the pupil–teacher dyad in *Propriété privée*, a foster mother in *White spirit* as well as the women-to-women relations in *Confidence pour confidence*. This chapter focuses on the specific connections between *Confidence pour confidence* and four of the earlier novels, *Ouregano*, *Propriété privée*, *Balta* and *La Fille du Gobernator*, making links between three female characters: Tiffany (a 7-year old in *Ouregano*, growing up to her teenage years in *Propriété privée* and an adult in *Balta*), Chrétienne, the little-girl character of *La Fille du Gobernator* and Aurore, a French writer and one of the four principal women characters of *Confidence pour confidence*.[1]

The parallels between the characters Tiffany and Chrétienne are striking: in *Ouregano* and *La Fille du Gobernator* respectively, both aged 7, they are taken to live in the Tropics when their fathers take up colonial appointments (Tiffany to the fictional Ouregano in Africa, Chrétienne to Cayenne, South America). During their stay, they are both marked for life by what is experienced as rejection and abandonment by their parents. In *Confidence pour confidence*, the adult Aurore has a somewhat different history but suffers a similar fate: born in Africa, she was orphaned as a child, both her parents killed in a bushfire from which she alone escapes. In all three cases, both parents are involved in the trauma suffered by their daughters, but it is always the loss of, or abandon by, the mother that is the most difficult to cope with. However negative the mother–daughter relationship, the strongest of emotions continue to be invested in it. If the three characters are connected by trauma associated with the mother–daughter relationship, all five novels under discussion are also linked by another loss: the leitmotif of a dying creature which has to be put out of its misery. In *Ouregano*, it is 'la petite bête' (the tiny wild animal), adopted by Tiffany, which escapes and, in the ensuing confusion, is trodden underfoot. Tiffany's mother's voice joins others in urging the 7-year old girl to finish it off, but she is quite unable to do so. Echoes of this episode haunt the following novel *Propriété privée*, most notably when Tiffany symbolically lays to rest the memory of her 'petite bête' by being the only one of her class to be able to kill a suffering guinea pig in the science laboratory. In *Balta*, the victim is human; here, it is the African boy Balta himself, dying of rabies, whose last moments are eased not only by an injection of morphine but also by the human warmth provided by the adult Tiffany who conquers her fear of the sick and dying to cradle him in her arms.

That this recurring motif is a trope for the psychological trauma endured by Constant's little-girl characters, and emblematic both of the loss of the self and of the mother that is at the heart of all the novels, is never clearer than in *La Fille du Gobernator*, in which Chrétienne secretly adopts a puppy against the express orders of her parents. When the animal falls ill, she is ill-equipped to look after it, and in a cruel punishment inflicted by her father, the little girl is forced to shoot the half ant-eaten creature herself to put it out of its misery. If Chrétienne had killed herself instead, the narrative suggests, it would have been preferable to the trauma of living with the memory of this scene for the rest of her life. It is most telling that this particular episode is juxtaposed with the departure of Chrétienne's mother to a leper camp, never to return; she has finally achieved the martyrdom she has been seeking: to become a leper. Significantly, these two events are described in the novel with the same vocabulary. According to Chrétienne's father: 'l'abandon d'un animal est un crime' (p. 153) ('it is a crime to abandon an animal' (p. 123)), while the narration goes on to reveal that Chrétienne's mother 'était partie pour toujours. Elle l'avait définitivement abandonnée' (p. 155) ('was gone for ever. She had abandoned her for good' (p. 125)). The use of the word 'abandon' for both episodes is noteworthy, since it programmes the judgement of the reader against the parents in favour of the little girl. In sacrificing herself, Chrétienne's mother has also made a sacrifice of her daughter, and if, in the view of Chrétienne's strictly Christian father, it is a moral crime to abandon an animal, it must surely also be one to abandon a child. What is more, Chrétienne's father subsequently 'abandons' her too as he goes on to abnegate responsibility for everything and disappears, shipwrecked, thus fulfilling his own desired destiny.

In *Confidence pour confidence*, Constant very explicitly reworks the motif of the suffering creature yet again, when the character Gloria squeezes to death a dehydrated pet jerboa (which she refers to as a 'rat') in order to put an end to its suffering. Here, the system of mirroring between the five novels is also turned in on itself to produce a *mise en abîme* that challenges the distinction between fiction and reality within the novel itself. Not only are multiple references made to a similar scenario from one of the books the character Aurore has written, but also memories resurface of an event in this character's own childhood, which, in turn, is strongly reminiscent of the *petite bête* episode in Constant's *Ouregano*. The fact that Aurore is portrayed as a writer in *Confidence pour confidence* is crucial in the forging of connections between Constant's individual novels and the construction of a cohesive œuvre. In a US lecture, Constant suggests that the character Aurore could actually have written both *Ouregano* and *La Fille du Gobernator*, the latter as a fictional autobiography.[2] This does not mean, however, that Tiffany, Chrétienne and Aurore are one and the same character; nor can they be read autobiographically, and related in a straightforward way to Constant herself, despite the fact that obviously autobiographical elements are included in her work: as a child, Constant lived in turn in Africa and Cayenne with her parents, and she makes no secret of the fact that *Confidence pour confidence* has its roots in her own US experiences. Rather, the metafictional aspects of *Confidence pour confidence* throw into relief the complex relationship between fiction and autobiography, and Constant's individual novels are woven ever more closely into a labyrinthine but connecting literary œuvre. The characters Tiffany, Chrétienne and Aurore are thus entwined, the thread which connects them, providing the key both to their evolution and to the progression of the mother–daughter relationship in Constant's work.

With the intention of following this thread, my focus now shifts to the endings of each of the five novels. The trajectory of the three different characters that is thus revealed unravels a psychological itinerary in which the mother–daughter relationship is deeply implicated. Constant's first novel, *Ouregano*, terminates on Tiffany's separation from her mother at the end of a desperately unhappy year in Africa, in which there is no place for the little girl in her parents' new colonial life. Rejected because of her scruffy appearance, because she does badly at school, and because she simply does not fit in, Tiffany's experiences of Ouregano are described as an 'absence [. . .] [où elle] s'arrêta de vivre' (p. 79) (absence [. . .] [where she] stopped living). The year in Ouregano culminates in her attempt to run away, whereupon she is sent back to France to attend convent school. Immediately branded 'une grande désordonnée' (p. 246) (an extremely untidy girl) by the nuns there, in the final paragraph of *Ouregano* Tiffany is left vomiting all over the dormitory floor. The next novel, *Propriété privée*, which charts Tiffany's difficult years through the convent school, ends on yet another separation or rather here, a whole series of separations: (a) the death of Tiffany's beloved grandmother, the grief of which renders her 'vide de tout et vide d'elle-même' (p. 209) (completely empty, even of herself); (b) the expulsion of Tiffany from the convent school for attacking her teacher, a maternal substitute whose overaffectionate advances she rejects, with an 'envie de vomir' (p. 218) (desire to vomit); (c) the subsequent return of Tiffany's mother from Africa paradoxically brings with it a renewed gulf between mother and daughter. Disgusted with Tiffany's behaviour, her mother rejects her once again: 'ne m'appelle pas maman . . . jusqu'à nouvel ordre, tu ne m'appelles pas maman?' (p. 233) (don't call me mummy again . . . until I say you may, don't call me mummy, do you hear?); (d) the sale of the 'propriété privée' (private property) of the title (Tiffany's grandparents' house), her only happy refuge. The novel ends with the emptying of the house, Tiffany's mother frenziedly throwing the last objects out of the attic window, and the removal lorry drawing away.

Thus, both novels in which Tiffany features as a child end on traumatic separation – and with symbols of purging. In each case (and indeed also in the third 'Tiffany' novel, *Balta*), the ambivalence of the mother–daughter relationship is echoed and reinforced by difficult relations between Tiffany and other adult women. *Balta*, the last Tiffany novel, also ends on a separation, although in this case with an arguably more positive outcome. As a young married woman, Tiffany has returned to what is now post-colonial Africa. She is shown to be unhappy, disconnected both from herself and others.[3] At the end of *Balta*, however, Tiffany appears to begin to move towards recuperation. Her ability to comfort the dying Balta turns out to be more than simply a generous gesture towards another. Opening the book that Balta has carried with him throughout the novel, she finds that it was originally hers. It is thus ultimately revealed (to the reader if not to Tiffany herself) that Balta's father, who gave him the book, is the same person as Moïse, Tiffany's only childhood friend in *Ouregano*. The last words of Constant's novel *Balta* are those that Tiffany reads in the front of Balta's book: '*Tiffany Murano, Ouregano*' (p. 258). At the end of this third novel, Tiffany is, then, in a sense, returned to Ouregano, perhaps to reconnect with her lost childhood self.

The character named Tiffany does not reappear in Constant's work, so we never discover what the outcome is of this potential psychological return. None the less, Tiffany's trajectory is to some extent reworked in *La Fille du Gobernator* through the character Chrétienne, albeit with a different outcome. If Tiffany's time in Ouregano was experienced as an absence, Chrétienne in *La Fille du Gobernator* leaves Cayenne, 'plus menu[e], plus maigre et surtout plus petit[e] qu'à l'arrivée' (p. 12) ('slighter, thinner, certainly smaller than when she had arrived' (pp. 1–2)). Almost dying from grief after her mother's departure, and from a fever which consumes her, she has not grown, her body has not developed. Rather than an absence,

Chrétienne's traumatic experiences in Cayenne have resulted in both physical and psychological regression. At the end of the novel, when the little girl (now an orphan) boards the ship which will return her to France, she has nothing left of her mother but the pair of shoes she is clutching which still bear the marks of her mother's toes:

> Elle pensait aux longues jambes, au ventre lisse que le tablier blanc serrait aux hanches. Elle voyait ses mains impatientes aux ongles courts, mais elle ne se rappelait plus sa tête, la couleur de ses yeux, la forme de son nez, l'épaisseur de sa bouche. Il n'y avait que le voile qui s'incrustait dans son front, qui flottait sur ses épaules. Quant à son odeur, il lui était impossible de la retrouver. (p. 183)

> (She thought about her long legs, her smooth belly squeezed tightly around the hips by a white apron. She saw her impatient hands with their short finger-nails, but she could not remember her head any more, the color of her eyes, the shape of her nose, the thickness of her lips. There was nothing there but the veil stuck onto her forehead and floating over her shoulders. As for her smell, it was impossible to remember.) (pp. 147–8)

Indeed, no photographs remain and memories are too painful; pitifully, the little girl can no longer even summon up the image of her mother's face.[4]

And thus to *Confidence pour confidence*. . . Here, the adult character Aurore might have a stronger sense of self than *Balta*'s disconnected Tiffany, yet a similarly difficult personal history is charted for her: trauma and loss, experiences of disconnection, uncertainty, emptiness and vagueness with respect to her self-identity, loneliness, a need to belong, the search for roots. Despite a successful public identity as a well-known novelist, and despite enjoying her other work in documentary filmmaking, Aurore is still desperately trying to reconnect with her childhood. Ultimately, it appears that she is successful since the very last words of the novel tell us that 'elle vit le visage de sa mère' (p. 234) (she saw her mother's face). In contrast to the traumatised Chrétienne at the end of *La Fille du Gobernator*, Aurore, after years of searching in vain, is, finally, able to picture her mother's face.[5]

The path traced through these five novels is cyclical rather than linear: in the Tiffany novels *Ouregano* and *Propriéte privée*, repeated instances of the trauma of loss and separation followed eventually in *Balta* by a possible return and reconnection; then in *La Fille du Gobernator*, a renewed cycle of loss and separation ending in trauma and regression; and finally in

Confidence pour confidence, a return – to the mother. This itinerary offers a
different way of reading the largely negative mother–daughter relations
in Constant's work. Rather than her novels simply portraying the well-
documented ambivalence of the mother–daughter relationship, or alternatively, rather than just blaming mothers for 'bad mothering' (rejection and
abandonment), the endings of these five texts, taken together, instead
suggest a long process – of mourning.

Melanie Klein's work on mourning is pertinent to this argument.[6]
Klein posits all mourning as the reworking of originary loss: that is to say,
separation from the mother. In Klein's thinking, this process of separation
involves, on the one hand, a conflict between the love and hate the infant
feels for the mother (which gives rise to good and bad phantasmatic
mothers) and, on the other, a conflict between both destructive and reparative impulses. Reparative impulses enable infants to rebuild internal phantasies of the good, loved object they feel they have destroyed in hate or
anger. It is this ongoing conflict between destruction and reparation that
gradually allows the child to separate psychologically from the mother and
to become an independent individual. For Klein, mourning of lost loved
ones throughout life reawakens and re-enacts these primary processes of
dealing with the loss of the first idealised love object. Furthermore, she
maintains that mourning cannot take place effectively unless either a secure
internal world has been established in infancy or the process is resolved
later in life. Effective mourning involves a creative, reparative process:
rather than simply purging painful memories, it entails re-experiencing the
loss, rebuilding and enriching the inner world – and strengthening the self.
Thus connection and reconnection play as much of a part in both individuation and mourning as separation. A return (to the mother) does not,
then, necessarily signify regression, but rather the process of working
through loss.

In Constant's harshly poetical work, we are reminded how intensely
children feel by the prevalence of violent images, the use of strong vocabulary and even by the typography which, in both *Ouregano* and *La Fille du
Gobernator*, conveys angry and sarcastic tones of voice in capital letters.
Moreover, Kleinian resonances are clear in the destructive impulses that
both Tiffany and Chrétienne direct towards their respective mothers: 'Ma
mère est morte' (p. 24) (My mother is dead), a broken Tiffany lies to a fellow
convent pupil at the beginning of *Propriété privée*. In turn, Chrétienne,
beaten by her mother and her father, wishes them both dead, while hastily
making reparation in order to retain the 'good mother' within: 'Elle désirait

la mort de son père et à un degré moindre – maman, je t'aime! – celle de sa mère' (*La Fille du Gobernator*, p. 94) ('She wanted her father dead and, though less (Mummy, I love you!), her mother too' (*The Governor's Daughter*, p. 72)). If the effects on Tiffany, Chrétienne and Aurore of the losses they suffer (of animals, people, places) are interpreted through the lens of Kleinian thought as repeated reworkings of the original infantile position, then Aurore's epiphanic memory of her mother's face at the end of *Confidence pour confidence* suggests that, ultimately, she attains effective mourning. To remember is creative; indeed, in the context of mourning, it is reparative. To be able to remember is evidence that grieving is giving way to successful mourning, and that the process of restoring the lost loved one in the bereaved psyche has begun.[7]

Klein argues that artistic production (including writing) can be part of this reparative process. It is highly significant then that Constant's Aurore is a writer. In *Confidence pour confidence*, writing is undoubtedly part of the way in which Aurore works through the process of mourning. But how and why does actual rememoration finally come about? At the very end of *Confidence pour confidence*, the new man in Aurore's life brings her a chimp from his zoo and it is at this very point that Aurore is able to break through the veil obstructing her memory and to picture her mother's face. The presence of the chimp is highly pertinent, since it was Aurore's mother who gave her Délice, the pet chimpanzee of her childhood. None the less, this moment of rememoration at the very end of *Confidence pour confidence* is the culmination of a long process in Aurore's psychological development, and thus it is also important to look more closely at what comes before.

It is true that bitter rivalries characterise relations between the women in *Confidence pour confidence*. This novel certainly does not offer an idealised portrayal of a feminist sisterhood. If Aurore's surname (Amer) connotes a return to the mother, it also signifies bitterness; Babette and Gloria detest each other; Lola loathes women in groups; Gloria is in the process of plagiarising one of Aurore's novels: purporting to translate and summarise it, she is making a collage of it and passing it off as a book of her own authorship. Gloria also assumes a mothering role vis-à-vis the other women, with all the resulting ambivalences that surround mother–daughter relations. On the other hand, however, the confidences the four women exchange during the morning they spend together mean that they reveal to each other something of the pain of the private selves behind their public identities: despite their mutual dislike, Gloria puts her arms round a tearful Babette in order to comfort her, Aurore looks after the alcoholic Lola, and, in turn, Lola helps Aurore to recognise the legitimacy of her own pain. Furthermore, the confidences the women share lead each of them on into self-reflection and to a degree of greater self-knowledge. Thus, there is a real sense in this novel of what women can do *for* each other – as well as *against* one another.

Klein's work is relevant to this aspect of the novel too: primary conflicts of love and hate are present throughout life in our relations with other people. The way we work through them in the infantile state influences all the relationships we have later in life. Although it is generally accepted that ambivalence is a common character of mother–daughter relations, Klein would undoubtedly argue that, to some extent, it is also to be found in all our relationships.[8] Constant's *Confidence pour confidence* points to different ways in which the identities of the four women are tied up with one another, and for Aurore this works in a positive way. During the course of the novel, Aurore herself never finds out about Gloria's outrageous plagiarism of her book.[9] On the contrary, Aurore's work is the centre of attention at the feminist conference, and, moreover, her self-identity is further strengthened in a more personal way. Aurore's sense of self has always been linked with Lola, whom she physically resembles. In her youth, Aurore was constantly mistaken for the slightly older actress, but here, in Gloria's house, Lola herself mistakes a photograph of Aurore for her own image. Thus, the dynamics of the relationship between the two women are changed, Lola's sense of self disintegrating in favour of Aurore's increasingly stronger identity. For Babette, Gloria's maternal demeanour is negative, but, in contrast, Aurore is happy for Gloria to care for her: 'elle continuait à frotter les pieds d'Aurore pour la réconforter, si incroyablement forte, si immensément forte. Aurore se laissait faire dans un abandon d'enfant en nourrice' (p. 59) (she continued to rub Aurore's feet to comfort her, so incredibly strong, so immensely strong. Aurore let herself go, abandoning herself like a child to a nurse).

These women-to-women relations are certainly pertinent to the apotheosis at the close of the novel, although in themselves they are only one crystallising element in the process which ends in Aurore remembering her mother's face, and other factors play their part. The death of the pet 'rat' in Gloria's kitchen is more than a real-life replay of an episode from one of Aurore's books, however much of a contributory factor that reworking in itself may be. Rather, it quite literally enables Aurore to re-experience childhood trauma: 'Et elle se rappelait, mais lointaine, étouffée, presque insensible comme une cicatrice, sa douleur d'enfant devant l'animal qu'on lui ordonnait de tuer' (pp. 177–8) (And she remembered, although it was distant, smothered, almost numb like a scar, the child's suffering when faced with the animal she was ordered to kill). To remember the pain of loss is an important stage in the mourning process, particularly for Aurore, who has been consciously seeking out connections with the sensations of her childhood: the sounds of wild animals, her mother's smell, the softness and warmth of her pet chimpanzee.

On the very last page of Constant's novel, the sense of return builds to a dizzying intensity as Aurore has an experience of déjà vu. Outside the church opposite Gloria's house, a little girl in a yellow dress is singing: 'Chrétienne est ressuscitée, Chrétienne est ressuscitée.' (p. 234) (Chrétienne is risen, Chrétienne is risen). Readers who are familiar with Constant's work are themselves returned here to her preceding novel, *La Fille du Gobernator*, where: 'Chrétienne fut pour la messe du dimanche dans la cathédrale jaune, jaune comme une baudruche en plein ciel; jaune, comme une fleur de tournesol; jaune comme le soleil' (pp. 73–4) ('Chrétienne was yellow for the mass in the yellow cathedral that Sunday. She was yellow as a balloon in midair, yellow as a sunflower, yellow as the sun' (p. 54)). This striking reflection between *Confidence pour confidence* and *La Fille du Gobernator* is all the more significant in the light of not only the epigraph to *Confidence pour confidence*, 'Il y a en moi une jeune fille qui refuse de mourir' (There is in me a young girl who refuses to die) but also the passage which recounts Aurore's rescue after the bushfire that killed her parents:

Les soldats, se souvint Aurore, avaient réussi à lui enlever Délice qui sentait déjà mauvais. Ils avaient desserré un à un tous ses doigts, ils avaient écarté son coude, soulevé son bras et retenu sa main qui voulait tout reprendre. Ils lui avaient enlevé les lambeaux *d'une robe jaune* qui restaient collés à sa peau. (p. 51; my emphasis)

(The soldiers, Aurore remembered, had succeeded in removing Délice who was already beginning to smell. They had prised open her fingers one by one, moved her elbow, lifted her arm and restrained the hand which was trying to grab hold of everything again. They had peeled away the shreds of *a yellow dress* that remained stuck to her skin.)

At the end of *Confidence pour confidence*, then, not only does Aurore remember her mother's face, but, through the little girl in the yellow dress outside Gloria's house, she also reconnects with a childhood self, a process that feminist psychologists Brown and Gilligan value for the positive psychological benefits it can have for adult women.

Links are thus also established between Aurore and Chrétienne, although the respective geographical and historical settings of the novels in which they feature confirm that they are not one and the same character, and so the nature of the actual connection between them remains ambiguous. Clearly, Aurore is not simply an adult version of Chrétienne, although, as we have seen, Chrétienne could be a fictional version of Aurore's childhood self. However, whatever the interpretation of the relationships between the three characters discussed here (Tiffany, Chrétienne and Aurore), it is evident that strong textual reverberations connect them. Following the trajectory I have traced through the five novels, each successive character is, in a sense, the latest version of the previous ones. Aurore's return to the mother, then, is no regression but rather can be seen as the beginnings of effective mourning and part of the process of constructing a stronger sense of self.

Aurore's ability to picture her mother's face is a coherent ending to *Confidence pour confidence* as a novel in its own right, but read in the light of earlier novels, its significance becomes greater, gaining real weight only if *Confidence pour confidence* is considered as an integral part of Constant's ongoing œuvre. In many of Paule Constant's novels, the mother is lost; in *Confidence pour confidence*, she is found again. Thus, Constant's characters evolve, but it is only by following the thread that connects them that we are able to understand to what extent her novels all examine and work through the problematic and complex connections between the mother–daughter relationship and women's identities.

Notes

1 Paule Constant, *Ouregano* (Paris: Gallimard, 1980); *Propriété privée* (Paris: Gallimard, 1981); *Balta* (Paris: Gallimard, 1983); *White spirit* (Paris: Gallimard, 1989); *La Fille du Gobernator* (Paris: Gallimard, 1994), *The Governor's Daughter*, trans. Betsy Wing (Lincoln: University of Nebraska Press, 1998); *Confidence pour confidence* (Paris: Gallimard, 1998). *White spirit* and *Le Grand Ghâpal* (Paris: Gallimard, 1991) can be fitted into the schema outlined here but in different and more marginal ways. In the interests of clarity, I have decided not to include them in this analysis.

2 Paule Constant, 'Echos et mirrors dans mes romans', unpublished lecture given at George Mason University, USA on 27 October 1999.

3 For the term 'disconnection' and its place in women's psychology, see Carol Gilligan's work, which finds that women frequently compromise their own needs

in favour of the relationships that are important to them to such an extent that they become disconnected from themselves; see especially Lyn Mikel Brown and Carol Gilligan, *Meeting at the Crossroads: Women's Psychology and Girls' Development* (Cambridge, MA and London: Harvard University Press, 1992).

4 In *Contre la dépression nationale* (Paris: Textuel, 1998), Julia Kristeva cites a similar manifestation of this kind of 'matricide' in women who have migrated to France (p. 96). Here, Kristeva links the loss of any image of the mother's face, on the one hand, to the destructive effects of a tyrannical father, and, on the other, to a change of language and culture. The key point that connects Kristeva's patients with Constant's character Chrétienne is that this blank is a symptom of trauma.

5 Aurore's highly connotative surname, Amer, itself indicates this trajectory: *à-mère* (to-mother).

6 See, in particular, Melanie Klein, *Love, Guilt and Reparation and Other Works 1921–1945* (London: Virago, 1988). Klein's concept of 'phantasy' is involved here. Different from 'fantasy', which in Freudian psychoanalysis is the expression or staging of unconscious desire, Klein's 'phantasy' is the process of psychical inter-action between inner and outer world.

7 For a sensitive analysis of the place of remembering in mourning drawing on Barthes's *La Chambre claire*, see Michael Worton, 'Thinking through photography, remembering to love the past', in Monique Streiff-Moretti, Mireille Revol Cappelleti and Odile Martinez (eds), *Il senso del nonsenso: scritti in memoria di Lynn Salkin Sbiroli* (Naples: Edizioni Scientifiche Italiane, 1994), pp. 733–53.

8 For such connections between mother–daughter relations, women's identities and women-to-women relations more generally, see Luce Irigaray, *Le Corps-à-corps avec la mère* (Montreal: Editions de la pleine lune, 1981); 'Body against body: in relation to the mother', trans. Gillian C. Gill, in Luce Irigaray, *Sexes and Genealogies* (New York: Columbia University Press, 1993), pp. 7–21. In *The Bonds of Love: Psychoanalysis, Feminism, and the Problem of Domination* (London: Virago, 1990), Jessica Benjamin argues positively for the maintenance of a certain degree of conflict, which in her view is necessary for the development of intersub-jective relations of mutual respect between two subjects rather than the hierarchi-cal subject–object relation which more usually characterises the mother–child relationship.

9 In the interview, 'L'entretien par Catherine Argand', *Lire* (April 1998), 36–41, Constant herself describes plagiarism as 'une négation complète de l'autre' (39) (a complete negation of the other) – a vicious assault on a writer's identity.

Puzzling out the fathers: Sibylle Lacan's *Un père: puzzle*

Sibylle Lacan's text *Un père*, published in 1994, bears the subtitle '*puzzle*', a term which the author describes as referring primarily to the fragmented nature of her writing.[1] However, it applies equally well to the subject of her text: the question of what kind of father Jacques Lacan represented for her is a puzzle wrestled with throughout the text. Behind this puzzle lies another. Is her text also primarily a testimony to her father's intellectual legacy? In taking up her pen, is the daughter merely confirming the law of the father? This intriguing text tables issues relating to autobiographical writing, to discourses of fatherhood and daughterhood and to the ways in which women's writing can be appropriated – or legitimised – by the dominant theoretical discourses of its day. I intend to consider these issues in three different stages of this chapter: first, what kind of writing project is entailed? Second, how does it explore and engage with discourses of the daughter–father relation? And third, can the text be reduced simply to a reading in terms of Lacanian theory, or are there alternative frameworks which can be productively brought to bear on the text?

However, it is first necessary to introduce the complex biographical nexus of relations with which the text sets out to deal. Jacques Lacan married Marie-Louise Blondin ('Malou') on 29 January 1934. During their honeymoon in Italy he sent a telegram to his mistress of the day; as Elisabeth Roudinesco remarks in her biography *Jacques Lacan*, husband and wife had entirely opposing notions of marital fidelity and, in her words, 'ce couple . . . s'engageait ainsi sur la voie du désastre' (the couple thus set out on the road to disaster).[2] Their first child, Caroline, was born in January 1937: her father gave her the nickname of 'Image', a reference to the theory of the mirror stage which he was elaborating at the time of her birth.

According to Roudinesco, Lacan was an adoring father made happy by the experience of paternity. However, twenty-one months after Caroline's birth, Lacan ran across Sylvia Bataille by chance in the café de Flore: she had refused to have a relationship with him some years earlier when she was still living with her husband, Georges Bataille. Now she was separated, and she and Lacan embarked on a relationship which would last the rest of Lacan's life.

Malou, meanwhile, had a second child, Thibault, born in August 1939, and in the autumn of 1940 was eight months pregnant with her third child when Lacan broke the news to her that Sylvia was also expecting his child. Malou's child Sibylle was born on 26 November 1940 in Royan; Malou became depressed and filed for divorce. Lacan and Sylvia moved into the rue de Lille in Paris, and on 3 July 1941 Sylvia gave birth to Judith, declared on her birth certificate as Judith Bataille, since she was still married to Bataille and Lacan had not yet been divorced from Malou. French law did not permit a married man legally to recognise a child born to anyone but his wife. A farcical situation had thus been created: Lacan was the biological and social father of Judith, but could not give her his name. Sibylle was his biological daughter and bore his name, but he had almost no contact with her in the early years of her life. Malou insisted that the truth be kept from the children, and when she moved back with them to Paris from Royan, Lacan would come to dine at the house every Thursday. The children were told he was busy with his work. They had no idea he had remarried (which he did in 1953) and they did not know of the existence of their half-sister Judith, or of that of Laurence, Sylvia's child by Bataille, to whom Lacan acted as a substitute father.

Thibault was let in on the secret and met his half-sister in 1956, but Sibylle, the youngest child, was only told in 1958, when her older sister Caroline was to be married and Lacan wanted the two families present at the wedding. Sibylle subsequently holidayed with her father and Judith in St Tropez and in Italy, and became painfully aware of what Roudinesco calls Lacan's 'véritable adoration pour Judith. Il souffrait amèrement de n'avoir pu lui donner son nom et lui voua un amour exclusif et passionné' (Roudinesco, p. 250) (veritable adoration for Judith. He suffered bitterly from the knowledge that he could not give her his name and loved her with an exclusive passion). Judith later married one of Lacan's most devoted disciples, Jacques-Alain Miller, and became Judith Miller. After the death of Georges Bataille, Lacan had taken the formal legal steps necessary to have her legitimised as Lacan, but, in the event, she bore the name Lacan for only two years, before becoming Miller. On Lacan's death in 1981, Malou and her family were upset by the will, which left most of Lacan's fortune to Sylvia and her family, and gave them the rights over his published and unpublished work. Legal battles between the two families went on for ten years after Lacan's death.

Sibylle Lacan's *Un père* was published in the period when the legal battles were coming to a close; the writing process is dated as having taken place over the period August 1991 to June 1994 and Sibylle was thus 51 when she began this written quest for the father. The text is brief, often brutally lapidary in style, and consists of thirty six unnumbered fragments preceded by a preface and followed by an epilogue, itself made up of three fragments. The preface makes a series of strong claims for the text's status as authentic. It opens, in high Balzacian style, with the following sentences: 'Ce livre n'est pas un roman ou une (auto)biographie romancée. Il ne contient pas une once de fiction' (p. 9) (This book is not a novel nor a fictionalised (auto)biography. It does not contain an ounce of fiction). She goes on: 'On n'y trouvera aucun détail inventé dans le but d'enjoliver le récit ou d'étoffer le texte' (p. 9) (The reader will find in it no detail invented to embellish or fill out the text). The text thus opens with three denials, before it comes on to a series of attempts to formulate the nature of her project as being to speak of Lacan in his relation to her as a father, and not as a famous psychoanalyst. Her method and materials are described as strongly privileging the process of memory, especially spontaneous and associative memory. She insists on the fact that the order of the text is the order in which the memories made their 'imperious' apparition in her mind; both the use of the word 'imperious' and the statement that she wrote 'à l'aveugle' (blindly), with no precise purpose, strongly suggest the comparison with the therapy session.

However, if the text is a kind of therapy, Sibylle plays the part of both patient and analyst, since the text we have in front of us is not a series of unadulterated memories presented in the order in which they came to her but, as she almost immediately concedes, a reordered and a 'corrected' set. Sibylle has assembled her puzzle pieces to make a whole – the link between them is not necessarily that of the associative process but of a set of later choices. From the outset, therefore, the project has a double face: on the one hand it is presented in a rather fiercely puritanical tone as a model of subjective authenticity, untouched by the desire to invent, to romanticise or to prettify. The 'perfect' writing, she asserts, is one which is 'spontanée, impulsive, sans corrections ultérieures. C'était pour moi une

question de principe' (p. 10) (spontaneous, impulsive, with no later corrections. That was a point of principle for me). However, this fierce
defence of rectitude, based on the notion of subjective memory as authenticity, is contradicted by the fact that what we actually have is a text
grouped and ordered according to a conscious logic which is not stated,
but about which the narrator appears to announce in advance her guilt,
since it breaks a lifelong principle.

The workings of this logic will be of particular interest as we turn to
the broad question of how the text explores the daughter–father relation,
and of what discourses of fathering it draws on. The title, *Un père*, with its
indefinite article, poses a blank space and, indeed, one of the first figures of
fatherhood the text stages is that of absence. The first fragment begins:
'Quand je suis née, mon père n'était déjà plus là' (p. 15) (When I was born,
my father was already no longer there). His absence was indeed so much
part of the structure of the family's existence that he could not be 'missed'.
In the second fragment she writes: 'Aucun manque [. . .] Nous savions que
nous avions un père, mais apparemment les pères n'étaient pas là' (p. 17)
(He wasn't missed [. . .] We knew we had a father but apparently fathers
were not present). Alongside the evocation of absence is immediately
raised the issue of the family name. In the last lines of the first fragment she
writes: 'nous étions, ma sœur aujourd'hui disparue, mon frère aîné et moi,
les seuls à porter le nom de Lacan. Et c'est bien de cela qu'il s'agit' (p. 15)
(my sister, no longer on this earth, my elder brother and I, we were the only
ones to bear the name Lacan. And that's what it's about).

The sense of portent emerging from the last sentence indicates the
extent to which holding onto the name becomes a talismanic symbol,
standing in compensatory relation to the absence of the father, and constituting the only form of superiority she has over her half-sister Judith – once
she has discovered the latter's existence. The arrangement of the fragments
indeed precisely ties the theme of the patronymic to the crisis of Sibylle's
discovery of Judith's existence: this discovery, and the realisation that
Judith and their father behave like 'lovers', are recounted in the tenth and
eleventh fragments. Fragment twelve draws particular attention to itself by
its extreme brevity. It consists of only two sentences in which Sibylle recalls
that when her mother, who had reverted to her maiden name of Blondin,
asked her children if they wanted to change their name to Blondin, they
had refused. However, this event actually took place earlier than the discovery of Judith; its positioning in the narrative here immediately following the
account of her discovery of Judith's existence indicates the significance she

attaches to it at the time of writing – or arranging – her text. The significance attached to the name of the father is thus beyond dispute.

The early fragments follow the images of absence with a number of images of the magical fantasy figure. The most striking is the recounting of an episode in which, during a visit to a fort in Brittany, her brother narrowly escapes falling to his death as the father catches hold of his clothing at the last moment. No other family member found the episode particularly memorable, but Sibylle is so transfixed by this heroic role for her father, that she reads her own attachment to the island of Formentera ('Fort-m'enterra' (fort buried me)) as a re-enactment of the incident. The following fragment again evokes her father in a saviour role – this time when he intervenes on her behalf against her siblings. The fragment ends on the following remark: 'Et si un père servait d'abord à cela: à rendre la justice...' (p. 27) (And perhaps that is a father's primary role: to dispense justice...). Also supporting these idealised versions of the father is the evocation of their visits to expensive restaurants: the mingled pleasures of *meringue glacée* and a sense of intimacy with her father produce 'le comble de la volupté' (p. 29) (the height of voluptuousness); she has her father's total attention and feels herself to be 'une personne à part entière' (p. 29) (a full and proper person).

These images are concentrated in the early part of the text, and form the main elements of what one might call the discourse of the 'magical' father. However, they connect to other discourses, of the father as provider and the father as guarantor of sexual identity, both of which are more problematic. The father is a positive provider when he opens the door to expensive restaurants, but he is a failing provider when, in Sibylle's account, he gives her mother only a small allowance which obliges her mother to make fitful and generally doomed efforts to seek work. Sibylle also expects her father to provide for her, and is deeply disappointed by her father's apparent lack of anxiety about who will provide for her after his death. His refusal to pay for an operation for her, when she is 40, leads her to break off relations altogether with him; Lacan died two years later without her ever seeing him again.

The sexuality issue is equally dichotomous. The 'height of voluptuousness' attained in the restaurant scene has obvious links with the sense of idyllic physical pleasure which emerges from one of the most evocative fragments of the text, in which her father sees her naked. The scene takes place in her father's country house, and she is describing the pleasures of washing in the bathroom connected to her bedroom, overlooking the garden:

J'y faisais ma toilette avec délices car elle était spacieuse, claire et avait un charme légèrement désuet propre aux demeures provinciales qui correspondait à mon sens de l'esthétique.

En fin de matinée, j'étais debout dans la baignoire, me passant le gant sur le corps. Soudain (il n'y avait pas de verrou), j'entends la porte s'ouvrir. Je me retourne en tressaillant, mon père était dans l'embrasure de la porte. Il marque un temps d'arrêt, me dit posément 'excuse-moi, ma chérie', et se retire tout aussi tranquillement en refermant la porte derrière lui.

Un coup d'œil, c'est toujours ça de pris. . .

(J'étais FURIEUSE.) (p. 61)

(I delighted in washing there, for the room was spacious, light and had the slightly old-fashioned charm of provincial houses which corresponded to my idea of the aesthetically pleasing.

In the late morning I was standing in the bath, passing the flannel over my body. Suddenly (there was no lock), I heard the door open. I turned round with a shiver, my father was in the doorway. He waited a moment, said calmly 'sorry, darling', and went away just as unhurriedly, closing the door behind him.

A glance, that's better than nothing. . .

(I was FURIOUS.))

The anger referred to in the last line is seriously undermined by the capitalisation and the use of parenthesis. The combination of aesthetic charm with the sensuality of the flannel passing over the body, the vocabulary of 'délices' and 'tressaillant' carry an evident sexual charge. The sense of having been looked at, conveyed in the penultimate line, is expressed with a more discordant brutality: 'un coup d'œil, c'est toujours ça de pris' clearly implies a relation of power between looker and looked at. This worm in the apple becomes dominant in most of the other representations of femininity and sexuality in the text. Sibylle stresses the way in which her father's sexual interest in his mistresses intervenes in her own relationship with him on a number of occasions: on one, he has been urgently summoned to discuss Sibylle's illness and, as she waits for him on the balcony, she sees him emerge from a local house of ill repute preceded by a woman. She is suffocated by indignation that he should satisfy his own sexual desires when she is waiting for him, and in her own street. Later, Lacan agrees to find her an analyst, but she discovers after a number of years that the analyst in question is his mistress. Once again she tries to draw closer to her father through illness but finds herself obliged to pass through her father's sexual relations to others.

However, the main thread of both sexual and sibling rivalry is centred around the existence of her half-sister Judith. In the ninth fragment Sibylle recounts the events of 1940: 'Alors que je venais de naître (ou bien maman était-elle encore enceinte de moi?), mon père annonça joyeusement à ma mère, avec la cruauté des enfants heureux, qu'il allait avoir un enfant' (p. 33) (When I had just been born (or was my mother still pregnant with me?), my father announced to my mother with the cruelty of a happy child, that he was going to have a baby). Sibylle then evokes her mother's 'effondrement intérieur, l'impression d'avoir reçu le coup de grâce, la mort qui envahit l'âme' (p. 33) (interior collapse, the feeling of having received a mortal blow, death in the soul) and her father's extraordinary remark to her mother: 'Je vous le rendrai au centuple' (p. 33) (I'll make it up to you a hundred times over). The narration of this event is a clear violation of the promise made in the preface that her own memories will form the materials of her narrative. But it allows her to stress the horror of this betrayal, and, furthermore, it is used as an introduction to the account of her meeting with Judith, a meeting portrayed as a crushing blow to her sense of feminine identity:

> Ma première vraie rencontre avec Judith m'écrasa. Elle était si aimable, si parfaite et moi, si maladroite, si gauche. Elle était la socialité, l'aisance, j'étais la paysanne du Danube. Elle avait l'air d'une femme, j'avais encore une allure enfantine. Ce sentiment dura longtemps. Depuis, j'ai rencontré ce spécimen féminin et je sais à quoi m'en tenir. Mais à l'époque j'étais accablée, coupable [. . .]
>
> Un souvenir halluciné est la vision de mon père et de Judith dansant comme des amoureux dans un bal populaire à Ramatuelle. Mais dans quel monde étais-je tombée? Un père n'était-il pas un père? (pp. 37–8)

(My first real encounter with Judith crushed me. She was so nice, so perfect, and I was so awkward, so gauche. She was all sociability, at ease, I was the peasant woman from the Danube. She looked like a woman, I still had a childish air. That feeling lasted for a long time. Since then, I have come across this feminine specimen and I know how to deal with it. But at the time I was overwhelmed, guilty [. . .]

A haunting memory is the vision of my father and Judith dancing like lovers at a local dance in Ramatuelle. What on earth was this? Was a father not a father?)

The rivalry with Judith and the sense of struggle for a daughterly identity cumulates in two particularly painful fragments, situated in the heart of the text, in fragments eighteen and twenty-three. The eighteenth fragment is

perhaps the most significant and stands exactly halfway through. It
recounts her discovery, via a friend, that her father is listed in *Who's Who*
as having only one daughter – Judith. Stupefaction is followed by hatred:
the next fragment is a pure indictment of Lacan as father, beginning with
the statement: 'J'ai haï mon père pendant plusieurs années' (p. 57) (I hated
my father for several years) and declaring him responsible not only for the
collapse of her family but for her own psychological crisis which began at
the end of adolescence. Four fragments later, we come to the episode of the
photograph:

> Aussi loin que je remonte dans mes souvenirs, j'ai toujours vu dans le
> cabinet de mon père, trônant sur la cheminée, une grande photographie
> de Judith jeune fille, en position assise, vêtue sagement – pull-over et jupe
> droite –, ses longs cheveux noirs lisses peignées en arrière de manière à
> dégager le front.
> Ce qui me frappa d'emblée quand j'entrai pour la première fois dans ce
> cabinet fut sa ressemblance avec papa. Comme lui, elle avait le visage
> ovale, les cheveux noirs et le nez allongé (mes cheveux sont châtain clair,
> j'ai le nez retroussé, le visage triangulaire et les pommettes saillantes). Ce
> qui me frappa ensuite, c'était sa beauté, l'intelligence de l'expression, l'élé-
> gance de la pose.
> Dans la pièce aucune autre photo.
> A ses patients, à nous, à moi, pendant plus de vingt ans, mon père a
> semblé dire: Voici ma fille, voici ma fille unique, voici ma fille chérie. (p. 65)

> (As far back as I can remember, I have always seen in my father's consult-
> ing-room, in pride of place on the mantlepiece, a large photograph of
> Judith as a girl, seated, neatly dressed in a pullover and straight skirt, her
> long black hair combed back revealing her forehead.
> What struck me straight away when I went to the consulting-room for
> the first time, was her resemblance to my father. Like him, she had an oval
> face, black hair and a long nose (my hair is light brown, my nose is turned
> up, my face triangular shape and my cheekbones prominent). What struck
> me afterwards was her beauty, the intelligence of her expression, the ele-
> gance of her pose.
> There was no other photo in the room.
> To his patients, to us, to me, for over twenty years, my father seemed to
> be saying: Here is my daughter, here is my only daughter, here is my
> beloved daughter.)

The photograph is indeed a very *daughterly* portrait, with Judith dressed
'sagement', hair brushed back, and bearing a strong resemblance to the

father. It appears to exclude Sibylle as daughter through the comparative list of features – even physically, it appears, Sibylle has difficulty in asserting her status as daughter. The message of the last line is a reinforcement of the *Who's Who*. Judith is not just *one* of Lacan's daughters, she occupies the whole place of daughterhood in relation to him.

These two episodes, of the photograph and the missing recognition in *Who's Who*, appear to be springboards for the text of *Un père*. In writing and publishing her text, Sibylle Lacan publicly asserts her name and her relation to her father, filling the gap, the missing piece in *Who's Who*. On the front of the volume is a photograph of Sibylle, labelled as having been taken at 16 in Brittany, which stands in complete opposition to the photograph of Judith. It dates from the period of Sybille's life in which she knew nothing of her rival for daughter status and it recalls the magical father who saved her brother's life in Brittany. It also displays a very boyish mode of femininity: short, unevenly cut hair, an immature yet determined-looking face, gaze directed pensively into the distance. It bears a strong resemblance to the determination expressed in the preface that nothing should be prettified or be inauthentic. It represents her portrait of a daughter, addressed to a public who have heretofore been presented with the portrait of Judith. She no longer appears to be crushed by Judith but to be asserting her own claim to daughterhood.

Thirteen fragments of the text remain, after the evocation of the *Who's Who* episode and Judith's portrait. The two dominant discourses are that of the mildly ridiculous 'drôle de père, un peu "zinzin"' (p. 70) (a weird father, a bit 'barmy'), with a host of stories of his social *hauteur*, and his inadequacies on the sporting and mechanical front, and that of the criminal father, source of her psychological breakdown. Eventually Sibylle forces her entry into her father's world, through her need for therapy. Contrary to her own claims, little seems to be resolved: she fails to visit him in his final illness and the account of the funeral is marked by recriminations and bitterness.

However, there is a final fragment of the main text in which Sibylle visits her father's grave and undergoes an experience of magical reconciliation, strongly recalling the description of the restaurant visits in an early fragment. She seeks a private, intimate rendez-vous with her father, and is rewarded by a physical sense of rapprochement so strong, that she is finally able to declare 'tu es mon père' (you are my father) a recognition which at last goes beyond the generic title *Un père*. It is supported by three very brief fragments of epilogue, focusing on dreams and memories in which she evokes images of closeness to him, even a sense of an 'histoire d'amour, de passion' (p. 101) (a story of love, of passion) between them. The final shape of the text therefore, which seems to be on a downward spiral from the *Who's Who* episode onwards, moves back up in the very last pages to a recapturing of her early sense of a passionate tête-à-tête with the father.

What then, in the end, is this text all about? A public recognition of her father as father, is clearly central: a public staging of her own name as Lacan is an assertion of daughterhood, made necessary because among his failures as father has been his failure publicly to recognise her as his daughter. The shape of the reordered narrative which drives downward into the heart of her sense of betrayal and disappointment but which moves upwards at the end towards reconciliation and reintegration suggests that the writing process may have succeeded where her therapy has failed. This is less true of the problematic feminine identity staged in the text, graphically illustrated by the photograph, mirrored in the insistence on an unvarnished writing style, and focused through the narrative of the rivalry with her half-sister Judith. In many ways, this set of issues about names, about a passionate but largely disappointed yearning for the absent father, and about gender identity look ripe for a Lacanian theoretical resolution. This is indeed a line explored very successfully by Martine Delvaux, who sees Sibylle Lacan as experiencing a 'forclusion du nom du père' (a forclusion of the name-of-the-father), the famous concept which Lacan began to elaborate in Sibylle's early childhood.[3] In this reading Sibylle's illness is caused by a rejection of the name of the father; writing and publishing the text allows her to accept her name and move towards an acceptance of herself. This is indeed a highly plausible reading, but I would like to raise the issue of what is at stake when we read the text in this way. In Simone de Beauvoir's *Les Belles Images*, Laurence falls ill when the emotional and intellectual lure of the father becomes evident to her, and she both recognises this and simultaneously rejects a Freudian explanation as a neat formula which can certainly be applied to her case, but which resolves nothing. Keeping her daughter out of therapy, and encouraging her friendship with another girl, are the most positive steps Laurence takes.[4] In the case of Sibylle Lacan, reading her text through a Lacanian framework risks reducing her account of an emotional and fragile journey towards a belief in the self, via her father's apparent rejection of her, to an illustration of the intellectual authority of the father, whose fame and eminence she stresses in her text. The effect is circular: she escapes the emotional bind in which she has been placed only to fall into the intellectual bind. Is there, then, any other way of reading the text which takes us outside the authority of the fathers?

Two other paths through the text seem to me to be worth pursuing. The first centres on the figure of the mother, whose presence in the text is often inextricable from that of the father. Jessica Benjamin argues that instead of seeing the daughter's turn to the father as the desire for the phallus, the rejection of the mother's lack (as Freud and Lacan do), we can instead understand the girl's desire for the father to be driven by a desire for freedom from dependency on the powerful mother of early infancy.[5] When we turn back to Sibylle Lacan's text we find that the mother, depicted as a poor abandoned wife in relation to the father, is nevertheless seen as an extremely powerful figure in relation to the children. Stressing her father's complete absence during the earliest years of her life, Sibylle writes: 'ma réalité à moi, c'est qu'il y avait maman, un point c'est tout [...] Maman était tout pour nous: l'amour, la sécurité, l'autorité' (p. 17) (my own reality was that mother was there, and that was that [...] Mother was everything to us: love, security, authority). The last term is especially significant. Her mother ran the household on a system of rights which accompanied age and it is this hierarchy which allows Sibylle's elder siblings to bully her – earlier I drew attention to the way in which the father comes into this scenario as saviour and justice figure. When Sibylle first becomes ill her entire family pushes her to spend a year in Russia: her father advises her that she needs to get away from her mother. In the fragment in which Sibylle considers this possibility she again draws attention to the primordial role played by her mother in her life, and evokes her mother's beauty. 'Grande, svelte et blonde' (p. 46) (tall, svelte and blond) – nothing could be more different from the photograph on the front cover of the text. It raises the possibility that Sibylle's sense of being crushed by Judith in the femininity stakes simply reflects her sense that she will never look like her mother. In a more identifying move, Sibylle spends most of her adult life apparently incapable of working, echoing her mother's desultory attempts to take up a variety of professions which all fizzle out. Also like her mother, who never remarried despite a number of opportunities, Sibylle remains unmarried. Reconsidering the role of the mother in the text places the daughter's pleasure in a rare escapade to a restaurant with her father in a different light, and may also explain why 'instinctively', she and her siblings refuse when asked if they wish to take their mother's name of Blondin. If it is indeed the discourse of the *mother* which in reality remains unresolved, the failure to resolve the feminine identity issue also becomes more explicable.

A second path involves another woman who can perhaps also be regarded as a quasi-maternal figure – Elisabeth Roudinesco. Roudinesco has a textual existence in the final fragment of the text, where Sibylle Lacan cites from Roudinesco's biography of Lacan the paragraph which describes Lacan's final moments. As he was in excruciating pain, it was decided that he should be given enough morphine to allow him to die. According to Roudinesco, Lacan was fully conscious of what was happening at the moment of death and stared into the eyes of the doctor who gave him the final injection. Sibylle Lacan describes the emotional storm which reading this paragraph unleashed in her, and its role in allowing her to come to terms with her father's death. The text ends: 'C'est ce jour-là [i.e. the day she read Roudinesco's paragraph] que je me suis sentie le plus proche de mon père. Depuis je n'ai plus pleuré en pensant à lui' (p. 106) (It was that day that I felt the closest to my father. Since then, I no longer cry when I think of him). Roudinesco's text is thus given a central role in Sibylle's final sense of identification with her father, and her acceptance of his death.

This appears all the more significant when we look further into the links between Roudinesco's biography and Sibylle Lacan's text. Roudinesco's biography was published in September 1993; Sibylle's text, written between August 1991 and June 1994, was therefore begun before the appearance of the biography. However, Roudinesco interviewed members of the Lacan family extensively in preparing her book, and the dates cited of interviews with Sibylle show that the interviews began as early as November 1989, and continued throughout 1990 and 1991. The beginning of Sibylle's writing process thus follows on from the interviews and Roudinesco has confirmed to me in conversation that she encouraged Sibylle to write. Sibylle's text can be considered, in this light, as having strong intertextual links with Roudinesco's biography, which itself draws on Sibylle's memories. In a further twist, Roudinesco's account of Lacan's development of the concept of the *nom-du-père* is a firmly biographical one. In her account, Jacques Lacan detested his paternal grandfather Emile, a family dictator of such ferocity that Jacques's own father Alfred was unable to exercise his paternal authority. Roudinesco goes on:

> Partant de l'abaissement de la condition paternelle dont il avait souffert dans son enfance, il [Jacques Lacan] faisait surgir le concept de *nom-du-père* de l'horreur que lui inspirait encore la figure d'Emile: le *père du père*. Et au souvenir de cette humiliation d'Alfred s'ajoutait le poids de sa

propre expérience de la paternité. Se sentant coupable de n'avoir pu donner son nom à sa fille, Lacan théorisait l'idée que seul un acte de parole – une nomination – pouvait permettre à un père d'authentifier sa descendance. (Roudinesco, pp. 373-4)

(Starting out from the abasement of the condition of fatherhood from which Lacan had suffered in his youth, he conjured up the concept of the name-of-the-father from the horror which the figure of Emile – the father's father – still inspired in him. And his memory of the humiliation of Alfred was further exacerbated by the weight of his own experience of paternity. Experiencing guilt at not having been able to give his name to his daughter, Lacan theorised that only a speech act – a nomination – could allow a father to authenticate his descendants.)

In sum, for Roudinesco, Lacan's theory recounts in her words 'ses affaires de famille' (Roudinesco, p. 373) (his family affairs). Theory and biography are turned on their heads. Instead of Lacanian theory being used as a reductive tool on Sibylle's life writing, Lacan's family life becomes an explanation of his theory. Sibylle is not so much the prisoner of Lacanian discourse as part of one of its sources. In both cases we have discourses of paternity which mask other discourses that lie beneath them or are entangled with them.

In the end, Sibylle Lacan's *Un père*, Roudinesco's *Jacques Lacan* and Jacques Lacan's *nom-du-père* become embroiled in an intertextual whirl in which notions of paternity, origins and authority lose their footing. Seen in this light, however, Sibylle's puzzle of a text escapes the reduction to simple confirmation of her father's intellectual legacy. The discourse of the daughter remains tightly enmeshed with a discourse of the father but is more than the subject of patriarchal law. Indeed, the most enabling figure of the text may be that of Roudinesco, who acts as godmother to the writing of the text, and hence to the partial resolution of the traumatic relation with the absent father. What is left far more unresolved is the challenge of the idealised and powerful femininity of the mother and half-sister, to which the portrait of the adolescent on the front cover of the book offers a painful response and a clue to the puzzle of this fragmented text.

Notes

1 Sibylle Lacan, *Un père: puzzle* (Paris: Folio, 1994), p. 10. Subsequent page references are given in brackets in the text.

2 Elisabeth Roudinesco, *Jacques Lacan. Esquisse d'une vie: histoire d'un système de pensée* (Paris: Fayard, 1993), p. 110.

3 Martine Delvaux, 'Who's who? *Un père* de Sibylle Lacan', in Lucie Lequin and Catherine Mavrikakis (eds), *La Francophonie sans frontière* (Paris: L'Harmattan, 2001), pp. 225–35. Delvaux also makes use of Derrida, Marie Maclean and Judith Butler among others in her interesting set of explorations of the text.

4 Simone de Beauvoir, *Les Belles Images* (Paris: Folio, 1966).

5 Jessica Benjamin, *The Bonds of Love: Psychoanalysis, Feminism, and the Problem of Domination* (London: Virago, 1990), p. 94.

II

Writing the dynamics of identity

Anatomical writing: *Blasons d'un corps masculin*, *L'Ecrivaillon* and *La Ligne âpre* by Régine Detambel

'Régine Detambel is a monster' claimed the September 1999 issue of the French magazine *Marie-Claire*, referring to her prolific output, which includes over 20 novels (over 30, including her books for children) by the age of 36.[1] The excess implied by this label is, however, modified in the same article where her 'monstrosity' gives way to descriptions of the writer of 'the world of childhood sensations', the perfectionist religiously tending to the secret garden of childhood and her own 'holy' literary fields or 'jardin de curé' (144) (priest's garden).[2] She has also been compared with the OuLiPo group because of her numerous texts written, *à la* Queneau or Perec, according to self-imposed rules.[3] Detambel herself stresses that she is influenced by music:[4] her series of stylistic exercises in *Les Ecarts majeurs* is a virtuoso rewriting of *La Marseillaise* in the vein of Gainsbourg's (sub)version.[5]

Might it be said, to use recent, somewhat reductive labels, that Detambel belongs to the so-called 'écorchée(s) à confesse' – women whose texts 'confess' that they are hypersensitive (literally 'flayed') and 'folles de leur corps' (mad about their bodies) – alongside Marie Darrieussecq, Lorette Nobécourt, Claire Legendre or Christine Angot?[6] Detambel, as a professional physiotherapist, author of *L'Amputation*, certainly offers a twist to the trend of sadomasochism.[7] As Pascal Quignard underlines, anatomical enquiries generate a pervasive feeling of malaise linked to the combination of uncanny familiarity and sadism, involving our fears, desires and fundamental uncertainties.[8]

Detambel's chosen genre is a complex one: the *blason anatomique* (anatomical blazon). Alison Saunders, in her seminal study of the sixteenth-century *blason poétique* (poetic blazon), argues that it is difficult to give 'a neat definition' of the literary genre of the blazon in all its variations (*blason poétique, blason-médaillon* (medallion blazon), *blason satirique* (satirical blazon)), especially since it was a short-lived form: 'the *blasons anatomiques du corps féminin* [anatomical blazons of the female body] have been regarded by sixteenth-century scholars as an ephemeral vogue springing into existence in the 1530s with Clément Marot's *Beau tetin* [beautiful breast], only to disappear into obscurity again, a few years later as suddenly as it had appeared'.[9] Saunders also reminds us that *blason*, a heraldic term which usually denotes the combination of illustration and accompanying text, is ambivalent when applied to titles of poems: it may well be commonly understood as praise of a woman's body, but that does not explain why the term 'contreblason' (counterblazon) was coined simultaneously to designate its negative opposite. Saunders sums up the difficulty of the *blason poétique*, a poetic form previously considered so minor that du Bellay himself 'disdains to mention such a genre which he would presumably have ranked among the "episseries qui corrumpent le goust de notre Langue" [spices which corrupt the taste of our Language]' (p. 11). No wonder, therefore, that the same ambiguity and complexity can be traced in Detambel's version of the *blason poétique*, where she takes on the challenging task of redefining the relationship between language and the body. Detambel's strikingly clinical writing of the body, a clear leitmotif in her work, is in fact persistently intermingled with an analysis of the writer's role, a questioning of her tools, history, function and future. Under Detambel's sharp pen or scalpel – or at the end of her fingertips typing on a computer, to use one of her up-to-date images of the writer's accessories – anatomy and desire become fused with the desire for writing. Desire is inscribed as the desire for a new dissection of the writer's body and mind.

How 'new' is Detambel's writing of the body or her re-presentation of the writer? The discussion which follows will offer potential answers and raise further questions on this subject. It is evident from Germaine Greer's *The Whole Woman* or Michel Serres's *Variations sur le corps*, or indeed from the exhibition 'Spectacular Bodies' (London, Hayward Gallery, 2000), that the body, the battlefield and old war-horse of feminist theory, is also on the current philosophical and cultural agenda.[10] Like Susan Faludi in *Stiffed: The Betrayal of the Modern Man*, Detambel turns her gaze in *Blasons d'un corps masculin* (blazons of a male body) to the representation of masculinity.[11] It is not easy to say, however, who or what is 'betrayed' by Detambel's text: the image of the modern man, the phantasms of a modern woman writer, or the desire for different images, as explicitly emphasised by Detambel's new blazons.

Corpus and body parts: writing the body

As a means of exorcising millennium anxiety, *Libération* published a special supplement on 31 December 1999, asking 200 writers, artists and intellectuals what was on their minds. Christine Angot's answer may have surprised readers when she said that she was thinking about Régine Detambel and about writing under oulipian constraints.[12] Detambel herself answered that she was thinking of writing according to self-imposed rules, adapting the classificatory scheme of chemistry as a means of opening up more possibilities and combination rules for her texts. Her reflection on 'the potential structure of an electronic novel' (*Libération*, p. 40), far from distancing herself from the dual theme of the body and identity, brings back anatomy, the emblem of the body flayed alive, and the dynamics of classification. As in a medical dictionary, the sum total of what we are physically, a list of classified body parts, may look limited, but it can be expanded to describe all the components of the physical universe. Even though the elements available for combination are by essence restricted, the rules of combination and literary creation can be played with, distorted, recycled, and endlessly renewed.

In *Blasons d'un corps masculin* (1996), Detambel writes specifically for a project launched by the medical association Via Voltaire in Montpellier. Her aim is to describe the sick body differently, as belonging to subjects, who deserve to recover not only their health, but also their 'freedom to act and to think'.[13] Respecting this ethical rule, and refusing therefore to reduce the hospitalised individual to a passive body, an object at the mercy of doctors or scientific discourses, Detambel adds extra rules – the literary codes of the blazons of the female body – only to distort them in order to offer us new images of the body. If her title, *Blasons d'un corps masculin*, refuses generalisations ('*un* corps'), it also diverts the gaze to a masculine body and genders voyeurism differently.

The traditional survey of human geography begins with the removal of underwear and subsequently cuts the body into fetishised parts. Detambel avoids such fetishisation. In her text, for example, male pubic hair is seen as flat and non-eroticised, 'un pelage ras, une toison usée' (the short hair of a threadbare coat), which ultimately reveals a triangular shape, 'une tente de chair jaune' (p. 14) (a tent of yellow flesh), which looks like a 'feminised' sex, adorned with hair and stereotypical images of 'femininity' such as earth and sea shells. The wet pubic hair is divided by the bisexual 'fente close du sexe' (p. 37) (the closed slit of the sex):

> Mouillés, ils avaient la consistance facile du terreau et les racines fortes du chiendent. Elle les suivait des yeux comme les mauvaises herbes ramifiées. Elle façonnait les boucles en coquille. Elle les arrachait pour le voir sursauter. (p. 14)

> (The wet pubic hair resembled moist compost and had strong roots like couch grass. Her gaze would follow this network of weeds. She would knead the curls into shell shapes, and tear them out to startle him.)

The sadistic gesture described above reveals that an aggressive 'contre-blason' is present within the text from the start. The ruthlessness of the medical gaze illuminates the so-called repellent or dangerous insides of the nostrils, the anus, the mouth and its 'dents tueuses' (p. 19) (deadly teeth) – reminiscent of the more familiar figure of the deadly *vagina dentata*. All the orifices are presented without signs of preference, hierarchy, or taboo, thereby showing the same freedom of expression seen in the addition of the (in)famous 'contre-blasons' to the Renaissance 'Blasons du corps féminin'. The bisexual image of the 'fente close du sexe' chosen by Detambel may also have an earlier echo. The potential exchangeability of sexes might be seen in the 1550 edition of the 'Blason du cul' (blazon of the backside), if we read 'venir' (to come) as 'devenir' (to become) in the line praising the 'clever', transsexual tricks performed by the bottom, which '(de)vient' ((be)comes) female when held tight.[14] The confusion of the syntax permits a freer interpretation because 'serrant' (holding) is also transcribed as 'servant' (serving). This intertexual reference highlights one of the sources Detambel might have used when rewriting her own blazons which also allow for indeterminacy and fluidity between the genders.

The originality of Detambel's blazons lies in the way images are super-imposed. Whereas medical scrutiny of close-ups gives a hyper-realistic impression, Detambel plays on extensive metaphors about nature which add humour and artifice. For instance, the rugged image of the 'outdoorsy' type of man is constructed with pebble muscles and 'une haleine boisée' (woody traces on his breath). This good old-fashioned hunter even has 'des animaux fabuleux dans l'abdomen' (fabulous creatures in the abdomen) or 'un ventre peluche' (a furry belly) which can turn into 'un jouet d'enfant qui couine' (a child's squeaky toy) or 'une carte postale sonore' (a musical postcard) (p. 33). Detambel plays with our expectations and literary references too. For example, Baudelaire's ghost appears in the precious jewellery adorning the man who is greatly attached to his 'chaîne d'or' (p. 38) (gold chain). Elza Adamowicz has highlighted the dual pleasure of recognition and displacement experienced by the reader of surrealist blazons in Breton's 'L'Union libre'.[15] Detambel makes the familiar images truly uncanny: the return of stereotypes of female roles in the text recalls the Freudian joke because of the latent malaise it creates. Detambel displaces the clichés of gendered identity and activities as a means of giving an ambivalent sex to the male: the man's foreskin is washed 'comme un col de chemise' (p. 42) (like a shirt collar), but his hair is washed too and his head wrapped up in a turban ('elle l'enturbannait' (p. 42)) so that he might pose, in front of the television, as an odalisque by Ingres. She also fleshes out the male breasts and highlights their mineral or 'metallic' flavour, to borrow Brenda Hillman's adjective on the subject of 'male nipples',[16] as part of a rare description of male breasts: 'Ses mamelons étaient entourés de poils. Ils lui saisissaient la langue comme l'eau gazeuse' (p. 42) (His nipples were surrounded by hair. They stung her tongue like sparkling water.)

For Detambel, language makes the body visible and makes it new: exploring words means rediscovering the body:

> Et savoir l'aida beaucoup à sentir. Avec l'abaca, elle osa évoquer les arbres. Abandonnique lui fit penser à ce qu'elle était. Aréole lui donna, pour la première fois, l'occasion d'illuminer le sein d'une femme et celui d'un homme et fit surgir par la même occasion des épaules, un visage.[17]

> (To know helped her a great deal to feel. With abaca, she dared to think of trees. *Abandonnique* (fearing abandonment) reminded her of what she was. Areola gave her the opportunity, for the first time, to highlight a woman's and a man's breast, and at the same time to make shoulders and a face loom up.)

Blazons of the masculine body occur less often than might be expected. The enigmatic Diane wrote hers in 1995, in a rather conventional style which mimics old-fashioned syntax and vocabulary, set in rhyming couplets, while she adopts a more modern terminology for her 'Contreblasons'.[18] Paradoxically, if she states that she aims to glorify the 'neglected, male body' (p. 9), she also expresses disgust at the 'queue' 'pendouillant(e)' (dangling tail) with its indescribable 'bouts de peau-là' (p. 26) (bits of foreskin). Diane's ultimately negative and dismissive tone echoes the preface to another edition of *Les Blasons du corps féminin*, which not only removes the overmoralistic blazons, but also censors the 'risky' counterblazons of shameful private parts.[19] If we are to catch more than a glimpse of or an allusion to the male body, assessing the value of height, hair or colour of his eyes, we must go back to Louise Labé's frank lines in sonnet XXI.[20]

Recent book covers can be very revealing and even more deceptive. For instance, *Le Grand Livre du Mois's* edition feminised Marie Darrieussecq's *Naissance des fantômes* by exhibiting on its cover a series of alluring, naked female figures whose bodies are cut in half by the 'female' gaze of a pair of made-up eyes. However, Darrieussecq's female narrator asks, at the very end of a clever novel dealing with the weight of memory and ghosts: what would her vanished husband look like, if he were naked, what about his weight, his skin, his smell, wondering 'avait-il encore un sexe?' (did he still have a penis?).[21]

Detambel combines a clinical, unflinching gaze and unflattering scrutiny focused on blackheads, moles and boils, cuts and scars with the sensual lyricism of metaphors borrowed from nature. In this her writing strikes us as 'original', but it clearly also contains echoes of Colette, one of her acknowledged role models, whom she subverts through the addition of medical brutality.[22] If the image of a nurse in *Blasons d'un corps masculin* could be seen as a stereotype of the 'maternal', gentle female figure, we must remember that this woman ends up looking like 'la hyène, le vautour qui l'épie' (p. 45) (the hyena, the vulture preying on him) in the eyes of the man who will leave her, ironically enough, because 'elle lui contemple le nombril' (p. 47) (she contemplates his navel). We are told that this nurse also had cannibalistic tendencies – she would eat or smoke the man's letters – and she gradually becomes closer to the figure of the *femme fatale* (one might think of Deneuve turned into a dangerous nurse in Truffaut's *La Sirène du Mississippi*, manipulating letters, identity papers, and poisoning Belmondo slowly but surely).[23] It is the same double edge which proves unsettling in the work of Detambel. She keeps both the reader and her texts oscillating between seriousness, subversion of stereotypes, and the humour of self-derision – a situation that is most striking in her version of a portrait of the artist as a young and passionate body that has been flayed alive.

Anatomy of one's art: inscribing the writer

Detambel's symptomatic interest in series, oulipian distortions, and her own 'écarts majeurs' (major deviations), in which she seeks to penetrate beyond appearances to reach the inner folds that lie 'beneath the skin of words', has been highlighted by Sjef Houppermans.[24] In *La Ligne âpre* (1998), Detambel revivifies the genre of the blazons of female and male bodies by dissecting and reassembling the bone structure of the body.[25] The ghost of the writer haunts many of her novels and creeps between her lines, taking an anatomical shape: the emblem of the body flayed alive. Detambel's dissection of the writer's body, with its attention to precise definitions, refined and renewed adjectives, and striking metaphors, is in fact a dissection of language.

It comes as no surprise that the writing of the writer's vocation in the novel *L'Ecrivaillon ou l'enfance de l'écriture* is intermingled with the writing of body parts, focusing on the writer's hands, the veins and the passion and pain flowing through the long apprenticeship of the literary profession.[26] The stigmata are shown in the 'poignets tellement simples, si bleus' (wrists, so simple, so blue) of the 'écorché vif' (p. 14) (writer flayed alive), as well as in the books he wants to write, seen as 'blue veins' on the whiteness of church marble (p. 62). More unusual is the perfect equivalence established in *Graveurs d'enfance* between pens and computers – which are seen as autonomous bodies – and the writer's hands and arms, her muscles, bones and veins.[27] Objects are treated like body parts, thus avoiding the repetition of clichés through displacement. For instance, 'pen envy' is hinted at, counteracted and deflated by the transfer of disgust from the implied penis to the pen. In *L'Ecrivaillon*, the pen, a slobbering pen with its fat ink which is far from being desirable, turns out to be doubly 'dégouttant' (p. 96) (leaking/disgusting). Computers have a healthy shape and 'un écran lumineux, net et sans empâtement' (p. 99) (a bright, clear and slim screen); however, they are not always seen in such a favourable light. The deficiencies and limitations of the magic 'spell check' are revealed and exploited in a humorous vein which questions the writer's desire for absolute control. Nobody is spared and even modern computer technology is criticised for failing to identify, and attempting 'to correct', La Fontaine's fables (p. 100).

Even more striking is the insistence and persistence of the 'stripping bare' or *mise à nu* of the writer. In *Le Vélin*, Detambel shows the connection between text and skin.[28] She strokes the velum page and makes the writer's mouth open in order to investigate the origin of language and to insist that language in the Hugolian 'bouche d'ombre' (mouth of shadow) is first linked with the tongue and the teeth: 'Ce matin, dans la glace, j'ai regardé ma langue parler allemand. Ensuite ma langue a parlé français. Et ma bouche s'est tordue différemment et parfois mes dents cliquetaient' (p. 26) (This morning, in the mirror, I looked at my tongue speaking German. Then my tongue spoke French. And my mouth twisted differently and sometimes my teeth were chattering). This recalls what Hector Bianciotti writes about the impossible nudity of the body: only the voice can be naked.[29] Detambel adds contradictions to her comparisons and spices them up with self-mockery: poetry, she also says, is not a simple matter of 'des lèvres coriaces et musclées' (tough and muscular lips), or 'souffleuses de vers' (breathing poetry [with a pun on glass blowing]) (*L'Ecrivaillon*, p. 27).

While Detambel focuses her text on the bones, the veins and pain–passion of writing, she does not remystify the sacred image of the writer. 'La ligne âpre' may be the symbolic hard line of the writer's trade – our lifeline, a double line of destiny and death, or even our 'true' face inscribed in our legs, as Detambel suggests in a curious image which displaces body parts – but it is also the name of 'le fémur' (femur) and, curiously, a synonym or sign of unglamorous writing, a mere 'obscene graffiti' (*La Ligne âpre*, p. 71). The writer is not only a celebrated 'voleuse de langue' (tongue snatcher), she is the not so glorious 'voleur, mendiant, emprunteur, ravisseur, retoucheur et copieur' (*L'Ecrivaillon*, p. 54) (thief, beggar, who will borrow, snatch, patch up, or copy).[30] Detambel warns readers that she steals shamelessly, appropriates or distorts images from Colette (*Colette*, p. 9): a strategy which is seen in her 'langue de muguet' (lily-of-the-valley tongue) blooming repeatedly in many texts.[31] Reading through her essay on Colette, *Comme une flore, comme un zoo*, and examining the index of floral and animal metaphors, it becomes apparent how Detambel's texts owe as much to 'la leçon de Colette' (Colette's lesson) as they do to the anatomy lesson. Viewed in this light, Detambel's *Blasons d'un corps masculin* can be read in order to hear, see and taste the colours, smells and textures of the body parts, starting from the olive and walnut bitterness to be found in the ear.

On occasion, Detambel recycles her own texts. Whole chapters of *L'Ecrivaillon* can be found in the text entitled *L'Avarice*, written for the exhibition at the Pompidou centre on the Seven Deadly Sins. The character of 'l'avaricieuse' (the avaricious woman) is an alter ego of the 'écrivaillon' or 'écrivaillonne' (male or female scribbler). In other words, the writer can be – and be written – in both interchangeable genders. The same demystification accompanies the telling of the vocation and the inspiration of the writer. She is worried about her short-sightedness, her deformed and ink-stained hands, but even more terrified by the double trap of predictable 'first novels' and readers' expectations. Such 'young' books overflow with introspection, oozing bumps, and desires which smell of 'wet fingers' and wet dreams (*L'Ecrivaillon*, p. 72). In order to avoid this trap, the young writer starts by examining stamps to see how words and images can circulate differently in the hope that this slightly obsolete pastime will, paradoxically, set her imagination free.

Slight variations in 'l'avaricieuse' and 'l'écrivaillon' play with other symptomatic images of adolescence. A poster of a rock group changes names on the wall, from *Deep Purple* to *Status Quo*, but its proximity to an élitist quote by Goethe, highlighting the 'god-given gift of literature' is ironic and points to the relative values attached to high and popular culture (*L'Avarice*, pp. 11–12).[32] What is undermined is the naïveté or pomposity of the juvenile writer, gazing at rock and roll stars or romantic words with absolute faith or blindness and the same lack of distance. The clichés of the Romantic ideal of storms, inner turmoil, and an ethos of pain are irremediably twisted into a modern-age fear with an added 'frisson', due to the 'thrill' of potential computer crashes at 'dangerous hours' (*L'Avarice*, p. 21). What remains is the classic image of hunger and literary desire: a hunger for words, an appetite for language and control of knowledge that is shown in a dual light. The writer's body, according to Detambel, is the body described by Montaigne: unavoidable, familiar or suddenly strange when it falls into a coma. The body remains omnipresent with an inner 'skeletos' which reminds us of the essence of our being: our mortality.[33]

Flaubert's influence is equally inscribed in *L'Ecrivaillon ou l'enfance de l'écriture*. The *écrivaillon/écrivaillonne*'s attempts and temptations recall the Bouvard et Pécuchet approach to the digestion of dictionaries – a futile excess which brings the hungry, writing learner to the point of nausea as she/he remembers the torture of childhood meals (p. 128). Overfed with volumes of words, the curious *avaricieuse* prescribes herself the remedy of a paradoxically healthy anorexia. She refuses to finish up her own texts as if they were meals, and 'savour[e] son inappétence' (p. 128) (savour[s] her lack of appetite). The trauma and the taboo of female anorexia are thus both inscribed and questioned in an insistent 'inappétence' which is linked to both genders. Detambel's irony shows her readers that one can distort anorexia and joke about what has become appropriated and perceived as a 'female' illness par excellence.[34] Could this disease become even more problematic if it were to remain a sacrosanct topic, an irrefutable proof of feminine essentialism? This uneasy question, about a very serious disease, can also be read between Detambel's humorous lines.

Conclusion: readers and fetishes

Detambel's passion for classification and the unveiling of structures is reminiscent of Roland Barthes. In *S/Z*, Barthes highlights how blazons are
caught in the trap of language, since fetishised body parts escape from
patient lists and never fulfil the artist's dreams of unity.[35] Pascal Quignard
insists not only on the sadism of the 'Blasons', but on the need for the other
that they represent: the only way to 'see' our invisible backs is to read the
'blason du dos', and even this reading will never be enough (p. 141). In parallel to Quignard, Detambel's practice of the blazon is applied to the other
and returned onto the self: 'Morceler et fragmenter m'intéresse. Le corps
donne une leçon d'humilité à l'écrivain' (I am interested in splitting up, in
fragmentation. The body teaches the writer a lesson in humility).[36] In the
same extract, she underlines the relative nature of common 'ignorance',
through a series of paradoxes and differences of priorities: readers and
writers who cannot name their bones or veins will strive to locate Chechnya
on a map, but they won't worry if they don't know where Jupiter is. The
hierarchy between priorities of knowledge that Detambel proposes is
shocking but seems to contain some truth. But are we really so distanced
from our bodies that human anatomy sounds as obscure and unreachable
as the geography of the stars?

    Detambel implicitly asks whether readers are guilty of ignorance or
indifference. François Dagognet too, having written extensively on the
body in philosophical essays, still wonders what kind of readers to address
in *La Peau découverte*.[37] Which reader is Detambel talking to or talking
about? Reading means another substance, texture, body and presence: 'Le
livre n'est pas seulement demande d'évasion et d'oubli, il réclame, il néces-
site la saine présence du lecteur' (p. 36) (A book does not only answer a
need to escape and forget, it demands and requires the healthy presence of
its reader). What types of reader has Detambel classified? Which one has
she inscribed in her words and metaphors? The 'perfect' reader has
already been trapped in one of her lists of fetishised 'objets d'écriture'
(objects of writing), an ambivalent list of children's stationery in *Graveurs
d'enfance*, which is not as nostalgic as it may seem. There the reader is portrayed as a thirsty piece of blotting paper which might also escape our definitions or expectations:

> Le Buvard est le lecteur authentique. A ne pas confondre avec l'éponge!
> Grand amateur d'impressions mouillées, il est le premier à toucher la page

finie, et ce qu'il garde de ce contact neuf avec la phrase fraîche, il s'en couvre le corps. Regarder de près, malgré ses couleurs pénibles, les veines du Buvard. Sacrifier un Buvard en le déchirant. (*Graveurs d'enfance*, pp. 207–8)

(The Blotting Paper is the true reader. Don't confuse it with the sponge! He is a connoisseur of wet sensations, the first one to touch the written page. What is kept from the initial contact with the fresh page is spread onto his body. Look closely at the Blotting Paper's veins, despite their sickening colours. Make a sacrifice by tearing it up.)

We can never be too careful. Detambel is already working on our own dissection. Should we welcome or avoid the potential 'sacrifice', 'déchirement' (tearing up) and the in-depth analysis?

Detambel also leaves us with some traces of hope, positive definitions of fears and 'écorchés' (flayed bodies). While her readers had just finished reading her perplexing *Blasons d'un corps masculin*, she was already working on the primary blazons, the blazons of the child's body or 'Blasons d'un corps enfantin'.[38] Here she takes us further back in the subversion of the genre of the blazons, deeper and closer to the roots of the problem – in the mathematical sense applied to the child, 'un être mathématique' (p. 166) (a mathematical being) and to the rules of 'l'écriture sous contraintes' (constrained writing). Bearing in mind that everything superficial is 'disastrous' (p. 168), we might as well accept Detambel's deeper incisions and 'éraflures' (scratches) to our reassuring definitions. Detambel cuts remorselessly through our masks, façades and protective closures, while inventing new, irresistible puns and musing about our blood-thirsty/blood-fearing nature. The star-shaped hole, or 'petit trou en forme d'étoile' she scratches at the surface and beyond appearances, reveals an inner darkness which matches the blindness in which we would rather remain comfortably enveloped: 'L'écorchure est une fenêtre soudain en soi [. . .] Il [l'enfant] a pénétré dans ce lieu étranger qu'il habite seul, qu'il prenait pour un abri, et qui n'en est pas un' (p. 169) (The scratch is a window suddenly flung open onto oneself [. . .] He [the child] has entered a world in which he lives alone, which he thought was a shelter, but which is not).

Notes

1 *Marie-Claire*, 565 (September 1999), p. 144.

2 The metaphor of the medicinal 'priest's garden', used to describe her work, might be an echo of the title of her novel, *Le Jardin clos* (Paris: Gallimard, 1994).

3 The OuLiPo (Ouvroir de Littérature Potentielle (Workshop of Potential Literature)), founded in Paris in the early 1960s, consisted of a group of mathematicians and writers who imposed constraints on their writing (e.g. concerning plot, structure, use of letters of the alphabet) as a means of fostering creativity.

4 Régine Detambel, *Le Mystère de la dame de fer* (Paris: Gallimard Jeunesse, 1998), p. 93.

5 Régine Detambel, *Les Ecarts majeurs* (Paris: Julliard, 1993); in 1979 Gainsbourg recorded a notoriously irreverant reggae version of the French national anthem.

6 Claire Devarrieux, 'L'écorchée à confesse', *Libération* (5 March 1998); Eric Loret, 'Les vits de Jésus', *Libération* (25 August 1999); 'Folles de leur corps', *Les Inrockuptibles*, 139 (18–24 February 1998).

7 Régine Detambel, *L'Amputation* (Paris: Julliard, 1990).

8 Pascal Quignard, 'Postface', in *Blasons anatomiques du corps féminin* (Paris: Gallimard, 1982), pp. 141–4.

9 Alison Saunders, *The Sixteenth-Century Blason Poétique* (Bern, Frankfurt am Main and Las Vegas: Peter Lang, 1981), pp. 9–11.

10 Germaine Greer, *The Whole Woman* (London: Doubleday, 1999); Michel Serres, *Variations sur le corps* (Paris: Le Pommier, 1999); *Spectacular Bodies: The Art and Science of the Human Body from Leonardo to Now*, catalogue of the exhibition which charted the relationship between art and dissection (London: Hayward Gallery, 2000).

11 Susan Faludi, *Stiffed, the Betrayal of the Modern Man* (London: Chatto & Windus, 1999).

12 *Libération*, special supplement, 'A quoi pensez-vous' (31 December 1999), p. 6. For 'oulipian' see note 3 above.

13 Régine Detambel, *Blasons d'un corps masculin* (Montpellier: Via Voltaire, 1996), p. 8. All translations are my own.

14 Anon., 'Blason du cul', in *Blasons anatomiques du corps féminin*, pp. 107–10. My thanks to Jennifer Britnell and Alison Saunders for their expert advice.

15 Elza Adamowicz, *Surrealist Collage in Text and Image: Dissecting the Exquisite Corpse* (Cambridge: Cambridge University Press, 1998), p. 176.

16 Brenda Hillman, *Loose Sugar* (Hanover, NH and London: Wesleyan University Press, University Press of New England, 1997), pp. 29–31.

17 Régine Detambel, *L'Avarice* (Paris: Centre Pompidou, 1997), pp. 16–17.

18 Diane, *Les Blasons du corps masculin* (Paris: Caractères, 1995). No last name is given.

19 Jean-Clarence Lambert (ed.), *Les Blasons du corps féminin* (Paris: Club des Libraires de France, 1963).

20 'Quelle grandeur rend l'homme venerable?/Quelle grosseur? quel poil? quelle couleur?/Qui est des yeux le plus emmieleur?/Qui fait plus tot une playe incurable?' (What figure, height and shade of hair are fittest/To make a man admired? and what complexion?/What colour of eye most sweetens the affection?/Which

deals the heart a deadly wound the quickest?), in Louise Labé, *Sonnets*, introd. and commentaries Peter Sharratt, trans. Graham Dunstan Martin (Edinburgh: Edinburgh University Press, 1973), pp. 40–1.

21 Marie Darrieussecq, *Naissance des fantômes* (Paris: Le Grand Livre du Mois, 1998), p. 155.

22 Régine Detambel, *Colette. Comme une flore, comme un zoo. Un répertoire des images du corps* (Paris: Stock, 1997), pp. 7–14.

23 François Truffaut, *La Sirène du Mississippi*, 1969 (Video, Warner, 1996).

24 Sjef Houppermans, 'Le jardin clos de Régine Detambel', in Michael Bishop (ed.), *Thirty Voices in the Feminine* (Amsterdam and Atlanta, GA: Rodopi, 1996), pp. 151–65 (p. 162).

25 Régine Detambel, *La Ligne âpre* (Paris: Christian Bourgois, 1998).

26 Régine Detambel, *L'Ecrivaillon ou l'enfance de l'écriture* (Paris: Gallimard, 1998).

27 Régine Detambel, *Graveurs d'enfance* (Paris: Christian Bourgois, 1993).

28 Régine Detambel, *Le Vélin* (Paris: Julliard, 1973).

29 Hector Bianciotti, 'La voix et la nudité', in Marie-France Castarède (ed.), *La Voix et ses sortilèges* (Paris: Les Belles Lettres, 1987), p. 166.

30 See Claudine Herrmann, *Les Voleuses de langue* (Paris: Des femmes, 1976).

31 See Régine Detambel, *Album* (Paris: Calmann-Lévy, 1995), p. 70 and *Blasons d'un corps masculin*, p. 16.

32 See *Colette*, p. 7, for the autobiographical dimension of this quotation.

33 Michel de Montaigne, *Essais* (Paris: Gallimard, Folio, 1965), p. 70. See Louis Marin, *La Voix excommuniée* (Paris: Galilée, 1981), p. 156.

34 See Susan Bordo, *Unbearable Weight: Feminism, Western Culture and the Body* (Berkeley and Los Angeles: University of California Press, 1995).

35 Roland Barthes, *S/Z* (Paris: Seuil, 1970), pp. 118–20. My thanks to Elza Adamowicz for reminding me of this passage.

36 Letter from Detambel to the author, 30 November 1999.

37 François Dagognet, *La Peau découverte* (Le Plessis-Robinson: Laboratoire Delagrange–Synthélabo, collection 'Les Empêcheurs de penser en rond', 1993), p. 111.

38 Régine Detambel, 'Blasons d'un corps enfantin', *Nouvelle Revue Française*, 552 (January 2000), 166–72.

'On ne s'entendait plus et c'était parfait ainsi' (They could no longer hear each other and it was just fine that way): misunderstandings in the novels of Agnès Desarthe

In the first three of the four novels Agnès Desarthe has published at the time of writing – *Quelques minutes de bonheur absolu* (1993), *Un secret sans importance* (1996), *Cinq photos de ma femme* (1998) and *Les Bonnes Intentions* (2000) – the binary opposition understanding–misunderstanding stands out as a central issue, particularly with regard to identity. What emerges is a relentless impulse on the part of the characters to be understood and to understand, or, more precisely, to be defined by, and to define, the other in absolutist terms. However, their dependence upon what are shown to be society's generally accepted, commonly exploited, but largely unreliable methods for projecting and perceiving identity only succeeds in establishing a network of misunderstandings and it is these which shape the various relationships, for example, between the two sexes (husband and wife, male admirer and female object of admiration), between members of the same sex (sisters, mothers, daughters), and also the relationship that the individual has with him or herself. If Desarthe's observation of signalling behaviour undoubtedly owes much to her formal training in linguistics, her analysis of communication extends well beyond a mere interest in semantics.[1] Rather, as this article will attempt to demonstrate, her illustration of the understanding–misunderstanding dichotomy, and the solution which she proposes to the interpretative dilemma, reveal a broader existential concern with the notions of truth and identity.

Identity/eye-dentity and the inexorable desire to fix

What emerges in the first three novels is a tension between two divergent approaches to interpretation which have given rise to much debate in the fields of semantics and philosophical hermeneutics: on the one hand, an objectivist attitude which sees identity as transparent and univocal; and on the other the view that there can be no purely objective interpretation because of the interpreter's inability to transcend his own subjectivity when reading the emitter's signals, with this inescapable subjectivity obtaining also when the interpreter and emitter are the same person.[2] In *Quelques minutes de bonheur absolu*, this tension is manifest in the uneasy relationships between a solitary, complex midwife, Cyrille Grossmann, and her friends, patients and family. If Cyrille is highly conscious of the difficulties of both understanding the world around her and particularly of making herself understood, she does, none the less, subscribe to the view that identity is an accessible absolute. This is demonstrated clearly by her interpretation of how Jacob, the husband of one of her patients, has categorised her during their very brief encounter at the theatre:

> elle distinguait son visage en tout petit dans l'iris miroitant de Jacob et connaissait ses pensées, comme si sa présence reflétée dans son œil lui avait permis de lire ce qui se passait derrière. Je suis une femme fatale, se dit-elle sans trouver l'ivresse qu'elle croyait pouvoir attendre d'une telle révélation. Pourquoi fallait-il que les hommes la voient autrement qu'elle était? Il aurait été si simple de lire par-dessus son épaule le sens de sa vie dans la glace éclatée qui finissait de souiller le couloir du Châtelet. Il n'y avait rien de mystérieux là-dedans. Il suffisait de la prendre telle qu'elle était.[3]

> (She could make out her face mirrored in miniature in Jacob's iris and could read his thoughts as if her reflected presence in his eye had allowed her to decipher what was going on behind it. I am a *femme fatale*, she said to herself without experiencing the headiness she thought she could expect from such a revelation. Why did men have to see her other than how she was? It would have been so simple to look over her shoulder and read the meaning of her life in the splattered ice-cream which was contributing to the filth in the corridor at Châtelet. There was nothing mysterious about it. She just had to be taken for what she was.)

Cyrille's analysis of Jacob's eye and of the reflection it carries – an obvious symbol of the defining process whereby we both categorise and are categorised – her refusal of his perceived identification of her and her view that she should just be taken at face value convey the idea that identity is located exclusively in the subject's intended identity and that successful communication of that identity consists in a straightforward linear transaction between the emitter's intended signal and the reproductive consciousness of the receiver/interpreter. What Cyrille fails to entertain is that, just as Jacob may have misinterpreted her sexual identity, it is equally possible that she may have misinterpreted his appraisal of her (and, of course, other expressions of his identity), and indeed her own true identity.

The episode also illustrates one of the mechanisms whereby the subject appraises her own identity. On numerous occasions, the person whom Cyrille is interpreting functions as a sign system in which she reads her own identity, as in the above example, where Jacob's interpretation of her as a *femme fatale* strengthens her conviction that she is *not* a *femme fatale*. This use of the other to understand the self also characterises Cyrille's relationship with her parents. She seeks her identity within them, as if there should necessarily be a common identity between parent and off-spring, but is disconcerted to find no physical or psychological resem-blance. Compounding this (thwarted) expectation of finding herself in her parents is Cyrille's attachment to her childhood: her greatest happiness, we are told, comes from rummaging through childhood clothes in her parents' cupboards because of the highly personal, though indistinct, associations which they trigger (p. 190), and she yearns again for the 'quelques minutes de bonheur absolu' (few minutes of pure bliss) which concealment in their wardrobe afforded her as a child (pp. 50, 124). These two pleasures, situ-ated as they are in the childhood family home, clearly connote her desire both to locate and fix her identity in the past and in the parents, but in fact offer her no clarity about herself.[4]

Despite believing herself to be accurate in her perception of others, Cyrille is, it is strongly implied, extremely subjective in her judgements, an unconscious tendency on her part which is highlighted by the narrative style. The processes by which she arrives at her judgements (and she is far from neutral) are not always made explicit to the reader and, when they are, they are not highly analytical, as evidenced, for example, by her various appraisals of her sister (pp. 92, 94), her mother (p. 56) and her friend Viviane (p. 77). Moreover, the narrator does not intervene to confirm or contradict Cyrille's interpretations. This narrative discretion, together with the exten-sive use of free indirect discourse to foreground her perspective, and a vocabulary connoting the subjectivity of perception – expressions such as 'avoir l'impression' (to have the impression), 'avoir la sensation' (to have the feeling), and 'se sentir' (to feel) abound in the text, and, indeed, in Desarthe's two following novels – highlights the arbitrariness of her inter-pretation of the world around her, thus placing an implied question mark over the accuracy of her appraisals of both herself and other characters.

In *Un secret sans importance*, the relationships of two distinct groups of people form the framework in which the understanding–misunderstanding dichotomy is explored. On the one hand, there is a group of linguisticians, Emile, Dan, Harriet, Gabriel and Frédéric, and, on the other, there are two women who are far from academic: Violette, a widow recently released from a psychiatric hospital, and Sonia, Dan's dying wife. Moreover, in contrast to *Quelques minutes de bonheur absolu*, an omniscient narrator leaves the reader in no doubt as to whether the truth, or at least the intended meaning, is being eluded or grasped.

The linguisticians believe that they may objectively interpret identity through an analysis of signalling behaviour, and that they may equally objectively translate their conclusions into language, an aspiration and confidence in their ability to transcend their subjectivity which is highlighted by the titles of their various projects. Gabriel, for example, is writing a thesis entitled 'Opérations énonciatives sous-jacentes aux mal-entendus' (Enunciative operations underlying misunderstandings), Emile has written an article entitled 'Détermination et modalité dans les langues indo-européenes' (Determination and modality in the Indo-European languages), and Harriet has written an epistemological dissertation, 'De l'animisme au vitalisme, les apports des conceptions aristotéliciennes aux travaux de Claude Bernard: Contre une définition cartésienne de l'humain' (From animism to vitalism, the contribution of Aristotelian conceptions to the work of Claude Bernard: against a Cartesian definition of the human). However, despite being officially recognised as experts in language, they are often shown both to be unable to communicate their ideas clearly and to misunderstand signals, a comment on the inadequacy of language (both linguistic and paralinguistic) to convey intended meaning.

A notable example of such problems with language is seen in the episode in which Emile and Gabriel, analysing their respective history in relation to Irina, Gabriel's mother, a dancer with whom Emile once had a fleeting affair, come to the conclusion that they must be father and son, and indeed the text implies that this is the case. It is only in the final few pages that we are told that this is not so, but Emile and Gabriel are not enlightened, confidently believing that they have accurately deciphered the past and redefined their relationship with each other. As Gabriel comments, unconsciously highlighting the error of his judgement and the precariousness of interpretation generally: 'C'était très facile. Tout est écrit. Il suffit de savoir lire' (It was very easy. Everything is written. You just have to know how to read).[5]

This impulse to define and fix identity within recognisable, but not necessarily accurate, contours is a marked trait in Emile which is reflected in his reliance upon flagrant stereotypes to categorise, for example, Americans (p. 72), and female sexuality (p. 91). His sense of shame that his mother did not fit into the sophisticated intellectual world to which he wished to belong is, we are told, the reason for his choice of girlfriends: they all conform to one type, a type diametrically opposed to the image he has of his mother (p. 92), but with none of them does he enjoy a harmony.[6] He is confused and discomfitted by his attraction to Violette because she does not conform to the usual model, and indeed seems to elude definition. As he tells her: 'Il me semble que vous appartenez à une espèce à part' (p. 180) (It seems to me that you belong to a different species). He is shown to have become so mannered with regard to women that he has lost all spontaneity, as evidenced by his inability to express his attraction to her when several appropriate opportunities present themselves. Similarly, Sonia too remains opaque before him because she does not conform to a familiar type, and this prevents him from being able to communicate with her (pp. 12–13).

In contrast to the linguisticians, Violette and Sonia are sceptical about the ability to communicate and to interpret situations objectively through language. Quite apart from their various comments to the linguisticians, this is shown when they meet each other at a reception held at the Institute. A degree of empathy is quickly established between the two women which arises from their mutual and tacit *refusal* both to communicate verbally and to attempt to interpret each other in detail:

> Sonia aurait aimé la questionner … Mais la différence d'âge lui paraissait infranchissable. Elle avait l'impression qu'elle et Violette ne parleraient pas la même langue. Violette, de son côté, avait envie de lui demander ce que ça faisait de porter une perruque. Toutefois, elle s'estimait déjà assez heureuse de pouvoir être assise à côté d'une femme perruquée. (p. 133)

> (Sonia would have liked to ask her some questions … But the age difference seemed unsurmountable to her. She had the impression that she and Violette would not speak the same language. As for Violette, she wanted to ask her what it was like to wear a wig. However, she considered herself happy enough just to be sat next to a woman in a wig.)

So it is that when the music starts up 'On ne s'entendait plus et c'était parfait ainsi' (p. 133) (They could no longer hear each other and it was just fine that way).

In *Cinq photos de ma femme*, the central character, Max, displays a contradictory approach to understanding which recalls that of Cyrille in *Quelques minutes de bonheur absolu*. If at times he is very much aware of the difficulties of both making himself understood and of understanding others, at other times he presumes that truth is a transparent absolute. It is this presumption which makes him believe that the identity (both physical and psychological) of his dead wife, Telma, is an eternal absolute which can be perceived and communicated by three artists from each of whom he commissions a portrait of her, even though he believes that while alive she eluded definition by him and, indeed, by other artists, namely the photographers who tried to photograph her:

> Max pensa que c'était une femme démoniaque et qu'elle avait soigneusement évité de se faire tirer le portrait. A présent qu'elle n'était plus là pour protester, *il se réjouissait à l'idée de la fixer enfin, de caler son joli visage triangulaire dans un cadre doré* et de passer des heures, en son immobile compagnie, à discuter en silence.[7]

> (Max thought she was fiendish and that she had carefully avoided having her portrait taken. Now that she was no longer there to protest, he took pleasure in the idea of fixing her once and for all, of capturing her pretty triangular face in a golden frame and of spending hours in her motionless company talking in silence. (p. 9))

Like Cyrille and the linguisticians, Max is oblivious to his own role in the mediation and construction of the other's identity. In what may be considered a reworking of the Zeuxis story,[8] he provides each of the artists, who have no first-hand experience of Telma, with five images of her. Their access to her identity is therefore through the photographers' interpretation of her, and this interpretation has been subjected to a further interpretation by Max who, from among all the photos and slides he has of her, selects only five, his criterion being that 'il fallait choisir les plus significatives' (p. 16) ('he had to choose the most revealing ones' (p. 8)). We are not informed why the ones he chooses are the most 'revealing', and this omission, together with the emphasis on his inability to understand Telma – who is frequently evoked as enigmatic and secretive (pp. 25, 26, 48) – highlights the opaque subjectivity and the arbitrariness of his choice, as indeed does the selection of just five photos and the commissioning of three portraits as opposed to any other number (as the character Nina points out (p. 142)), and the random selection of the artists: Angus from the telephone directory, Virginie from a newspaper advertisement, and Marion by chance encounter at the Ecole des Beaux-Arts. Moreover, in the case of the materials which he provides for the artists Virginie and Marion, he has transposed the original photos onto different media (slides and photocopies respectively), which constitutes a further reinterpretation, a further layer of subjectivity, separating them from the original subject. This entire project whereby Telma is reproduced by Max in different media, only to undergo a further series of interpretations in different media again, highlights the malleability of identity at the hands of the interpreter.

As the artists reveal their respective approaches and finally their understanding of Telma, we recognise a recontextualisation of the debate central to the two earlier novels on the role of the perceiving subject in relation to the object. Virginie and Nina's aspiration to reproduce Telma's physical appearance as Max knew it implies that, in their opinion, they may find the key to her identity through him, a confidence expressed by the detail in which they explain to Max the sensitivity of their respective interpretation (pp. 159, 179–82). Moreover, by relying upon Max to define Telma's physical attributes, as if he is an objective appraiser of Telma, the two artists signal to the reader how far removed their interpretation is from the object (pp. 74, 180). In contrast, Angus and Marion try to capture her essence in more abstract and figurative terms which flaunt the subjectivity of their interpretation. However, none of these approaches produces a portrait in which Max recognises the version of Telma he wishes to capture:

> A chacun d'eux, il avait parlé de la petite étincelle dans le regard et n'avait rencontré, les trois fois, que l'indifférence la plus sourde. 'Ce que je veux, précisait-il, c'est ce petit air, qu'elle a, enfin, qu'elle avait. On ne se rend pas compte sur le photos, c'est pour ça que je vous en parle. La petite lumière dans les yeux. Vous voyez ce que je veux dire?' C'est ça, cause toujours, papy. Il les aurait mangés tout crus. Comment pouvait-on accepter une commande si l'on n'en saisissait pas tous les termes? Une bande de malhonnêtes. (p. 164)

> (He had spoken to each of them about the little twinkle in her eye, and on all three occasions this had been greeted with nothing but dull indifference. 'What I want', he had specified, 'is that little look that she has, well, that she had. You can't really see it in the photos, that's why I'm telling you about it. The little light in her eyes. Do you see what I mean?' That's right, Grandpa, you keep chatting. He could have eaten them for breakfast. How can you accept a commission when you haven't grasped all the conditions? Bunch of crooks. (p. 144))

As Max realises when he collects the first painting from Virginie, the portraits, far from eternalising Telma's identity, serve only to efface it for him, because they do not correspond to his idea of her as a still vibrant force (p. 162). He decides to destroy the three commissioned portraits because of their failure to interpret objectively his own subjective appraisal of her identity. As for the fourth portrait, an unsollicited one by Nina, he does not feel angry and disappointed in it because he realises now that Telma's identity cannot be transposed into a material representation (p. 157). It is Nina's portrait in particular which highlights the extent to which the subjectivity of the observer prevails in the interpretative process: she unwittingly presents him with a portrait not of Telma, but of herself (p. 183). By contrast with Zeuxis, then, the sum of the parts, the five photos and their four reinterpretations, do not make up the perfect whole, the 'perfect whole' being Max's specific idea of Telma.

Picasso, an icon of art's diversity,[9] appears to him in a dream (connoting Max's subconscious), and explains that Telma's identity is eternalised not through someone else's unavoidably subjective interpretation, but through Max's own personal idea of her:

Qui mieux que vous pourrait faire ce portrait? Car vous l'avez aimée cette femme, n'est-ce pas? Les photos, c'est bien mignon, mais vous savez comme moi que ce sont elles les coupables. Des miroirs déformants . . . Concentrez-vous, Max. Vous la revoyez. Il suffit que les lettres de son prénom s'agencent pour qu'aussitôt son image s'offre à vous. (p. 173)

(Who could do this portrait better than you? Because you loved this woman, didn't you? Photos are all very sweet, but you know as well as I do that they're at fault here. They're distorting mirrors . . . Concentrate, Max. You can see her again. All it takes is for the letters of her name to appear in the right order and a picture of her comes to you immediately. (p. 153))

As Picasso implies in the dream, the signifier, the name Telma, holds for Max particular associations accessible only to him. The name does not and cannot have the same resonance for others because they do not share the same experience of Telma, an idea articulated earlier in the text, albeit more implicitly, by the particular associations which Telma's name has for Virginie (a packet of soup sold in Monoprix (p. 62)) and which her son's name, Paulo, has for Max (a brand of sweets (p. 63)). This location of identity in the subjective idea and experience is in fact a key notion of conceptual art which argues that perception is subjective. It could, therefore, be argued that the interpretation of Telma by Angus, the conceptual artist, is the most authentic of the four portraits, because it does not aspire to being an objective representation of her, but to being a representation of how Angus conceives of her. Conceptual art emerges, then, as a metaphor for the subjectivity and instability of all communicative and interpretative processes.

'*Sous le pont Mirabeau*' (Under the Mirabeau bridge): towards an absolute identity

Despite the catalogue of misunderstandings and tensions in which Desarthe's characters become embroiled by attempting to fix identity in absolutist terms, a number of them come to a new and reassuring understanding of the people around them, and of their own place in the universe. The reasons for this shift are not explicated in the text, and the characters themselves seem to have no idea of its exact provenance, which would imply that it is both intuitive, rather than rationalised, and randomly triggered. The process is defined clearly by Violette as 'une sorte d'intuition . . . L'impression que l'on sait ce qui se cache derrière les murs. On sait exactement ce qu'on doit faire, on n'a pas besoin de réfléchir' (*Un secret sans importance*, p. 186) (a sort of intuition . . . the impression that you know what is hidden behind the walls. You know exactly what you have to do, you don't need to reflect).

In *Quelques minutes de bonheur absolu*, Cyrille acquires this new understanding in the final pages of the novel, and it may be seen as a redefinition of her 'quelques minutes de bonheur absolu' (few minutes of pure bliss). If, up until now, she has sought both to locate and fix her identity largely in the past and particularly through identification with her parents, she suddenly realises that her childhood is gone for ever, that she cannot fix herself in the past, but must look forward because life is fluid, constantly in flux, and she is a part of this larger momentum, in the same way as everybody else (pp. 190–2). Similarly, Violette's apparently random realisation while digging the garden that death is a part of the natural cycle makes her understand that she must now begin a new life and lay to rest the memories of her dead mother and husband, memories which have paralysed her with depression (*Un secret sans importance*, p. 169). Finally, Max suddenly realises that he should shift his focus from his dead wife to the shared living legacy in which they perpetuate themselves, namely, their two children (*Cinq photos de ma femme*, p. 186). The only certainty, it appears, is that death awaits everyone, and so Cyrille, Violette, Max, all individuals, have simply to submit to this absolute existential truth, the common keystone to everyone's identity. The rest, it is implied, is meaningless. As Cyrille realises:

> Il valait mieux s'y attendre et s'y préparer. Elle ferma les yeux afin de signer le pacte qu'elle venait de passer avec elle-même. Sous le pont Mirabeau coule la Seine, récita-t-elle avec un sentiment d'apaisement inconnu. Il suffisait de se laisser flotter, sans lutter contre le courant, d'un pont à l'autre, la tête juste assez hors de l'eau pour admirer les changements de paysage. (*Quelques minutes de bonheur absolu*, p. 192)[10]

(It was best to expect it and to prepare for it. She closed her eyes in order to sign the pact which she had just made with herself. Under the Mirabeau bridge flows the Seine, she recited with a sense of peacefulness which she had not experienced before. She just had to let herself float, without battling against the current, from one bridge to another, with her head just slightly raised out of the water to enable her to admire the changing landscape.)

In these three novels, then, the tension between subjectivity and objectivity is central to the construction of identity. The recontextualisation of this problematic in each text has a twofold effect. First, it creates a schematic effect which serves to emphasise that it is a commonplace not confined to one universe. Second, it unites the three texts in a tryptych, each panel of which foregrounds the understanding–misunderstanding issue. The characters are shown to have difficulty understanding themselves and others when they fail to recognise their inescapable subjectivity in the interpretative and communicative processes. Consequently, ideas and identities in their absolute form remain remote, never seized in their entirety, only partially glimpsed and understood,[11] and largely eclipsed by the interpreter's subjective reconstruction of them. However, Desarthe's universe is not relentlessly bleak and continually self-deconstructing because at the centre of it is an absolute truth which humankind may grasp through intuition. This absolute truth is that life and death are the only certainties, and so, as nothing may be accurately comprehended by man and his interpretative rationalising methods, he should live according to nature's law which connects him to a more spiritual understanding of his identity, and that of others, in the universe. In this respect Desarthe's philosophy rescues character and reader alike from the deconstructionist postmodern wilderness of an entirely uncomprehending and incomprehensible world.

Notes

1 Desarthe holds one of the highest French academic qualifications, the prestigious *agrégation*, in linguistics.

2 This is what Hans-Georg Gadamer calls 'inescapable situatedness': our ability to understand and interpret is limited by our particular horizon or range of vision which is in itself fixed by prejudices which are not chosen freely or arbitrarily but arise from our particular social, historical situation and of which we are not fully aware. According to this theory, one cannot then disregard oneself and one's own situation in trying to understand others, one cannot comprehend a situation as another person comprehends it. On this notion, see in particular Hans-Georg Gadamer, *Truth and Method*, trans. Joel Weinsheimer and Donald G. Marshall (London: Sheed and Ward, 1975).

3 Agnès Desarthe, *Quelques minutes de bonheur absolu* (Paris: Seuil, 1993), p. 147. Unless otherwise stated, all translations are my own.

4 It is certainly tempting to see Cyrille's thwarted search for her self in her childhood and parents as an ironic allusion to, and indirect criticism of, psychoanalytical emphasis on the role of the childhood in determining identity.

5 Agnès Desarthe, *Un secret sans importance* (Paris: Olivier/Seuil, 1996), p. 206. Emile and Gabriel would, however, seem to be father and son in the figurative sense given their similar confidence in their ability to interpret objectively. Their physical resemblance to each other strengthens the parent–child analogy.

6 This rejection of the mother image is a variation on the search for identity in the parent encountered in *Quelques minutes de bonheur absolu*.

7 *Cinq photos de ma femme* (Paris: Seuil, 1998), p. 17, my italics. Translations of this work are taken from *Five Photos of my Wife*, trans. Adriana Hunter (London: Flamingo, 2001).

8 Just as Zeuxis painted a composite Helen, based on the various parts of five of the most beautiful girls in Crotona – the theory being that the sum of the perfect parts must add up to a perfect whole – so too does Max wish a painting to be made of a composite Telma. On the Zeuxis story, see Cicero, *De Inventione*, II, I.I; Pliny, *Natural History*, XXXV, xxxvi. 61.

9 Moreover, the fact that, in Picasso's extensive experiments with pictorial language, much of his work was inspired by women, and that he frequently executed the same subject in multiple styles and media, makes him an appropriate commentator on the diverse images to which artistic interpretation of Telma gives rise. Ironically, Max states earlier that the last thing he wants is a portrait in the style of Picasso (p. 64), and so highlights his view of identity as a transparent absolute and of painting as objectively representational. His similar rejection of the Impressionist, Renoir, has embedded in it the same aesthetic view that art should put a line round a concept (p. 64).

10 Certainly the intertext, 'Le pont Mirabeau', Apollinaire's poem on the transience of all things, especially love, implies the solitariness of this stoical understanding of life. See Guillaume Apollinaire, *Alcools* (Paris: Gallimard, 1920), p. 15.

11 Like the concept of the hermeneutic circle whereby in order to understand the whole one has to understand the parts, while in order to understand the parts one has to understand the whole, this partial understanding may be said to constitute misunderstanding.

Textual mirrors and uncertain reflections: gender and narrative in *L'Hiver de beauté*, *Les Ports du silence* and *La Rage au bois dormant* by Christiane Baroche

Un roman est un miroir qui se promène sur une grande route. (Stendhal)

(A novel is a mirror travelling along a highway.)

L'écriture *est la possibilité même du changement*, l'espace d'où peut s'élancer une pensée subversive, le mouvement avant-coureur d'une transformation des structures sociales et culturelles. (Cixous)

(Writing is precisely *the very possibility of change*, the space that can serve as a springboard for subversive thought, the precursory movement of a transformation of social and cultural structures.)

Christiane Baroche was acclaimed in France first as a short-story writer, although her œuvre as a whole now comprises not only short stories but also poetry, novels and essays.[1] She has published many well-received volumes of realist 'slice of life' stories, beginning with *Les Feux du large* in 1975;[2] several of her collections have been awarded literary prizes. The triptych *Un soir, j'inventerai le soir*, published in 1983, is in a somewhat different vein, each of the three stories being original and playful treatments of the theme of myth, while functioning together as a comment on the diverse ways in which myth operates on identity formation. The motif of the mirror which structures this latter volume connects it with the novels I discuss in this chapter.[3] Baroche's first novel *Plaisirs amers* was published in 1984, but it was her second, *L'Hiver de beauté*, first published in 1987, that really marked a new departure in her writing career.[4] *L'Hiver de beauté*, which was repackaged in 1990 for the *Folio* edition and augmented with the addition of a *postface* by the author and new material (in the form of a short story), is, in one sense, a sequel to Choderlos de Laclos's

eighteenth-century novel *Les Liaisons dangereuses*. The principal character of Baroche's novel is a rewriting of Laclos's intriguing Mme de
Merteuil. Baroche picks up the character where Laclos left her in the last
letter of *Les Liaisons dangereuses*: that is, having lost an eye because of
smallpox, disfigured from the disease, ruined financially and socially as
well as physically. In another sense, however, with the introduction of a
twentieth-century female narrator-protagonist, *L'Hiver de beauté* is
resoundingly contemporary, a powerful novel in its own right. *Les Ports du
silence* and *La Rage au bois dormant*, both published in the first half of the
1990s, and *L'Homme de cendres*, which appeared in 2001, are likewise all
substantial novels dealing with major contemporary and universal themes:
life and death, war, memory, love.[5]

In *L'Hiver de beauté*, the motif of the mirror functions on several different levels and as such lays the foundations for the readings of both *Les Ports
du silence* and *La Rage au bois dormant* which follow here. Deeply implicated in the construction of identity, the effects of the mirror motif are multiple, operating, in all these novels, in particularly creative ways on the
representation of gender. In *Les Ports de silence* and *La Rage au bois
dormant*, the mirror-object itself disappears, yet it still continues to function in figurative terms at the level of form. Stendhal's metaphor of the
mirror, quoted in my epigraph, still holds true today, although it can of
course only ever be a partial explanation of the way the novel works as a
reflection of the society it portrays. Baroche's textual mirrors, however,
operate in a rather different way. They proffer uncertain reflections which,
on the one hand, *pace* Stendhal, are images of reality. On the other, however,
following my second epigraph (Cixous's liberating description of literature
as a *precursor* of social change), these novels also function as 'un ailleurs',
an 'elsewhere' or 'somewhere else', in which it is possible to envisage escaping from the dominant scheme of gender identities and sexual politics.[6]

Three moments highlight the importance of the mirror in *L'Hiver de
beauté*:

> J'ai levé les yeux vers le grand miroir de Venise qui renvoie mille lumières
> pour une, qui m'a renvoyé dix mille morts pour la ruine de mes traits. A
> vingt-cinq ans, j'entrais dans l'hiver de beauté. (p. 15)

> (I raised my eyes to the large Venetian mirror, which reflects back a thou-
> sand images instead of one. My ruined face stared back at me and I died
> a thousand deaths. Twenty-five years old, and I had already entered the
> winter of my beauty.)

'Je me contemple. Je n'ai jamais fui la vérité, tu le sais bien, ou si peu de temps...' [...] j'étais redevenue, ou plutôt j'étais rentrée dans une humanité banale, j'étais laide, c'est tout. (p. 50)

('I am contemplating myself. I have never tried to deny the truth, as you well know, or only fleetingly...' [...] I was, or rather I had become, ordinary, I was just ugly, that's all.)

Isabelle se regardait dans le miroir de l'Etude qu'elle avait emporté [...] Je ne suis pas belle, je suis mieux que cela. Vivante. (p. 318)

(Isabelle looked at herself in the Study mirror that she had brought with her [...] I'm not beautiful, I'm better than that. I'm full of life.)

On the first occasion, Baroche's Mme de Merteuil-character, now named Isabelle, looks into the Venetian mirror at her sister's house and is confronted with multiple images of the full horror of her scarred and disfigured face. Some months later, when the scabs from the smallpox have disappeared and the worst of the scarring has begun to fade, she contemplates herself in a similar mirror in her own house, concluding that she is no longer the frightening monster she once was – she is now simply ugly. And at the end of Baroche's novel, on board ship, about to embark on a new life in the New World, Isabelle once again looks into the mirror that she has brought with her, and discovers that inner vitality is more seductive than superficial beauty. These three occasions when Baroche's Isabelle (the ex-Mme de Merteuil) looks at her reflection in the mirror mark important stages both in her recuperation from the living death in which Laclos had left his character and in the reconstruction of Isabelle's own identity that Baroche's novel effects.

The mirror, then, has a primary role in the construction of identity in *L'Hiver de beauté*, but not only as content: the mirror is also central to the form of the novel. Not only does *L'Hiver de beauté* exist in an explicit intertextual relationship with Laclos's *Les Liaisons dangereuses*, setting up reflections and echoes between eighteenth and twentieth centuries, but it is also a metafiction. The twentieth-century character Queria reads the diaries Isabelle has written in order, in turn, to write a book about the eighteenth-century woman's life. Thus, the Venetian mirror, framed by small mirror panes, in which Isabelle sees her ruined face reflected a thousand times over, becomes a trope for the multiple mirroring which structures Baroche's novel: writing about writing, writing about reading, reading about writing, reading about reading. The result is a series of reflections between writers (Baroche, Laclos, Queria, Isabelle) and between readers (Baroche (especially via the *postface* which tells of her reading of Laclos's novel), Queria, readers of Queria's work within the novel and Baroche's own readers).

Dual narratives create a system of alter egos and elicit a dialogue between characters, between historical periods, between text and reader. None the less, this is no straightforward *mise-en-abyme*, and it is here that the comparison between the Venetian mirror and Baroche's text begins to founder. In the eighteenth-century, Venetian glass was the clearest it was possible to obtain, but the reflections Baroche's novel relays to the reader are uncertain, unstable and fragmented. Cloudy images permeate the text – harbour mists, flickering candlelight, dimly lit rooms, grey seas, soapy water – and these images echo and reinforce the fluid and uncertain nature of the narrative. Narration, reconstruction and fictionalisation alternate and interweave in a complex way. Narration is in both the first person and third person, and, despite typographical distinctions, it is at times difficult to tell who is speaking – eighteenth-century Isabelle or twentieth-century Queria. Just as Queria pieces together Isabelle's life, Baroche's readers have to construct their own versions – of Isabelle, of Queria and of other characters in the novel. Isabelle comes into being within the diegesis as a combination of what Queria's historical research unearths and the woman Queria imagines Isabelle to be. For Baroche's readers, the character Isabelle is also likely to carry traces of her intertextual self and other, Laclos's formidable Mme de Merteuil. Queria (the twentieth-century woman) is a shadowy persona who becomes a character in her own right only in the course of reconstructing Isabelle as a powerful, empowering figure in her book.

The uncertainty that is thus inscribed into the very texture of Baroche's text is none the less particularly fruitful and enabling, especially as far as gender is concerned. Seductive albeit ugly and disfigured women; emotional men; independent, active and violent women; passive men; women as desiring subjects; men as sexual objects; a raped woman emerging triumphant from her ordeal:[7] these are some of the ways in which conventional gender identities are undermined in *L'Hiver de beauté*. The Mme de Merteuil that Laclos originally created was like a siren of classic Greek mythology – fascinating men and leading them to their destruction. Baroche's Isabelle is singularly different. She becomes 'la sirène borgne' (the one-eyed siren), assuming an identity which includes her disfigurement within a seductive persona: like the sirens, Isabelle's singing fascinates men but rather than destroying them, it moves them to tears, putting them in touch with their own emotions. Here, women are described as 'un peu virile(s)' (slightly virile) and men 'un peu féminin(s)' (slightly feminine). The 'un peu' (slightly) is crucial: it signifies that men's so-called 'femininity' co-exists with conventional masculinity, and women's 'masculinity' with their more traditional femininity. Baroche's men have qualities that are usually assigned to the feminine, but their femininity is considered to enrich their masculinity rather than to take anything away from it: they are neither emasculated nor are they androgynous. Thus the binary opposition of masculinity and femininity, that works to imprison real men and women in stereotypical gender roles, is clouded in Baroche's novel and a different dynamic between the terms is accommodated within individual characters.

None the less, despite the fact that stereotypical gender identities are problematised in *L'Hiver de beauté*, the narrative does not offer any clearly defined alternatives, and this is actually where the strength – and the generosity – of Baroche's writing lies for readings that are attentive to gender. Indeed, it is not so much the actual representations of men and women as the uncertainty that suffuses their portrayal that works to bring about a compelling questioning of gender identities in Baroche's work. Thus her readers are left to speculate, for example, on what the different, slightly feminine, sort of masculinity, that Baroche's novel points to, might actually be like in practice.

In the two later novels *Les Ports du silence* and *La Rage au bois dormant*, the literal Venetian mirror of *L'Hiver de beauté* has completely given way to complex systems of *textual* mirroring. Both novels are metafictional (they are themselves about reading and about writing), both have multiple narratives, in both, layers of textuality work explicitly to problematise single meanings and to contribute to the open-ended nature of the texts. As in *L'Hiver de beauté*, narrative uncertainty is a prime player and it impacts on the portrayal of gender in similar ways. Although binary oppositions are dismantled, multiple narratives work against any fixing of alternative identities. The two main characters in *Les Ports du silence*, Jaime and Elodie, are seen through the eyes of a number of different characters, as well as their own, so that the picture that the reader puts together from these various perspectives is not only necessarily fragmented but also contradictory. Moreover, Jaime and Elodie mirror the principal characters in *L'Hiver de beauté*: like Queria and Isabelle, Elodie is both 'laide' (ugly) and 'vivante' (full of life), and she is a woman who is both active and passive, masculine and feminine. Jaime, described as 'a real man' by his housekeeper, is also 'un peu féminin' (slightly feminine) – sensitive, a dreamer, passive.

In *La Rage au bois dormant*, the mirroring motif works rather differently. While, in *L'Hiver de beauté*, it is as if Queria and Isabelle each have different sides of the same face, so it is, in *La Rage au bois dormant*, that the two principal women characters, Adèle and Judith, manifest two different sides of women's identity. Similar pairings are to be found elsewhere in Baroche's novels – in Isabelle and her sister Madeleine in *L'Hiver de beauté* and in the sisters Marthe and Magdelène in *Les Ports du silence*. In *La Rage au bois dormant*, Adèle, first a prostitute, then a wife and mother, is largely passive and unquestioning. For example, she remains blissfully ignorant of her husband's illegal business activities until long after his death. This is all the more surprising since, not only was the couple forced to flee to South America because of it, but also Adèle herself is a real gossip – at least as far as other people are concerned. Judith, on the other hand, is a passionate, independent and active woman: also a wife and mother, she is, however, first a committed resistance fighter, and then a successful business woman, her work and her love of horses sustaining her in the face of repeated tragedy. None the less, the relationship between the two women ultimately complicates any straightforward mirroring structure and works against the fixing of their identities, as it becomes clear that gossip, fantasy and embroidered memories are part and parcel of the life stories that are being told within the diegesis. Adèle does not really know much about Judith; the stories she tells are attempts to save her own life story from the failing memory of old age; they are one set of stories among many possible stories, the many possible narratives of what it means 'to be a woman'.

It is in (hetero)sexual politics that the radical potential of the gender identities suggested in Baroche's novels can be seen most clearly. Heterosexuality has long been critiqued as a normative institution by various forms of feminism and more recently by queer theory,[8] but contemporary feminist analyses of heterosexuality itself that take on board changing practices and the diversity within it have been fewer.[9] Sexual politics are a key determinant of individual heterosexual relations and the ways in which gender identities are lived in turn impact on social and sexual relations between men and women. In Laclos's *Les Liaisons dangereuses*, Mme de Merteuil is a female Don Juan, and thus, for a while at least, reverses traditional sexual politics. Baroche's novels go further, and, rather than simply reversing the binary oppositions man/woman, masculine/feminine, active/passive, they disrupt them, as we have seen, and relationships

between men and women go against the grain. Leaving behind the rigid eti-
quette and hierarchies of French court society (*Les Liaisons dangereuses*)
and the conventions and proprieties of bourgeois Rotterdam (*L'Hiver de
beauté*), Isabelle and the man she loves (Armand-Marie) will, it is intimated
in the latter novel, develop their relationship, each on their own terms. A
new life in the New World, to where they are bound at the end of the eighteenth century, functions as a promise of different possibilities for living out
both social and sexual relations.

Similarly, in the same novel, Queria embarks on her own love affair
(with Barney) at the same time as she embarks on a whole new way of life.
She flies to South America to be with him, but this is no romantic walk into
the sunset, since, before leaving, she makes firm plans for a new career on
her return. The couple's rendez-vous on the beach at Rio problematises
romantic clichés further. Each enjoying their solitude, they defer the
moment of their meeting which in romantic genres would have been a conventional 'happy end' in itself. Queria wants Barney to love her, 'mais pas
trop', to be there, 'mais pas trop' (p. 289) (but not too much). The sexual
politics between Barney and Queria that are sketched out in Baroche's
novel are thus sufficient to signal that their relationship will not conform to
conventional patriarchal formulas, but the way in which this is to be lived
out is not actually represented in the novel. It is left for the reader to work
with the pointers in the text.

Les Ports du silence arguably gives its readers a little more practical
detail on the subject of heterosexual sexual politics. The relationship
between Jaime and Elodie is suffused with silence and mutual respect: 'je
reste où je suis, je ne franchis pas sa frontière. . .' (p. 82) (I stay where I am,
I don't invade her territory. . .). They are 'deux solitudes' (p. 254) (two solitary people), a 'fils' and a 'fille du vent' (pp. 127, 207) (son and daughter of
the wind), independent, with different lives, different desires. Jaime loves
Elodie for her vitality, for the life she has in her; Elodie, in turn, will love
Jaime 'une fois pour toutes' (p. 254) (once and for all). They love but they
do not need – each other, anyone. Again, here, there is little explicit detail,
but there is no sense given in the text that they depend on each other for
anything. None the less, they have a child; Jaime leaves and returns; they
have another child; but never do they constitute a conventional nuclear
family. Although it is Jaime who goes away to work and Elodie who stays
behind, a situation that may, on the face of it, seem to reinforce conventional
gender roles, this arrangement is none the less open to positive feminist
readings. In fact, the traditional male/female split between active and

passive or between public and private does not apply. Nor is it just reversed in the way it is elsewhere in the same novel – in the opposition between the busy activity of Jaime's housekeeper, Louise, and the immobility of her passive, inert husband. Elodie has her own life and work. Moreover, the parenting arrangements, love and mutual respect between Elodie and Jaime are shared by another woman, Flore. Yet, even so, the three adults do not form a *ménage à trois*. When Jaime returns from travelling once and for all, the three of them continue to live separately: 'Le bonheur. Pas tout à fait celui qu'on pratique, mais quoi! En plus, il n'y a rien à en dire, les gens heureux n'ont pas d'histoire' (p. 270) (Happiness. Not exactly the way we'd go about it, but so what! Anyway, there's nothing more to say, happy people have no story). The narrator's gossipy tone, the uncertainty that surrounds the relationships being commented on and the silence about the way of life that is gestured at here are all part of the fabric of the narrative. They make space for the reader's interpretation even as they offer scope for the characters to live differently within the diegesis. At the end of the novel, we are left with the possibilities of the different kinds of sexual politics and alternative family arrangements that are hinted at. The reader must flesh out the representation from the bare bones sketched out in the text. Moreover, the 'alternative' nature of that sketch may well lead us to speculate on the sort of gender identities that will become possible for the next generation, in the persons of the two young daughters of Jaime and Elodie.

In *Les Ports du silence*, therefore, Baroche points optimistically to workable alternatives to the nuclear family, and indeed, in the wider breadth of her work, the number of women who for various reasons mother children who are not their own is noteworthy. The diffusion of mothering roles and relations in Baroche's fiction is significant and forms a creative input into contemporary feminist analyses of changing theories and prac-tices of parenting. Yet positive portrayals of alternative parenting in Baroche's novels are certainly not restricted to heterosexual arrangements. Homosexual or bisexual parenting is not uncommon in her work and includes, as the gossipy narrators of *Les Ports du silence* would have it, Elodie's own adored (and adoring) father, Basile: 'Il n'a pas eu d'enfant de son sang. Des bruits ont couru qu'il ne pouvait pas, qu'il y a des mariages commodes quand ce sont les garçons qu'on aime. . . En vérité, Basile ne voulait pas plus des gars que des filles, même s'il a usé des deux à ce qu'on murmure' (p. 183). (He had no children of his own. They said that he couldn't, that marriage is convenient for men who like boys. . . In truth,

Basile didn't want boys any more than girls, even if, as the story goes, he'd
made use of both.) Basile is not Elodie's biological father, but he married
her mother, brought her up and she carries his name, and as Basile himself
argues: 'un enfant, c'est un enfant. Et le père, celui qui l'élève . . . "Qu'est-
ce que c'est qu'une semence, Louise? Trente secondes de plaisir, et encore
c'est parce que je ne trouve pas d'autre mot. Tandis que vingt ans de
patience, de soins, d'amour. . ."' (p. 219) (a child is a child. And the father
is the one who brings her up . . . 'what is fertilisation, Louise? Thirty
seconds of pleasure, and I use that word because I can't find a better one.
While twenty years of patience, of care, of love. . .'). Here, biological paternity is contrasted with years of fathering, immediate sexual pleasure with
long-term care and affection, and found lacking.[10]

Parenting by homosexual men is also to be found in Baroche's *La
Rage au bois dormant*. Here, Judith is marked for life by the hatred shown
her by her father, who, as she discovers when she finds him in bed with
another man, indeed uses marriage and fatherhood as a respectable cover
for his homosexual activities. Judith's father serves as an example of negative homosexual parenting, but this is set against a positive one in the same
novel. Two other gay men (Bernard and François Esposite) become
Judith's 'chosen family'. Not only does Judith choose, as a teenager, to live
with them herself but she also chooses to leave her much-loved young son,
Emmanuel, in their care during the greater part of his childhood. The
arrangements Judith has with the Esposites are particularly interesting in
terms of the implications they have for gender identities as well as for the
intrinsic issue of gay parenting itself. Controversially, the term 'mothering'
is used in the narrative, albeit passingly, to describe the two men's parenting role: 'Pour qui d'autre les Esposite feraient ce qu'ils font, du matern-
age?' (p. 249) (For who else would the Esposites do what they do – the
mothering?) However, the context of the enunciation is uncertain. Because
of the multiple narrative and the metafictional layering of the text, it is
impossible to tell for certain from which character, or even from which historical period, the term 'mothering' originates. Moreover, the structure and
style of Baroche's narrative means the reader cannot know whether this
description is just gossipy, or whether it is homophobic (implying that gay
men are like women), or, alternatively, whether it makes direct reference to
the type of care the Esposites provide (although there are very few details
given in the text of Emmanuel's life with the two men).

If, however, this chosen family arrangement is to be set up as an interesting alternative to the norm – or normativeness – of the heterosexual

nuclear family, the key question to ask must be to what extent the example of stable family life provided by the Esposites in *La Rage au bois dormant* differs from that norm. The first point to note is that the most telling comparison in Baroche's novel is not actually between homosexual and heterosexual parenting, but between different kinds of parenting by homosexual men. Moreover, aside from the fact that Judith's own (homosexual) father fathers (negatively) precisely within what is overtly a standard nuclear family set-up, if the Esposites can be perceived to form a nuclear family, it is in a reconfigured version. As a couple, Bernard and François Esposite do not assume conventional heterosexual gender roles or functions: neither one of them is more 'masculine' or more 'feminine' than the other; nor does one of them take on the conventional paternal role and the other the maternal one. Instead, according to the narrative, they both mother – which means that in *La Rage au bois dormant*, Judith's son Emmanuel arguably has three mothers. . . And two of them are men!

As I have argued throughout this chapter, Baroche's novels, shot through with uncertainty, offer food for thought, rather than providing fixed and complete representations. In itself, the reference to the care the Esposites give Emmanuel as mothering raises a series of questions about gender and parenting, although it does not go as far as answering them. Can we really use the term 'mothering' for the care men give to children? What does it actually mean to say that men mother? What are the differences between mothering by men and fathering? What then are the implications for heterosexual parenting, for gay and lesbian parenting? What does 'mothering' mean these days anyway? What will it come to mean in the future?

Despite some challenges to the novelistic conventions of character, chronology and form, Baroche's novels are not, however, obviously radical, revolutionary works. Instead, her writing is resoundingly realist and, in many respects, conforms to convention. In terms of content, patriarchy as a system is certainly not dislodged, nor is it much shaken, although, as I have argued here, frequently the dominant scheme of gender identities, of sexual politics, of family arrangements is subverted by individual practice. The author herself maintains that the men and women she creates in her fiction and the relationships between them are simply reflections of changing reality, based on the lives she sees around her.[11] Hence, on the one hand, Baroche's fiction shows us the value of individual agency: it *is* possible to live our gender identities differently; it *is* possible to work out alternative relational models. Moreover, individual interventions into the social order such as those inscribed in her novels can gradually modify attitudes, practice, social structures, on a wider scale. On the other hand, Baroche's novels in themselves foreground the reader's part in contributing to the representations they adumbrate. The textual mirroring, in the three novels discussed in this chapter, functions both as a *mise-en-abyme* that impacts on the text–reader relationship and as a vehicle of uncertainty that is inscribed into the narrative. These functions work together to engage the reader's interaction with the text. The most creative challenge to conventional gender identities comes not simply in the way the characters are represented in Baroche's texts, nor only in the readers' interpretations of them, but rather in the potential for speculative readings engendered by the mirroring structure of the text.

Thus, Baroche's novels demonstrate that fiction and reality are interdependent, but the multiple mirroring and uncertainty that are a key part of their character go even further than this and have a twofold effect. On the one hand, these texts act as mirrors of reality, reflecting, however, not only the dominant order of things, but also newly emerging experiences and innovative practices. On the other hand, the uncertain reflections they offer mean they also act as Cixousian textual 'elsewheres', pointing to alternative (still-to-be-represented) concepts and ways of living, of loving, of being. Compared with the arguably more utopian but equally empowering visions of, say, Cixous's own textual elsewheres, Baroche's more realist writing has certain strengths. This is because, although the alternative forms of gender identity discussed here are never fully represented, they are eminently representable, and as such suggest new directions and examples of what future practice might become.

As sociologist Stevi Jackson argues, in order for change to come about in reality, we need 'to *imagine* social relations being radically other than they are' (*Heterosexuality in Question*, p. 182).[12] Baroche's thought-provoking novels initiate this sort of imagining. Her Venetian mirrors and the uncertainty of their multiple reflections are both provocative and full of promise, initiating a sort of dialogue with the reader, facilitating a speculative engagement with the text. Baroche's work does not offer set alternatives that may well be as alienating to some readers as they are empowering to others. Rather, it challenges us to think, to rethink gender identities, loving relationships and sexual politics for the contemporary world in which we live.

Notes

1 See, for example, the special issue of the journal *Sud* devoted to Baroche, 'A la tour abolie: rimes intérieures II', *Sud*, 105 (1993).

2 Christiane Baroche, *Les Feux du large* (Paris: Gallimard, 1975).

3 Christiane Baroche, *Un soir, j'inventerai le soir* (Paradou: Actes Sud, 1983). See Gill Rye, 'La ré-écriture mythologique: tradition, originalité et identité dans *Un Soir, j'inventerai le soir* de Christiane Baroche', in Johnnie Gratton and Jean-Philippe Imbert (eds), *La Nouvelle hier et aujourd'hui* (Paris: L'Harmattan, 1997), pp. 159–65.

4 Christiane Baroche, *Plaisirs amers* (Paradou: Actes Sud, 1984); *L'Hiver de beauté* (Paris: Gallimard, 1987; extended *Folio* edition, 1990).

5 Christiane Baroche, *Les Ports du silence* (Paris: Grasset, 1992); *La Rage au bois dormant* (Paris: Grasset, 1995); *L'Homme de cendres* (Paris: Grasset, 2001).

6 For the text as an *ailleurs*, see Hélène Cixous and Catherine Clément, *La Jeune Née* (Paris: UGE, 1975), p. 132; *The Newly Born Woman*, trans. Betsy Wing (London: I. B. Tauris, 1996), p. 72.

7 For a discussion of the rape episode in the context of reading in/of Baroche's novels, see Gill Rye, *Reading for Change: Interactions between Text and Identity in Contemporary French Women's Writing (Baroche, Cixous, Constant)* (Bern: Peter Lang, 2001), pp. 79–81, 107–8, 190–1. For a wider discussion of Baroche's women characters, see Michael Worton, 'Le chant de la sirène: les romans de Christiane Baroche', *Sud*, 105, 73–85.

8 Seminal texts for this kind of critique are Adrienne Rich, 'Compulsory heterosexuality and lesbian existence', *Signs*, 5 (1980), 631–60; Judith Butler, *Gender Trouble: Feminism and the Subversion of Identity* (London: Routledge, 1990).

9 But see Lynne Segal, *Straight Sex: The Politics of Pleasure* (London: Virago, 1994), which argues for the need to consider heterosexualities in the plural; Nancy Chodorow, *Femininities, Masculinities, Sexualities: Freud and Beyond* (London: Free Association Books, 1994), which accommodates plurality; Stevi Jackson, *Heterosexuality in Question* (London: Sage, 1999), which identifies the importance of seeing heterosexuality 'as a site of struggle and contested meanings for those who *are* heterosexual as well as those who are not' (p. 165).

10 See also Elisabeth Badinter, *XY: de l'identité masculine* (Paris: Odile Jacob, 1992), who in her discussion of fatherhood reiterates this thus: 'Nous entendons par "père", non seulement le géniteur de l'enfant, mais tout substitut paternel qui donne amour et soins à un enfant' (p. 247) (We understand by 'father', not only the child's biological parent, but also all paternal substitutes who love and take care of a child).

11 Unpublished interview with Gill Rye at Cerisy-la-Salle (26 August 1995).

12 It is noteworthy that the importance of being able to imagine difference is recognised here even from a sociological and materialist feminist perspective such as Jackson's.

The articulation of *beur* female identity in the works of Farida Belghoul, Ferrudja Kessas and Soraya Nini

In view of the relatively recent literary success of works by second-generation Maghrebis born and brought up in France and the self-designatory origins of the term *beur*,[1] this chapter examines the work of three *beur* women writers in order to establish the extent to which the highly specific socio-historical locus of the *beur* writer, when combined with her female subject position, may produce narrative similarities, whether formal or thematic. *Beur* literature only began to enjoy commercial success in the early 1980s, when a substantial number of the children of North African immigrants first reached adulthood. The designation *beur* is considered an example of *verlan* – a form of French slang involving the inversion of syllables – stemming from the term 'Arabe'. The term itself has become problematic in that its common currency in France and appropriation by the French media have endowed it with many of the pejorative, Occidental associations of its precursor. Alternative modes of designation refer to the *beur* population as the offspring of North African immigrants or – since this is generally the case – as second-generation Algerians, alternatives which are not only rather cumbersome but inadequate in that they fail to acknowledge the specific problematics of the French locus these individuals inhabit. Therefore, this chapter will continue to employ the – at least succinct – term *beur* to refer to these writers who are the offspring of Algerian immigrants who came to France during the 1950s and 1960s.

While seeking to identify some common ground in *beur* women's writing, this chapter does not wish to play down the variety and hybridity of *beur* narratives in a quasi-colonialist drive for uniformity and categorisation. Indeed, the very recentness of the emergence of this writing makes any endeavour to characterise its expression of identity politics tentative. Given the diversity of the writers who are conventionally grouped under the umbrella term *beur* – some writers classed as *beur* were born in North Africa then came to France, others were born in France of, say, a French mother and Algerian father – this chapter will focus on texts by writers who most closely conform to *beur* criteria, in that all three were born in France of Algerian parents. The works to be examined are *Georgette!* by Farida Belghoul, *Beur's story* by Ferrudja Kessas and *Ils disent que je suis une beurette* by Soraya Nini.[2] These works are all autobiographical and are written by authors of working-class origin – which would seem to be an inevitable component of this particular permutation of 'Beurness', in that the first-generation Algerian parents of these writers came to France as unskilled workers.[3] They are also the first publication of the writers in question, and, in two out of three cases, the only publication at the time of writing. Indeed, one 'extraneous' characteristic of the articulation of identity in *beur* writing is that many writers limit that articulation to one, generally autobiographical, work, continuing with their chosen profession after publication.

The autobiographical nature of much *beur* writing accounts for its commonly first-person narrative voice and oral expression, an expression which may encompass examples of *verlan*, English and Arabic terms, or regional and slang vocabulary – in other words, the polyphonic textual language mirrors the hybrid identity of the protagonists. The emphasis on orality in *beur* women's writing is particularly appropriate given the limited access of first-generation Algerian women to written language and the recentness of their daughters' own exposure to it in the form of French literature. If the 'orature' of texts by *beur* women writers reflects the urgency of the narrators' desire for self-expression, the incorporation of non-literary language can also be read as a positive assertion of female otherness or as a form of protest, in that the perceived violence inflicted on the colonised economically and culturally is reciprocated linguistically – what Ketu H. Katrak, in describing the oral traditions of much post-colonial women's writing, refers to as 'effective tools of resistance against neocolonial tendencies and against women's particular oppressions'.[4] However, as this chapter argues, the protagonists of Belghoul's, Kessas's and Nini's works also foreground the necessity of consciously assimilating the French language in both its oral *and* written forms – and the consequent importance of the education system – in articulating their cross-cultural position. The interdiction on uncensored female expression within the family home and the narrators' underconfidence in French outside it may also contribute to the need for a narrative outlet in which they are given a voice: unable to experience the freedom of their brothers and fathers, *beur* female protagonists are shown to experience it vicariously through the reading, and, subsequently, the writing of, narratives. In the dedication to *Beur's story*, Ferrudja Kessas makes the personal and political impetus behind the act of writing clear: 'Je dédie cette histoire à mes sœurs maghrébines pour que nous cessions d'être cette entité négligeable qui hante l'arrière-plan des romans de nos jeunes écrivains maghrébins' (I dedicate this story to my Maghrebi sisters so that we may stop being that negligible entity which haunts the background of the novels by our young Maghrebi [male] writers).

Kessas's reference to *beur* women's developmental anteriority to their male counterparts in literature may further account for the predominance of first-person autobiographical narratives in the texts examined, in that autobiography often provides narrative entry for marginalised groups mis- or non-represented by the dominant culture. It is perceived to constitute a means of countering the 'inauthentic' voices or forms of ventriloquism imposed by the dominant group on the subaltern. Two of the three texts are written in the first person, with only *Beur's story* written in the third person. While Kessas's work adopts a more 'classic' narrative approach, in which ambiguities in textual development are minimal, *Georgette!* is the most formally interesting of the works in that it combines a first-person narrative account – and one which, like Nini's and many other *beur* narratives, resembles a form of oral diarywriting – with a more inventive, quasi-fantastic narrative, in which the reader is frequently unsure whether the narrator is relating or imagining events. These tangential narrative meanderings follow the narrator's thought processes before returning to the 'real' present, meanderings which can partly be attributed to the age of the narrator – she is only 7 – and the consequently more permeable dividing line separating her worlds of fact and fiction, as well as to her desire to transgress the constrictive limits which circumscribe the locus of her identity. Indeed, this desire to avoid being easily categorised – and dismissed – accounts for the common portrayal of *beur* female protagonists as social chameleons, assuming whatever façade is most appropriate to the particular circumstances or milieux they inhabit.[5]

In all three texts, the role played by the narrators' imagination or imaginative fantasies – what Nini's narrator Samia terms 'une échappatoire' (p. 263) (an evasion/means of escape) – enables them to tolerate the experiential constraints of *le vécu* more easily. In *Georgette!*, these fantasies serve to nourish the narrator's self-perception in the face of the French education system's drive for homogeneity (as well as her family's religious strictures), whether the narrator imagines herself as an old man – indicative of her desire to be respected by the other, a situation denied her by her age, race and gender; a cat – which points to her continuing independence behind her apparently domesticated appearance; or an American Indian – the symbol of the colonised since time immemorial, and, for the narrator, of her internal resistance to French acculturation. If the Indian is to preserve his identity and culture, he must outmanœuvre the cowboy, and never allow his 'real' self to be exposed: 'La carte d'identité des indiens est un secret de guerre [. . .] Personne connaît la vraie figure des indiens. Encore heureux! Sinon, le cow-boy les massacre tous, un par un' (p. 72) (The identity card used by Indians is a battle secret [. . .] No one knows the true face of the Indians. Just as well! Otherwise the cowboy would massacre them all, one by one). The symbolic value with which the narrator accredits the Indian accounts for her refusal to watch the end of westerns on television; she endows the Indian with an immortality she does not wish to see contradicted by 'real-life' cultural representations of him.[6]

Georgette! has the shortest timespan of all the works: while the narrative covers a year, it focuses principally on twenty-four hours in the life of the protagonist. *Ils disent que je suis une beurette* relates the experiences of a 12-year-old girl, Samia, through until the age of 17, while *Beur's story* is set during the year of the *baccalauréat* for Malika. By their focus on the education system, all three texts point up the pivotal role played by the socialisation process and formation of identity in *beur* women's writing, as the narrators attempt to negotiate the influences of their French and Arabic cultures, cultures habitually portrayed as antithetical in their Occidental/Christian and Oriental/Muslim traditions. The problematic marriage of these two cultures in *beur* women's writing, paradoxically, may also account for its commercial success, in that the bi-cultural focus of these works serves to defamiliarise the familiar for the reader – in the case of French culture – and familiarise the unfamiliar, in the case of Algerian culture.[7] These female protagonists inhabit the 'border zones' of culture, or what may be viewed as a form of Homi K. Bhabha's 'Third Space', a hybrid intermediacy characterised by the indefinite renegotiation of identity.[8] If the temporal limits of the works are relatively tight – the texts are also written contemporaneously with events portrayed – all three take place within highly restricted spatial limits, restrictions closely linked to the gender of the protagonists. There is repeated mention of the interdictions forbidding *beur* girls to step beyond the experiential parameters allowed by the journey from home to school, and by their education itself. When not attending school, they are confined to the home – typically a highrise block of flats in a housing estate[9] – and are shown to lead a claustrophobic existence utterly lacking in privacy which centres on the drudgery of housework rather than on the potentially dangerous intellectual stimulation provided by homework.

These *romans d'apprentissage* represent the daily voyage made by the protagonists between the Algerian domestic culture and the French educational one. The narrators inhabit a cross-cultural position, marginalised because of their racial origins in the French public domain and because of their gender within the Algerian domestic domain: if French society is shown to desire the eradication of all ambivalence and multiplicity in favour of a monolithic national identity, the Algerian family unit similarly seeks to isolate its female members from French paradigms of womanhood. In both Nini's and Kessas's works, there is little sense of racial solidarity within the family, in that male members mistreat and physically abuse their sisters. Even in *Georgette!*, the narrator's predominantly sympathetic father hits her mother when she dares to speak her mind. Whatever the racism they encounter in French society, Arabic men are shown to perpetuate that oppression within the domestic domain, to duplicate the discrimination they themselves experience. Indeed, in *Beur's story*, the protagonist Malika's more radical sister Fatima maintains that the form of racial 'emasculation' which forbids Arabic men to exert authority outside the home intensifies their need to do so inside it: 'Et puis, justement eux qui ont tant de problèmes, ils devraient nous comprendre, nous aussi nous sommes de la deuxième génération, un jour ou l'autre on sera peut-être confrontés à pire que ça! Et au lieu de nous donner la main, ils nous tournent le dos! Et faute de jouer les caïds dehors, ils les jouent chez eux!' (p. 202) (And precisely because they [Arabic men] have so many problems, they should understand our situation. We're also second-generation immigrants, and one day we may have to face an even worse predicament! And instead of offering us a helping hand, they turn their backs on us! Since they can't play the big shot outside, they do it at home!).

The fundamental role played by identity and naming – whether indicating ethnic or sexual identity – is made clear in the titles of the works. If *Beur's story* points to the representative value which the narrator attributes to her *Bildung*, *Ils disent que je suis une beurette* immediately signals the narrator's distancing from the nominal politics which seek to categorise her as *beur*, a distancing apparent in the narrator's desire for integration into French society at the text's conclusion. The deliberate fluidity of the designation 'ils' points to the female narrator's sense of dual oppression at the hands of both French and Algerian men. *Georgette!* further foregrounds the problematics of identity by employing a traditional French name in its title, a name the nameless protagonist imagines her father calling her, thereby highlighting her degree of alienation from her culture of origin, and her sense of betrayal following her assimilation by the French education system. The inherent falseness French identity represents for the young narrator is given symbolic resonance when she is asked by an old French woman to write letters to her pretending to be her sons, a request which further reinforces the eradication of the narrator's Arabic identity initiated by her school environment.[10] The narrator draws attention to the significance the articulation of identity holds for her when she determines to teach her own mother to write her name as soon as she herself learns to write. As Kessas's dedication highlights, these daughters of first-generation Muslim women, women who are generally illiterate and unable to express themselves in French, seek to speak out against the tradition of silence in order to voice their own sense of identity and to legitimate their own life histories.

In all these texts, the female siblings are more educated and fare better at school than their brothers, due to their perception of education as empowering, as a means of extending the limited opportunities of their domestic culture, a perception surely intensified by the working-class origins of all three narrators. It is not surprising that constant exposure to the 'liberalising' individualism of Western values strikes a particularly resonant chord with *beur* adolescent girls on the threshhold of adulthood, an adulthood which their culture of origin typically represents as a diminishment of freedom and opportunities in the form of an arranged marriage, of being tied ever more firmly to the domestic.[11] Education also provides the female protagonists with the linguistic fluency they require to act as go-betweens – as both cultural and linguistic interpreters – for their parents and French society.[12] In *Georgette!*, the young narrator may dislike school and learning to read and write, yet continues with it in order to increase future professional opportunities: 'Pour l'instant, j'ai besoin d'apprendre à lire. C'est idiot de se presser et de se jeter sur un mauvais risque: je veux pas devenir clochard. Dès que je dessine une écriture magnifique, aussi belle que la voix de mon père, je m'en vais loin d'ici, je me sauve au ciel avec un bon métier' (p. 64) (For now, I need to learn to read. It doesn't make sense to rush things and to risk my future: I don't want to become a tramp. As soon as I can master beautiful handwriting, as beautiful as my father's voice, I'm going to leave all this far behind, the sky's the limit if I get a good job). *Georgette!*'s opening words which describe the end of a school break immediately signal the normative role played by the education system in teaching the protagonist French. An example of a *verlan*-type malapropism is swiftly replaced by its correct expression: 'La sonne cloche. . . Non, la cloche sonne' (p. 9) (The ring bells. . . no, the bell rings). The narrator has difficulty mastering spoken and written French, and this opening malapropism foreshadows a thematics in the work, in which her French schooling associates Arabism with being 'the wrong way round', as symbolised by her father's writing in her homework jotter at what is viewed as the back according to Western convention.

The narrator's acquisition of French language is the central thematics of *Georgette!*, and a principal subject in *beur* writing generally. References to pencils, pens and inkpots; to eyes (reading), hands and fingers (writing) and throats (speaking); and to the differences between Arabic and French modes of writing and reading abound in the work. It is perhaps unsurprising that the narrator's closest friend in *Georgette!* has a speech impediment, mirroring her own self-perceived difficulty in expressing herself. If the teacher is described as opening the narrator's book at the 'wrong' place towards the beginning of the work, the narrator's gradual assimilation of the values of French culture – or the efficaciousness of French 'internal colonialism' – is illustrated by her change in perspective when she later accuses her father of opening the book at the wrong place and dismisses his Arabic writing: 'Son écriture pourrie c'est des gribouillages. L'écriture à l'envers n'existe pas! En vérité, il sait pas écrire et il me raconte des histoires debout. Il est complètement marteau, ce bonhomme!' (p. 58) (His awful writing is nothing but scribbles. Back-to-front writing doesn't exist! If truth be told, he can't write and he tells me nonsense stories. He's completely nuts, this guy!). This dichotomised representation in which the culture of the father is set up against that of the female schoolteacher is also apparent in *Ils disent que je suis une beurette*. In this work, Arabic is the language of the father and of the male teachers, who, at her father's insistence, give Samia Arabic lessons, a language she cannot understand. It is French which produces an affective identification in the narrator, and which comes to be associated with the liberating feminine, both in the form of her schoolteacher Mme Sallibert, who provides Samia with a 'real-life' alternative female role model, and in the literature she recommends. As this chapter has suggested, literature is an important representative medium for the protagonists of these *beur* texts in that it allows them to experience vicarious liberation in the form of French protagonists, a paradigm of liberation their own texts implicitly hold out to other *beur* women readers. In all three texts, the narrators' gradual acculturation is reinforced by the role played by an older French woman who can be seen as partially usurping the Algerian maternal, whether Mme Sallibert in *Ils disent que je suis une beurette*, 'la vieille' in *Georgette!* who effectively asks the narrator to become her surrogate child, and both the bookshop owner Malika befriends in *Beur's story* and her schoolteacher, as an extract from one of her poems makes clear: '*Maîtresse, vous voulez bien être ma maman aussi/Ce sera facile, je vous aime déjà tant/Mais tant!*' (p. 95) (Miss, can you be my mummy too/It would be easy, I love you so much already/So much!).[13]

In none of the works is the protagonist's bi-cultural identity experienced as plenitude or enriching hybridity,[14] yet the degree of alienation varies from work to work with the most intense desire for integration expressed in *Ils disent que je suis une beurette*.[15] Samia offers the most condemnatory assessment of her Algerian heritage, yet, like Malika in *Beur's story*, acknowledges generational differences in attitude and the complex imbrication of her socialisation process and cross-cultural position. Malika attributes the rigidity of her parents' adherence to Algerian cultural beliefs to their need to have some sense of continuity in a society largely alien to them. All three narratives end on a note of loss or departure: *Ils disent que je suis une beurette* concludes with the departure of the protagonist for greater integration in French society and the (temporary?) abandonment of her endeavours to participate in the Algerian domain; in *Beur's story*, Malika's best friend and alter ego Farida is unable to accept the limitations of her role as an Arab woman and commits suicide. When Farida's ghost criticises Malika for her lack of intervention or action at the text's conclusion, the reader is clearly supposed to interpret this as a call for *beur* women to participate more fully in their fate.[16] If a positive assumption of *beur* identity can be seen as embodied in Fatima, Malika's sister, who decides to inform her classmates about Arabic culture and Algerian traditions, and perhaps to write a book about her experiences, as well as in Malika's own intention to continue with her education, the narrative ends on a note of desolation when Malika learns of the death of her best friend. *Georgette!* ends with the departure of the protagonist in that the reader presumes she has died under the wheels of a car, although the absence of a full stop after the work's final sentence makes such a conclusion ambiguous.

Ultimately, then, all three texts conclude by a form of inconclusiveness, a lack of resolution reflected in the uncertain sense of self experienced by their *beur* protagonists in contemporary France, and in the girls' status as cultural nomads never fully assimilated by either Algerian or French culture.

As a peripheral group within a peripheral group, *beur* women writers have the particularly acute sense of the split self or dual identity that W. E. B. Du Bois attributes to the African American, whose self-perception, he argues, is intrinsically linked to the other's perception of him, resulting in a form of 'double consciousness' or awareness.[17] This awareness is positively channelled in *Ils disent que je suis une beurette*, in which the narrator develops from being the perceived, objectified other in a television documentary about her housing estate to locating herself as perceiving subject of her own literary *histoire* (story/history). The previously subaltern position is abandoned thanks to the empowering mimicry of the coloniser's gaze, which, to quote Bhabha, may be seen as constituting one of several 'strategies of subversion that turn the gaze of the discriminated back upon the eye of power'.[18] Much *beur* women's writing demonstrates that texts which portray the unfamiliar subject of bi-cultural female identity within a more classic narrative framework (and thereby implicate an extensive readership) provide effective vehicles for the deconstruction of the racial and sexual selves imposed upon their female narrators in contemporary French society. As Martine Delvaux remarks:

> Le mimétisme, en ce qu'il constitue une représentation de soi-même qui récupère partiellement mais suffisament l'autre qui menace et ainsi l'encourage à se reconnaître en celui qu'il domine, permet l'articulation d'un tiers espace qui constitue le lieu d'une manipulation de l'organe de domination.
>
> (Mimicry, insofar as it constitutes a form of self-representation which partially yet sufficiently harnesses the threatening other, and therefore encourages him to perceive himself in the person he dominates, allows for the articulation of a third space which constitutes the place of manipulation of the organ of domination.)[19]

As intrinsically fluid, non-specular mirrors of the post-colonial white, middle-class, 'indigenous' French male subject position, the works examined in this chapter give voice to the previously unauthorised through their exploration of the complexities of *beur* female identity. At this particular socio-historical juncture, narratives by *beur* women can be seen to occupy a 'third space', a space which, if not yet characterised by a nourishing trans-cultural reciprocity, none the less represents a form of liberation: having long had their identities contained in ideological straitjackets, the female narrators in these examples of *beur* women's writing signal the importance of finding their own *voie/voix* (way/voice) for future representation.

Notes

1 It is generally accepted that the term *beur* was first employed in the 1980s by French-born children of North African immigrants living in Paris as a means of self-designation in order to escape the increasingly racist connotations of 'arabe'.

2 Farida Belghoul, *Georgette!* (Paris: Bernard Barrault, 1986); Ferrudja Kessas, *Beur's story* (Paris: L'Harmattan, 1990); Soraya Nini, *Ils disent que je suis une beur-ette* (Paris: Fixot 1993). *Georgette!* has been included in this study of *beur* women's writing since, while published in 1986, it remains one of the better-known *beur* texts. In view of the recent origins of *beur* writing, it would appear somewhat arbi-trary to exclude a text from the mid-1980s when seeking to establish common nar-rative tendencies.

3 While literary criticism of *beur* works tends to focus on issues relating to race or gender, the role of class, or the interface between class and race in *beur* writing, has received relatively little critical attention, in spite of – or perhaps because of – its ubiquity in the texts.

4 Ketu H. Katrak, 'Decolonizing culture: toward a theory for postcolonial women's texts', *Modern Fiction Studies*, 35(1) (1989), 157–79 (178).

5 One example of this inventiveness is the works' repeated references to the protag-onists' need for an endless supply of alibis if they are to achieve acceptance at school through their participation in extra-curricular activities. A common pretext given to parents is that the narrators require time to study in the library, which may further account for the significant role played by literature in their lives.

6 This analogy between the French/cowboys and the Algerians/Indians is also made in *Ils disent que je suis une beurette*, when the narrator compares her two Algerian aunts to Indians and gives them Indian names, Geronimo and Conchise. In *Beur's story*, the family also watches westerns, films which, whatever their colo-nialist attitudes, reinforce traditional masculine values and are deemed relatively free from corrupting Western mores.

7 The role of readers and their implied characterisation in these works is an ambiv-alent one. While a section of the implied readership is clearly *beur*, these works target a predominantly French audience, in that they provide explanations of Arabic terms and aspects of Arabic culture. This is particularly true of *Beur's story*, which includes footnotes informing the reader of the meaning and pronun-ciation of certain Arabic words.

8 'Border zones' is a term employed by Renato Rosaldo in his article 'Ideology, place, and people without culture', *Cultural Anthropology*, 3 (1988), 77–87 (85). In

his essay, 'The commitment to theory', in *The Location of Culture* (London and New York: Routledge, 1994), Homi K. Bhabha describes the benefits of a dynamic and enrichingly heterogeneous co-existence between politics and theory, or between different models of cultural identity, a 'Third Space' of ongoing negotiation.

9 Zola is probably the most frequently cited author in the texts of *beur* writers and the many descriptions of these highrise blocks in *beur* writing bring to mind the tenement block described in Zola's *L'Assommoir*, in that, like the latter, they are portrayed as self-contained (Algerian) villages.

10 The narrator's identity is literally eradicated by a representative of the French education system at the work's conclusion, when the reader is led to presume that the young narrator has been knocked down by a car driven by her teacher.

11 While some *beur* female narrators may highlight negative familial traits in order to justify their desire for integration into French society or, at the very least, to explain their vociferous criticism of the Algerian domestic domain, the quasi-stereotypical representation of the Arabic family in many *beur* texts may equally indicate these women writers' internalisation of the racist paradigms of French society.

12 The original title of Nini's text – *L'Entre-deux* – while foregrounding the cultural no man's land many *beur* individuals feel they inhabit, points to this role played by the children of Maghrebi immigrants.

13 If the mother figure in *Beur's story* is portrayed as cruelly conventional towards her daughters in her adherence to Arabic norms, she is something of a cypher in *Ils disent que je suis une beurette* – which can be interpreted as reflecting her submissiveness within the family unit – while in *Georgette!*, as in all the works, the mother's preference is clearly for her male children.

14 So pronounced is that bi-cultural identity in *Georgette!* that Michèle Bacholle in *Un passé contraignant: double bind et transculturation* (Amsterdam and Atlanta GA: Rodopi, 2000) perceives it as a form of schizophrenia.

15 It could, of course, be argued that Samia's integration into mainstream French society necessitates an inevitable broadening of the notion of Frenchness, and is therefore less politically pessimistic than it may first appear. Françoise Lionnet remarks that 'subaltern elements contribute to the evolution and transformation of the hegemonic system by producing resistances and counterdiscourses' ('"Logiques métisses", cultural appropriation and postcolonial representations', in Mary Jean Matthews Green (ed.), *Postcolonial Subjects, Francophone Women Writers* (Minneapolis and London: University of Minnesota Press, 1996), pp. 321–43 (p. 323)). Given that such a process is not unidirectional, Lionnet prefers the term 'transculturation' to 'acculturation'. The reciprocity and deconstruction of simplistic binary oppositions inherent in this concept has echoes of Bhabha's 'Third Space'.

16 This projected politicisation of the *beur* female reader can be seen as reflecting two of the three characteristics of minority literature posited by Gilles Deleuze and Félix Guattari in *Kafka: pour une littérature mineure* (Paris: Minuit, 1975); in other words, 'le branchement de l'individuel sur l'immédiat-politique, l'agence-

ment collectif d'énonciation' (p. 33) ('the connection of the individual to a political immediacy, and the collective assemblage of enunciation' (*Kafka: Toward a Minor Literature*, trans. Dana Polan (Minneapolis and London: University of Minnesota Press, 1986), p. 18)). The third characteristic, 'la déterritorialisation de la langue' (p. 33) ('the deterritorialisation of language' (p. 18)) is apparent in the linguistic polyphony already mentioned.

17 See William Edward Burghardt Du Bois, *The Souls of Black Folk*, ed. Henry Louis Gates Jnr and Terri Hume Oliver (New York and London: W. W. Norton, 1999). Susan Ireland's article 'Writing at the crossroads: cultural conflict in the work of *beur* women writers' first drew my attention to the relevance of Du Bois's work, and provided an invaluable introduction to many of the main concerns of *beur* women's writing generally. See *French Review*, 68(6) (May 1995), 1022–34.

18 Homi K. Bhabha, 'Signs taken for wonders', in *The Location of Culture* (London: Routledge, 1994), p. 112.

19 Martine Delvaux, 'L'ironie du sort: le tiers espace de la littérature *beure*', *French Review*, 68(4) (March 1995), 681–93 (688). The 'tiers espace' in *Georgette!* can also be seen as reflected in the tripartite structure of the work, in which, in Part 1 the narrator is most influenced by her home environment, in Part 2 by her school, and in Part 3 plays truant, inhabiting a type of no man's land both geographically and psychologically.

Saying the unsayable: identities in crisis in the early novels of Marie Darrieussecq

Introduction

When Marie Darrieussecq's first novel *Truismes* exploded on to the French literary scene it was clear that she was a young writer intent on taking the reader to disturbing places.[1] Set in a partially recognisable, dystopic France of the near future, this erotic, funny and inventive novel satirises right-wing extremism, repressive state mechanisms, new-age fanaticisms and political correctness gone mad. Its primary focus on gender and body politics is provocatively inflected by Darrieussecq's choice of narrator – a young woman who metamorphoses into a sow – and the novel reveals the author's penchant for probing the frontiers between the everyday and the fantastic, the mimetic and the marvellous. *Truismes* launched the single-minded fascination with identity crises and altered states which would be confirmed by the subsequent novels, *Naissance des fantômes* and *Le Mal de mer* and it gave the French publishing world its phenomenon for the beginning of the 1996 literary year.[2]

In contrast to this pyrotechnic *succès de scandale*, Darrieussecq's next two novels were more sober, more literary and more tightly focused. *Naissance des fantômes* is an introspective, sometimes hallucinatory study of loss which is minimalist in terms of character range and plot. It is another series of confidences from a young first-person narrator who feels she is losing touch with reality, but rather than charting beastly transformations and innumerable adventures it simply catalogues her attempts to define herself through the empty spaces left after the sudden and inexplicable disappearance of her husband. Expanding on the theme of separation *Le Mal de mer* follows a young mother as she embarks abruptly on an ill-defined voyage of discovery, taking her small daughter with her and leaving the novel's husband/father behind. Each of these major works is a forensic analysis of a particular trauma, a particular crisis of identity, and each provides variations on dominant areas of investigation one might already call Darrieussecquian. Painful metamorphoses, solitude and the incommensurability of the other, the resurgence of childhood fears, the existence of parallel worlds which encroach on and disrupt what we think of as 'reality' – these are the stuff her fictional universe is made of. Her determination to develop a distinctive, coherent set of metaphors for each altered state overrides other features such as plot or psychology. From *Truismes* onwards she attempts less to explain what is happening to her protagonists than to put the reader into contact with states of being which evoke shared experiences of trauma, growth and change.

A final point: the punchy presentation of gender relations in *Truismes* and Darrieussecq's assertion that she is a feminist should not lead us to the conclusion that she sees herself as a woman's writer in any militant or politicised sense.[3] Although in this first novel feminine identity is clearly explored within an oppressive, patriarchal context, the following works constitute much more elliptical examinations of the self in crisis with no overtly political dimension and Darrieussecq's ambitions are less ideological than literary. In other words, what she does want to challenge are the limits of language, and the clinical precision with which she anatomises fleeting states of being is testimony to her sustained attempt to 'dire l'indicible' (say the unsayable).[4] This chapter will develop the ideas expressed above by pursuing three themes: monstrous bodies, missing others and fantastic landscapes.

Monstrous bodies

A fascination with bodies is evident throughout Darrieussecq's work and bodies may be monstrous in less obvious ways than the freakish forms we encounter in *Truismes*. To begin with, however, I will explore the politicised idea of the monstrous body in this first novel, concentrating on the problems of interpretation it sets for the reader.

I have already suggested that the heroine's porcine transformations keep the struggle over the meanings of the female body firmly at the centre of this complex text. Cleverly standing in metaphoric relation to a wide range of experiences from puberty to menopause, they allow Darrieussecq to explore a collective sense of feminine identity through highlighting one woman's relationship – sometimes painful, sometimes joyous – with her physical self. They also exemplify to the point of caricature the monstrous or 'abject' body, a concept which permeates the novel entirely. The abject body is one which leaks and bleeds, is protean and uncontainable, and there are numerous manifestations of this such as the heroine's flood-like periods, ever-expanding breasts and buttocks, uncontrollable body hair, unaccountable appetites and increasing tendency to walk on all fours. The abject is said to engender dread and abhorrence in men[5] and to denote 'a realm outside culture . . . shapeless, monstrous, damp and slimy [and] threatening to reduce culture to chaos'.[6] It situates gender identities according to the dangerously essentialist culture–nature polarity, its corollary being the perceived necessity to 'civilise' and 'control' female bodies.

As the novel's punning title suggests,[7] Darrieussecq's primary purpose in *Truismes* is to accumulate commonplace perceptions and discourses such as these which have perennially sought to constrain and manipulate women. They are deeply entrenched and institutionalised in her not so brave new world, and rather than contest them her aim appears to be to reinforce them so thoroughly that their insidiousness and absurdity are consistently underlined. For example, her heroine is non-intellectual, narcissistic, predominantly interested in beauty products and entirely dependent for her sense of self-worth on masculine desire ('mon seul atout était mon côté *pneumatique*' (p. 29) ('my only asset was my *pneumatic* aspect' (p. 19))). She consents to the view of her body as a currency which is plummeting in value and to the pathologising of the female body which is perpetuated by her own diagnoses, those of her clients in the massage parlour, her dermatologist, the fantastic figure of the *marabout*, the gynaecologists and last but not least her partner who declares that 'les femmes, ça a toujours des problèmes de ventre' (p. 23) ('women always have problems with their insides' (p. 13)). In each case what comes to the fore are her increasingly acute sense of shame, negative self-perception and lack of autonomy as her body deviates from society's exacting gold standard of sexual desirability.

It is not possible within the scope of this chapter to explore every twist of *Truismes*'s picaresque narrative. Instead, if we are to establish what message Darrieussecq's novel holds for the collective body of women, we should turn to its end point. This involves no reversal of fortune and little enhanced comprehension on the part of the heroine. She remains a pig–woman and is resigned to exclusion since she has renounced human society altogether, leaving the patriarchal order of the city for the countryside and the company of pigs. The conclusion also sends us back to the start of the narrative since it foregrounds the heroine's decision to bear witness; the novel both begins and ends with a *mise en scène* of the writing project.

A positive reading of *Truismes*'s conclusion might point out that the heroine is no longer colluding with a society which was threatening to annihilate her, that she has learned how to obtain rather than simply provide sexual pleasure and that far from being repulsed by her monstrous body she now assumes it and delights in it:

> Je me laisse souvent aller. Rien n'est meilleur que la terre chaude autour de soi quand on s'éveille le matin, l'odeur de son propre corps mélangée à l'odeur de l'humus, les premières bouchées que l'on prend sans même se lever, glands, châtaignes, tout ce qui a roulé dans la bauge sous le coup de pattes des rêves. (p. 148)

> (I often relax and enjoy myself. There's nothing better than warm earth around you when you wake up in the morning, the smell of your own body mingling with the odour of humus, the first mouthfuls you take without even getting up, gobbling acorns, chestnuts, everything that has rolled down into the wallow while you were scrabbling in your dreams. (p. 135))

She is clearly finding a new, more poetic voice and above all she has begun to write, the first step to understanding the assumptions by which she has been framed, and itself an identity affirming exercise.

A negative reading of the conclusion might instead point out that the heroine, condemned to permanent hybridity, is still constrained by the misfortunes of biology. Neither human nor pig, she is doubly outcast and barely accepted by her new companions ('Je ne suis pas à la hauteur de leurs attentes' (p. 141) ('I'm unable to rise to their expectations' (p. 128))). Although her attempt to write could be seen through the lens of feminist thought and practice which links writing and the affirmation of subjecthood, Darrieussecq allows her heroine scant success in this domain. Lacking in analytic focus, her retrospective narrative could hardly be defined as a demonstration of understanding and the whole process is in any case shown to be jeopardised by the mud of the wallow in which she enjoys rolling, 'qui salit tout, qui dilue l'encre à peine sèche' (p. 11) ('which dirties everything and dilutes ink that's barely dry' (p. 1)). The competing fluids of ink and mud reactivate the misogynistic nature–culture, body–intellect cliché – one of the harmful truisms the author is supposedly attempting to destroy through satire – thereby casting a shadow over any indicator of change or emancipation the conclusion may otherwise have held.

In short, the identity crisis dramatised in *Truismes* does not lend itself easily to a single interpretation. On the one hand the novel seems deeply pessimistic, a study of the worst in women's experiences, riddled with soft-porn images and sexual violence, and with a narrator who is unpardonably light-hearted and too insouciant to denounce the social order. From this perspective the ultimate outrage is that as Darrieussecq takes us 'back to the future', she appears to indicate that bodies of feminist knowledge have not percolated down to ordinary women: it is as if they were an irrelevance of history. Reading the text as ironic, oppositional practice, however, *Truismes* could be said to exemplify Lidia Curti's equally persuasive argument that the freakish body can be 'a derisive counterpoint to stereotypes of the feminine'.[8]

Darrieussecq's following novels retain an intensive focus on the body, but in a less controversial and more ambitious way. They are almost entirely unconcerned with sexuality or erotic experiences and far from being a key to identity physical appearances become practically irrelevant. The metamorphoses with which these novels are concerned are invisible ones, and the bodily changes they describe are not a source of, but a response to, crisis. If bodies here may be defined as monstrous this is because they are shown to be beyond our control, eluding interpretation and eluding language. Darrieussecq's emphasis on the physical is a particularly original feature of her work. The novel, she contends, has focused too heavily on the psychological, on the mind at the expense of the body, and her own fiction shifts the balance with an unrelenting examination of trauma through close-up, slow-motion studies of the physical sensations to which it gives rise. Building on the ground cleared by the *nouveau roman*, Darrieussecq eschews conventional notions of plot and character. She gives her protagonists no face, no pre-history, no curriculum vitae and no name, and although we may sense that they are rounded, real individuals, their function is more important than their character; the author's aim is to give expression to generic experiences, not to leave us with indelible impressions of unforgettable personages. Thus in *Naissance des fantômes* the heroine's initial experience of unity as she watches swallows cut across the early evening skies is physical: 'j'avais l'impression d'être moi-même une grosse chose vibrante et chaude . . . entière, pleine et ramassée' (p. 13) ('It was as though I too were some large, trembling, hot thing' (p. 7)), and the transformation through which her sense of self is progressively splintered will also be described through the body. 'Ecrire "elle se sentait triste", non!' (Write 'she felt sad', no!) proclaims Darrieussecq,[9] 'mon roman est tout sauf psychologique' (my novel is anything but psychological).[10]

Missing others: disappearances, hauntings and holograms

Darrieussecq's protagonists are profoundly isolated and haunted by absence. Each novel creates a situation in which others go missing and are missed: the husband of *Naissance des fantômes* and the mother and daughter of *Le Mal de mer* disappear without warning, triggering crises in the lives of those they have left; the heroine of *Truismes* disastrously seeks out her estranged mother and gradually loses all contact with the social world as she herself – or at least her human incarnation – goes missing. Such literal disappearances are simply one way of highlighting what is in any case endemic in interpersonal relationships as described by Darrieussecq: however hard we try to communicate, we do not connect. We keep on missing each other.

It is to *Naissance des fantômes* and *Le Mal de mer* that we will turn in order to consider the idea of the missing other and the shaken sense of self which is its corollary. In the first of these, Darrieussecq's lucid and inventive meditation on the enduring theme of the disappeared distils the effects of a common grief within one woman's experience. Her choice of a missing rather than a dead husband is a key factor in this respect, embracing generations of women who have waited (Duras's *La Douleur* is clearly a precursor),[11] and reaching out to all those who attempt to reconcile themselves with unaccountable loss. If the disappeared cannot be located, what happens to the self? What happens to the memory of the other? And these questions also refer to the ghosts which haunt Europe's collective conscience: 'Comment écrire après Auschwitz quand "eux" sont partis et pas revenus? Comment dire le monde sans "eux"? Comment reconstruire autour d'un trou noir?' (How can we write after Auschwitz when 'they' left and did not return? How can we express the world without 'them'? How can we rebuild around a black hole?).[12]

Darrieussecq's determination to produce a detailed account of the physical effects of loss gives rise to one of the most original features of her second novel: its increasing reliance on tropes drawn from science. If this is a ghost story, it is one that refers us not to superstition but to quantum physics; if it is a love story, it is 'un roman d'amour vécu sous l'angle des molécules' (Garcin, p. 90) (a love story experienced from a molecular

point of view). In an irreversible paradigm shift consistent with the idea of
a life in pieces, physical objects and people alike are caught up in a terrifying dance of dispersed atoms and porosity: 'Mon mari était forcément
quelque part, gazeux peut-être, à la limite de sortir de l'univers, mais
quelque part forcément' (p. 94) ('My husband had to be somewhere,
maybe in form of a gas at the very outer edge of the universe, but he still
had to be somewhere' (p. 86)). The effort of will required to hold together
the contours of the world is tremendous. Microscopic examinations of
objects in the marital apartment reveal uncanny structural modifications,
and the heroine's own body is perceived biologically as a fragile collection
of barriers, 'un ensemble de digues, la peau, la derme, les muscles, l'en-
veloppe des organes, la barrière immunitaire' (p. 78) ('a system of dikes
(epidermis, dermis, membranes, muscles, immune barriers)' (p. 70)),
barely keeping disintegration at bay. In a striking *mise-en-abyme* of the
novel's repeated slippage between the graspable and the inconceivable,
the narrator attempts to give voice to her perceptions as she climbs the
familiar winding staircase to her apartment and contemplates the void of
the stairwell. Defeated in her attempt to probe the limitations of language,
she resorts to drawing and what she produces is a complex of spirals
within a spiral, a visual evocation of infinity and of the new space–time
which is the universe of loss.

The entry to this universe is deceptively ordinary. *Naissance des fantômes* begins with a steady reiteration of this ordinariness, setting up a
mystery in a manner reminiscent of detective fiction: 'Mon mari a disparu.
Il est rentré du travail, il a posé sa serviette contre le mur, il m'a demandé si
j'avais acheté du pain. Il devait être aux alentours de sept heures et demie'
(p. 9) ('My husband's disappeared. He got in from work, propped his brief-
case against the wall and asked me if I'd bought the bread. It must have
been around half past seven' (p. 3)). This nod to a more reassuring, plot-
based literary genre is also a feature of *Le Mal de mer*, and Darrieussecq
exploits it with a purpose over and above that of injecting her narratives
with suspense. Detective fiction is about finding people and finding things
out about people, and it usually does just that. In *Naissance des fantômes*,
however, the author's technique of adopting then abandoning some of its
generic traits is mimetic of the heroine's progressive loss of bearings.
Although she initially pursues her husband through conventional routes
(checking the *boulangerie*, contacting the police and tracing his last-known
movements) the 'script' soon fritters away. The investigation is abandoned
after a few pages to be replaced by inaction and the void, and the text yields

no answers concerning the husband's departure. In *Le Mal de mer* the detective strand is more structurally integrated within the novel, since the abandoned husband (whom we never see) hires a private detective to track down his wife and child, and Darrieussecq stops writing once this happens. The point is, however, that the novel is devoid of the psychological analysis proper to most detective fiction and little is resolved on the level of human understanding. The detective finds the fugitives, but he does not find anything out about them; the reader never discovers what impelled the young mother to leave in the first place, and the characters are no nearer to understanding each other by the end of the novel than they were at the beginning. This brings us to the second aspect of 'missing others.'

A dominant strand of Darrieussecq's work involves the existential question of the self and the other. Although the identity of the young wife in *Naissance des fantômes* disintegrates because no longer held together by the familiar presence of her husband, her attempts to piece together his traces paradoxically erase any certainty that she ever knew him and bring her to the conclusion that he was a phantom even before he disappeared. *Le Mal de mer* provides further studies in existential isolation. The fact that the novel is more peopled merely provides extra opportunities for Darrieussecq to accumulate 'ces moments où, même si l'on tend la main, on croit ne pas pouvoir atteindre l'hologramme qui se tient devant nous' (p. 32) ('those moments when, even if you reach out, you don't think you can touch the hologram standing in front of you' (p. 23)). The protagonists seem separated from each other as if by an invisible membrane and struck by aphasia. Whereas the first two novels are narrated in the first person and writing is both a theme and an element of the heroines' transformations, the characters here are dumbstruck. There is no dialogue or reported speech, for Darrieussecq is no longer working at the level of articulated thought. Instead, in Sarrautean fashion, she records the sub-currents of conflicting sensations experienced by a series of unnamed '*ils*' and '*elles*', creating an unstable universe of misunderstandings and intimate, identity-threatening crises which are generated by the other and never resolved. The distinctive and finely honed body of imagery through which Sarraute describes our shaken worlds, including references to plate tectonics, whirling planets, meteorites and monsters,[13] is matched by imagery of similar force, design and consistency in Darrieussecq.

Fantastic landscapes, frontiers and parallel worlds

If the abandoned husband in *Le Mal de mer* is 'sidéré par la porosité des frontières' (p. 41) ('amazed by how porous borders can be' (p. 32)), so is the reader of Darrieussecq. Her fiction, teeming with boundaries and thresholds, pinpoints the frontier places to which we are taken as we undergo violent change and the fissures through which we can tumble into alien parallel worlds. The metaphorical sense of place in her writing is idiosyncratic and highly developed, each of her heroines' identity crises unfolding in a psycho-physical environment which juxtaposes the comforting and the menacing, keeping the proximity of chaos uppermost in our minds. The postmodern, bomb-damaged, epidemic-ridden cityscape of *Truismes* – which is an integral aspect of Darrieussecq's socio-political satire as well as the backdrop for her heroine's trials – remains recognisably Parisian. In *Naissance des fantômes* the aquatic and the urban come together as waves lap around the walls of métro stations, and a mysterious and dangerous frontier is visible from the heroine's apartment. The slippage between the ordinary and the fantastic is so fluid, so skilfully operated, that any notion we may have harboured of a safe and ordered existence is placed under considerable pressure. This is particularly the case in *Le Mal de mer* where Darrieussecq does not allow us to forget for an instant that 'sous le sol familier, bitumé, rues, cour d'école, square, parking' (p. 58) ('beneath the familiar tarmac surface of streets, school playgrounds, public squares, car parks' (p. 48)) is a seething, formless magma which could erupt at any moment. Here we encounter another of Darrieussecq's parallel worlds which leaks into the quotidian at periods of crisis: the world of childhood and its monstrous terrors. Her writing, she claims, 'se nourrit de vieilles peurs enfantines' (Baudet, p. 21) (feeds on old childhood fears) which engulf us even in adulthood with all their original intensity. In *Le Mal de mer* she revisits childhood trauma through her intense examination of a mother/daughter separation which highlights particularly clearly the metaphorical importance of environment – in this case the seaside – in her work.

If Darrieussecq's hallmark is her focus on what we might call the disruptive moment, the wave is clearly an appropriate figure and the seashore, 'un endroit d'attache et d'abandon' (a place of attachment and desertion), a fitting locus for a series of ruptures and transformations.[14] The author's grasp of water, particularly in its destructive capacity, is Durassian and this eerily somnolent off-season resort is perhaps the most strange and terrifying of all her frontier places. This becomes clear from the novel's opening sentence – a powerfully anthropomorphic evocation of the Atlantic as seen for the first time by a disorientated little girl: 'C'est une bouche à demi ouverte, qui respire, mais les yeux, le nez, le menton ne sont plus là. C'est une bouche plus grande que toutes les bouches imaginables, et qui fend l'espace en deux' (p. 9) ('It's a mouth, half open, breathing, but the eyes, nose, and chin are no longer there. It's a mouth bigger than any mouth imaginable, rending space in two' (p. 1)). Darrieussecq's slumbering monster of a seascape, whose mythical proportions and apocalyptic capabilities assume Zolaesque proportions, is gradually made to embody the mother as an ambiguous, fearful force.

The frontier between sea and shore, self and other, is portrayed with particular intensity in the novel's opening section where twenty-one pages of mutual incomprehension begin the child's initiation to separation and to the impossibility of osmosis with the mother. The absence of dialogue and the juxtaposition of conflicting points of view establish the distance between the pair, and the prevailing images are the conflicting ones of home and womb on the one hand, and devouring, cannibalistic mouth on the other. The child, limp as a knitted doll or puppet and useless without the mother's hand to animate her, suffers nightmare visions of dismemberment, impotence and incompleteness. Remembering her first cinema visit (the film was *Pinocchio*) and her terror at the celluloid sea, she now wishes to 'glisser à nouveau dans le noir jusque dans le *ventre* de la baleine' (p. 17) ('[slip] once again into the darkness and even into the belly of the whale' (p. 9)). The blue tent in which the couple spend the night signifies both home and womb, but its security depends on the presence of the father: on mountain holidays it is he who bangs the tent pegs convincingly into the earth, creating a comforting structure, 'la jointure, endroit et envers, entre sa peau à elle et le monde' (p. 21) ('the membrane, within and without, between her own skin and the world' (p. 13)). Here in the unstable sand the tent heaves with convulsions, a *mise-en-abyme* of the sea, a formless parody of home and an unreliable womb. While the mother dreams of one form of symbiosis with the sea as a release from her depression ('La mer est une paroi verticale, à travers laquelle il suffirait de passer' (pp. 27–8) ('The sea is a vertical partition through which you need only to pass' (p. 20))), the child lives through a quite different one. Her breathing and sobbing are dictated by the rhythm of the waves, her tears taste of oysters and seaweed and later in the novel she will, under maternal instigation, learn to swim.

The seaside, then, is the place where both mother and daughter explore absence before their ultimate separation takes place and it is carefully selected by a mother who knows precisely where she wants to stage her daughter's first oceanic encounter. It is as if the place could account for something without her having to explain, as if it were some second baptism or a rite of passage in terms of understanding the adult world: 'sa mère le croit, qu'on le voit, sur le visage des gens, et particulièrement des enfants, ceux qui ont vu la mer et ceux qui ne l'ont pas vue' (p. 11) ('her mother believes that – that you can tell from people's faces, especially children's, who has seen the sea and who has not' (p. 3)). In her third novel, then, Darrieussecq's attention to fantastic landscapes provides a fresh gloss to the homonymic link that is now a cliché of literature ('mer'/'mère'). The novel's title refers to both the mother's unspecified 'sickness' and the vertiginous instability inflicted by her on 'la petite'. Finally, the title may also refer to the mother's wrongdoing and to the fact that her daughter will, at the end, be 'en mal de mère' (lacking a mother).

Conclusion

In a recent interview, Darrieussecq suggested that in spite of their obvious differences she has come to view her first three published novels as a trilogy.[15] Each of them develops metaphors to account for the violence inflicted upon women and girls by life changes and, while overly narrow biographical interpretations are unhelpful, the author nevertheless acknowledges that the novels were written during a period when she was herself learning to become an adult.[16] Her studies of crisis are open-ended and although in each case a degree of autonomy is gained there is no answer to the perennial question 'who am I?'. The narrator of *Truismes* remains in conflict with herself, the heroine of *Naissance des fantômes* learns that 'l'amour fusion' (Baudet, p. 21) (fusion love) is an adolescent fantasy, the child in *Le Mal de mer* is forced into painful self-reliance and the novel leaves her mother in the liminal space of an airport, on the threshold of a new life yet not free from her depression. To insist on a resolution would, however, be reductive and for Darrieussecq the question of identity is raised at a more fundamental level by the writing project itself than by the 'plot' of these three tales. Perhaps the most challenging of all her frontier places is that inhabited by the writer, 'cet espace indéterminé entre ce que l'on sent et ce que l'on veut nommer' (Gaudemar, p. II) (that indeterminate space between what one feels and what one wishes to name) and it is in this territory that the sense of self is most acutely at stake. This is why Darrieussecq has two of her heroines turn to writing and why she has not shirked from revealing the torment in which she sometimes writes[17] or the intensely personal elements woven through her studies of crisis. The ultimate interest for the reader of her works is not in any lesson to be derived from the search for the self, but in the moments of intense identification provoked by the astonishingly original outcomes of her resolve to say the unsayable.

Notes

1 Marie Darrieussecq, *Truismes* (Paris: POL, 1996); *Pig Tales*, trans. Linda Coverdale (London: Faber & Faber, 1997).

2 Marie Darrieussecq, *Naissance des fantômes* (Paris: POL, 1998); *My Phantom Husband*, trans. Helen Stevenson (London: Faber & Faber, 1999); *Le Mal de mer* (Paris: POL, 1999); *Breathing Underwater*, trans. Linda Coverdale (London: Faber & Faber, 2001).

3 Jean-Pierre Bourcier, 'Marie Darrieussecq: "Européenne, féministe et athée"', *La Tribune* (13 November 1996), p. 20.

4 Sebastian Le Fol, 'Marie Darrieussecq: "Je veux changer la langue!"', *Le Figaro* (11 March 1999), p. 79.

5 Julia Kristeva, *Pouvoirs de l'horreur: essai sur l'abjection* (Paris: Seuil, 1980); Mary Douglas, *Purity and Danger: An Analysis of Concepts of Pollution and Taboo* (London: Routledge and Kegan Paul, 1986).

6 Barbara Brook, *Feminist Perspectives on the Body* (London and New York: Longman, 1999), pp. 14–15.

7 '*Truie*' is the French for 'sow'.

8 Lidia Curti, *Female Stories, Female Bodies: Narrative, Identity and Representation* (London: Macmillan, 1998), p. 107.

9 M. Baudet, 'Marie Darrieussecq, auteur à haute résolution', *Libre Culture* (19 May 1999), p. 21.

10 Jérôme Garcin, 'Marie Darrieussecq: l'après *Truismes*', *Le Nouvel Observateur*, 1684 (19–25 February 1998), pp. 88–90 (p. 90).

11 Marguerite Duras, *La Douleur* (Paris: POL, 1985).

12 Antoine de Gaudemar, 'Darrieussecq, du cochon au volatil', *Libération (Livres)* (26 February 1998), I–III (III).

13 See, for example, Nathalie Sarraute, *Le Planétarium* (Paris: Gallimard, 1972).

14 Marie Darrieussecq, *Précisions sur les vagues* (Paris: POL, 1999), p. 10.

15 Unpublished interview with Shirley Jordan, 29 May 2001.

16 'A cette époque-là de ma vie j'étais en train de devenir adulte, entre vingt et trente ans, quoi.' (This was a period in my life – say, between the ages of 20 and 30 – when I was becoming an adult). Unpublished interview with Shirley Jordan.

17 See Daniel Mazingarbe, 'Marie Darrieussecq: *Naissance des fantômes*', *Madame Figaro* (28 February 1998), p. 31.

III

Transgressions and transformation

Experiment and experience in the phototextual projects of Sophie Calle

Born in 1953, Sophie Calle is both a writer and a photographer, and rarely one without the other. This double focus is accommodated in two main forms. The first, and the one that usually appears first, is the installation exhibited in an art gallery or museum, where photos hung at eye level or sometimes simply leaning against a wall are juxtaposed with framed printed texts. But Calle has also found a rewarding outlet in the form of book publications based on the same kind of text–photo juxtaposition – and, given the scope and objectives of this particular volume of essays, it is above all on the published work that I focus here. By virtue of being com-pacted into and redistributed across a sequence of pages, the published work tends all the more strongly to bear out the description of herself that Calle is said to favour: that of 'narrative artist' (which neatly sidesteps the more frequently bestowed label of 'conceptual artist').[1] Calle's work has become renowned for the stimulating and often controversial ways in which it crosses the boundary lines between public and private, detach-ment and involvement, life and art. In crossing such lines, Calle's work comes to bear a high degree of self-implication, a quality it shares with the work of many other contemporary artists, such as Christian Boltanski, Annette Messager and Orlan. What does it mean to be 'implicated in' one's work, as opposed, say, to being 'expressed by' it? In order to address this question, we first need to set Calle's work in its historical context: that of the shift from the modernist project of art to a postmodernist art of the project.

   The term 'project' may be used to describe the activities providing the raw material of Calle's installations and published works. A project involves thinking up and then setting up a situation that will be allowed to run its course under certain conditions. The external boundaries of the situation will be defined by preordained limits of time and/or space, while its internal dynamics will be defined by a further set of ground rules or protocols. The photographer remains acutely aware of limits, for delimitation accounts for every photograph, being a condition at once imposed (by the rectangular edges of the shot when first taken, edges themselves dictated by the format of the film in the camera) and assumed, changed into something chosen (by framing, trimming, cropping, etc.). In this respect, Calle may well be a postmodernist, but in her work thus far she has remained steadfastly pre-digital, an artist who likes to play with evidentiality rather than virtuality or computer-manipulated imagery.

As something 'set up' or staged, the project–situation is artificial, a quality reflected in Calle's use of terms such as *rituel* (ritual) or *pseudo-enquête* (pseudo-inquiry) to describe certain of her projects. By the same token, more or less all of her projects may also be described as experiments: experiments run not with a view to testing any particular hypothesis, but, far less teleologically, in order to 'see what happens'. This I take to be a suddenly resonant phrase as applied to Calle, given both her status as a photographer ('to see. . .') and her self-definition as a 'narrative' artist ('. . .what happens'). I shall argue in this chapter that, for Calle, 'seeing what happens' always includes seeing what happens to herself, tracking her own *experience* as primed and prompted by the context of the *experiment*. Her 'own' experience here is, we might say, an 'experimental experience', an experience of the kind made accessible in and through the promotion of what Celia Lury calls 'experimental individualism'. Conceived as a contemporary alternative to the norm of 'possessive individualism', this is a mode in which the individuality, identity or biography of the person can be prosthetically disassembled and reassembled using various forms of technological mediation.[2] As Lury herself remarks, in a comment that sounds tailor-made to evoke the case of Sophie Calle: 'the prosthetic biography requires significant new forms of authorisation and, in this respect, the image is combining with narrative to produce techniques of the self in new ways' (p. 24).

Calle's most compelling projects have typically taken the form of experiments in approaching the other, in 'entering into the life' of the other, as she herself put it when writing in *La Filature* about the private detective who tailed her around Paris on 16 April 1981 – a detective she had persuaded her mother to hire for this purpose as part of another engineered, experimental situation.[3] The book includes not only her own notes taken over the course of the day as she was being followed, but a copy of the detective's report and reproductions of the photos he had been instructed to take as evidence of his subject's movements and activities while under surveillance. Thus the *auto-portrait* is counterpointed by a kind of *allo-portrait*. Calle's own notes record how she recurrently found herself wondering whether the detective felt attracted to her: a show of affect which nods knowingly towards the romanticism of the mass-market *photo-roman*. Contrary to the scripts and scenarios of the *photo-roman*, however, there is never any question in *La Filature* of wanting actually to meet the man. The experience of feeling a 'personal' connection with him, to the point where the day in question is described by Calle with hollow poignancy as 'notre journée' (p. 118) (our day), is a product of the experiment, an 'experimental experience', which, as such, remains tied to the provisional, prosthetic identity of the woman under surveillance, and cannot therefore be transported outside the limits and protocols of the experiment.

By constantly making us unsure about the face value of her textual and photographic statements, Calle seems to encourage in those who read and view her work a sense of its own incipient fictionality, even where its most overt claims are documentary or, in photographic terms, indexical. At the same time, however, it continues to sound as though it could still be 'true': the effect of truth, whether autobiographical or ethnographic in its generic force, is not cancelled out. We are thus left suspended, uncertain. There are many reasons one could adduce for both the suspicion of *fictionality* in Calle's work and the sense of its ultimately *uncertain* status. I would like to suggest here that one of the most pervasive triggers of both responses is the recurrent instance of what I have chosen to call 'experimental experience'. Experimental experience takes the form of feelings, emotions, reactions, etc., which are not so much in and of an underlying self as signs announcing what Celia Lury, echoing Roland Barthes, calls the 'advent', indeed the 'adventure', of oneself as other (p. 76). And this sense of a self coming into view as other, at a remove from what it was, is easily – and often accurately – construed as a process of generating a fictional character out of autobiographical material. The principle of uncertainty is restored, however, if, along Barthesian lines, the strategy of 'experimental experience' is understood to offer a more self-protective way of reconstituting the division between public and private. In other words, might this strategy not provide Calle with a technique for fulfilling what was also Barthes's desire as a writer in *La Chambre claire*: 'Je veux énoncer l'intériorité sans livrer l'intimité' (I want to utter interiority without yielding intimacy)?[4] Another way of making the same point might be to say that the subject of 'experimental experience' in *La Filature* is not in fact the one I referred to earlier as the woman under surveillance, but, more precisely, the woman who *knows* she is under surveillance, the woman with the upper hand. In ethnographic terms, the 'observer' has merged with the 'participant'. What I call 'experimental experience', therefore, may well involve stepping into a role, but does not escape the self-implication of the one playing that role. And, ultimately, the romantic script which Calle finds herself reading aloud, and which superimposes an image of vulnerability onto that of the woman with the upper hand, must probably be read as something that joins the role to the player, something that is not played out in a purely ironic spirit. More generally, this is one example of the way experimental experience implicates Calle herself as the subject of certain fantasies, indeed as the subject of a certain kind of madness.

Since the late 1980s, Calle has explored more open, empathic and collaborative ways of 'entering into the life' of the other, notably by using interviews in order to garner raw material for the textual component of certain projects. Surprisingly, however, this more recent vein was illustrated by only one of the eleven phototextual projects included in '*Doubles-jeux*', a major exhibition of Calle's work shown in 1998 at the Centre National de la Photographie in Paris. A boxed set of seven books representing the exhibited works, and bearing the same title, was published simultaneously by Actes-Sud.[5] The exhibition was itself the fruit of a kind of meta-project inspired by the activities of Calle's fictional double, Maria Turner, the eccentric character from Paul Auster's novel, *Leviathan* (1992). Eight of the component works of the exhibition correspond, as Calle herself puts it, to rituals that Auster 'borrowed' from her to shape the character of Maria. Calle also used the exhibition as an opportunity to produce two new works based on rituals attributed to Maria for which she herself had not been the direct inspiration. Finally, Calle took this 'double-play' or 'double-ploy' one stage further by inviting Auster to do with her whatever he wished for a period of up to one year, as though she were no longer just a real model for a fictional character, but his own fictional creation. As she explains in the text repeated at the start of each of the seven volumes of the book *Doubles-jeux*, Auster declined her invitation, preferring instead to send her some 'personal instructions' for the improvement of life in New York. The resulting project eventually yielded *Gotham handbook* – the one component of *Doubles-jeux* that reflects, albeit in a rather jaundiced manner, the new, ethically correct Calle.

This, perhaps, is an appropriate point at which to offer a justification for the fact that, in a book about women's writing in French in the 1990s, I should have chosen to devote the remainder of this essay to an analysis of *Suite vénitienne* and *L'Hôtel*, two works by Calle first exhibited and published in the 1980s. I leave aside, for the time being, my contention that, in engaging with the other on a non-collaborative or intrusive basis, Calle's 1980s projects raise questions that were once more being strongly echoed in the late 1990s. What concerns me here is the question, or questioning, of temporal location. The project documented in *La Filature* took place in 1981 but did not become available as a published document until 1998, when it appeared as a component of the book *Doubles-jeux*. Somewhat differently, *Suite vénitienne* and *L'Hôtel* already existed in book form and were recycled in *Doubles-jeux*. There is no doubt, however, that, for many readers and spectators previously unfamiliar with Calle, all components of the exhibition and book had a 'firstness' – and indeed a sense of late 1990s contemporaneity – about them. Moreover, the 'doubleness' of *Doubles-jeux* arises not only through the phototextual interplay of document and fiction, experience and experiment, 'Sophie Calle' and 'Maria Turner', but through a temporal interplay of past and present. This occurs most obviously at the chronological level, where the inclusion of new work ensures that *Doubles-jeux* cannot be pigeon-holed into the comfortable format of the 'retrospective'. But it can also be seen to occur within individual components of the work. For example, in the book *Doubles-jeux*, the 1998 versions of both *Suite vénitienne* and *L'Hôtel* show changes in textual and photographic content, as well as general layout, when compared with the 'original' versions. Similar changes can even be noted when one moves from the 'original' French paperback version of *Doubles-jeux* to the larger, more lavishly produced English-language version, *Double Game*, published as a single hardback volume.[6] Different book formats will affect what Calle decides to select from her own archive and how she decides to present that selection, just as the different physical settings offered by different museums and galleries will affect the precise content and layout of her exhibitions. Calle's enthusiasm for demonstrating the permutability of her previously published or exhibited phototextual sequences indicates clearly that, for her, as for numerous other contemporary artists (and, increasingly, writers), there is no such thing as a definitive, unproblematically date-bound, realisation of a given project.

The phototextual projects that yielded *Suite vénitienne* and *L'Hôtel* take the form of essentially furtive attempts to engage with the life of a singular or serial other. One insight into this furtiveness is offered by Jean

Baudrillard when discussing *Suite vénitienne* in a 1994 interview: 'Pas de psychologie, mais une façon énigmatique d'entrer dans la vie de l'autre, non pas au sens où vous la violez, mais au sens où vous en êtes le secret' (No psychology, but an enigmatic way of entering into another's life, not in the sense that you violate it, but in the sense that you are its secret).[7] 'Being the other's secret' is a form of words prompted by Baudrillard's theory of seduction, but at the same time a euphemism meaning that the other remains unaware of being followed or spied on. The boundary lines separating private from public, and life from art, are variously crossed in most of Calle's work, but nowhere more dramatically, intrusively and therefore controversially, than in her projects of the early 1980s. These projects are not necessarily motivated by a humanist impulse of 'being-towards-the-other', as advocated by a Levinas or a Ricœur, and they are therefore not necessarily set up in any expectation of finally 'meeting' the other. Furtiveness is necessitated, if never fully justified, by the idea of entering into the life of another person without their knowledge, obliquely, by indirect means. In so doing, Calle also typically lays herself open to the advent of the aleatory within the situation established by her own ground rules. What I have called 'experimental experience' often results from striking interactions of choice and chance.

In turning now to *Suite vénitienne* and *L'Hôtel*, my analysis will focus not only on the 'furtive' nature of Calle's entry into the life of the other, but on the way she represents the modalities of her own self-implication in each project. I shall also try to highlight how Calle's propensity for thinking through photography impacts on the experimental and experiential dimensions of either project.

Suite vénitienne consists of the photographic and textual record, packaged as an illustrated diary, of two weeks Calle spent in Venice in 1980, first of all hunting down a man she had first met in Paris, and subsequently shadowing him. In so doing, she plays out what Whitney Chadwick calls 'an elaborate transference of agency, appropriating the "male gaze" and producing the woman, traditionally the object of others' looks in public, as the viewing subject'.[8] Venice itself, of course, is a charged site, guaranteed to intensify whatever is at stake in the project for Calle herself. By a happy coincidence, carnival time is approaching and masks are very much in evidence. In order to conceal her identity from her prey, Calle too has decided to disguise herself for the duration of the project by wearing a blonde wig (she assures us that in reality she is a brunette).

The whole artistic and literary mythology of Venice infects Calle from the outset, and indeed *affects* very directly the way she represents her own self-implication in this project. Calle's more personal comments in her diary are, rather unusually, given prominence and added urgency by being set in italics. One of the first occurrences of such italicised text is also one of the most dramatic: 'Arrivée place Saint-Marc, je m'assieds contre une colonne. Je regarde. *Je me vois aux portes d'un labyrinthe, prête à me perdre dans la ville et dans cette histoire. Soumise*' (I arrive at Piazza San Marco and sit against a column. I look around. *I see myself at the gates of a labyrinth, ready to get lost in the city and in this story. Submissive*).[9] Calle imagines she is on the threshold of a loss of self, an entering-in and giving-in to the labyrinthine destiny whose parameters are a city and a story. The city and story in which one volunteers to lose oneself, or to advene as other, are thus the site of an unusually intense 'experimental experience', a kind of danger zone. Indeed, the reflexive doubling of 'Je me vois. . .' (I see myself) briefly distinguishes experimental subject from experiential subject, the overseer from the undergoer, only to confirm at the same time that the two positions are co-referential. Given this image of seeing oneself, and the fact that the figure of self advening as other has its roots in one of Barthes's comments from *La Chambre claire* concerning our reactions to photographs of ourselves, it is clear that Calle's propensity for thinking *through* photography strongly informs the question of 'experimental experience' – as both envisaged and enacted.

Still two days before she eventually catches sight of the man called Henri B., Calle finds herself struggling to keep experimental experience at an appropriate remove, a safe distance:

> *12h 30.* Je vais me promener sur la plage du Lido. *Je pense à lui et à cette phrase de Proust: 'Dire que j'ai gâché des années de ma vie, que j'ai voulu mourir et que j'ai eu mon plus grand amour, pour une femme qui ne me plaisait pas, qui n'était pas mon genre.'*
>
> *Je ne dois pas oublier que je n'éprouve aucun sentiment amoureux pour Henri B. Ces symptômes, l'impatience avec laquelle j'attends sa venue, la peur de cette rencontre, ne m'appartiennent pas en propre.* (p. 57)

> (12:30 p.m. I take a walk along the beach of the Lido. *I think about him and about that sentence of Proust: "To think that I've wasted years of my life, that I wanted to die and had my greatest love for a woman who gave me no pleasure, who was not my type".*
>
> *I must not forget that I have no feelings of love toward Henri B. These symptoms – my impatience as I await his arrival, my fears about our meeting – don't really belong to me.*)

Her impatience and fear, she tries to persuade herself, are 'symptoms' that do not belong to her as such. By this, she presumably means that these symptoms are no more than effects produced by the experimental situation, little more than fictional implants. (Curiously, it is of course a fiction, Proust's *Un Amour de Swann*, that helps her see this.) By attempting to distance and disavow any feelings of amorous involvement with Henri B., the subject perhaps forgets that the experiencer is co-referential with the experimenter, and that co-reference implies both discontinuity and continuity. Baudrillard has argued tirelessly that Calle's work, as exemplified in the case of *Suite vénitienne*, has left psychology behind, abandoning the 'degraded' alterity of inter-subjective encounters and altercations in favour of something called 'pure' alterity (p. 147). It is no accident that Baudrillard hardly ever discusses the work as a concrete realisation. By contrast, what interests me is precisely the trace, at certain crux moments, of something like 'psychology' in Calle's efforts to manage the notion of experimental experience. Paradoxically, this trace is nowhere more evident than in her very efforts to escape 'psychology'. Psychology, or inter-subjectivity, determines here that, both before and during the time she first glimpses Henri B., both before and during the time he identifies and confronts her in a Venice street, the story launched by the experimental project is, as Calle writes in the penultimate sentence of the diary framing the photographs of *Suite vénitienne*, 'notre histoire' (p. 107) (our story). Irony swarms around this phrase, but never quite manages to sting it to death, even when we learn through the good offices of Baudrillard writing some fourteen years after the event that, due to legal objections lodged on behalf of the filmmaker Henri B., Calle was in fact obliged before publishing or exhibiting her work to return to the scene of her potential crime and restage all her photos featuring Henri B. and his female companion, but now with two stand-ins (p. 145). To be privy to such information is to appreciate that the temporal staggering of Calle's work from its initial completion as project to its eventual, multiple and frequently remixed realisations in exhibited and published form can be more complex than at first appears to be the case.

What does effectively cancel out the story *qua* 'our' story is the decision to discontinue the experiment. 'Our' story will have no future beyond the limits of the project, outside the space of disguise, carnival and labyrinth, which proved so conducive to the cultivation of experimental experience. Such, it seems to me, is the import of Calle's parting words in *Suite vénitienne*: 'Je le photographie une dernière fois alors qu'il franchit l'enceinte de la gare. Je n'irai pas plus loin. Il s'éloigne, je le perds de vue. *Après ces treize jours passés avec lui, notre histoire s'achève. 10 h 10.* Je cesse de suivre Henri B.' (p. 107) (I photograph him one last time as he passes through the station gate. I shall go no further. He walks away, I lose sight of him. *After these last thirteen days with him, our story comes to an end. 10:10 a.m.* I stop following Henri B.).

First published as a book in 1984, *L'Hôtel* is the phototextual record of a project undertaken by Calle, again in Venice, and once more around carnival time, between February and March 1983. This book too, moreover, is presented in the form of an illustrated diary. And yet another common feature with other works of the early 1980s is that *L'Hôtel* opens with a brief outline of the nature of the project behind the book. Here, Calle explains how, in February 1981, she finally managed to find a temporary three-week job as a chambermaid in the 'Hotel C.'. Having been entrusted with twelve rooms on the fourth floor, she then tells us how she proceeded to examine the 'personal effects' (in context, a very resonant phrase) of the occupants of those rooms, furtively observing in a detailed way 'des vies qui me restaient étrangères' (lives that remained foreign to me).[10] The precise details anticipate a key quality of the diary, for it is written not only day by day, but room by room. In ascribing sequences of days to each room visited within the delimited experimental field of three weeks and twelve rooms, Calle invites us to perceive the structure of both the book and the project in terms of a grid. As for the accessibility of the rooms in question, what better way to gain indirect entry into the lives of others than to get oneself hired as a hotel chambermaid? These others will be available to Calle only through their 'personal effects' and through a variety of 'signs' left behind in their rooms. Present effects, absent causes; signs unaccompanied, and in a sense unburdened, by the makers or leavers of those signs. Hence the delicate balance of intimacy and distance in the assertion of having observed in detail 'lives that remained foreign to me'. Hence also, perhaps, our uncertainty as to whether, for Calle, this enduring strangeness represents a frustration or a kind of ideal.

Just how Calle carried out her inquiry is something we only discover as we read on. Each day, we soon learn, she concealed a camera and a tape recorder in her bucket, smuggling these into the various rooms she was due to clean. This is how she came to take the photos and compile the often detailed on-the-spot observations that would merge into the form of an illustrated diary. The diary reveals how Calle not only observed what was on display, but searched in drawers and rummaged through suitcases, frequently removing articles and spreading them on the floor or bed in order to photograph them as if they constituted some kind of forensic evidence. She delves into diaries, letters, passports and other identity papers, often recording whole pages *verbatim* for later transcription into her own diary and eventual exhibition and publication. Another group of signs that catches her eye, and her lens, is that made up of crumpled bedsheets, items of clothing strewn across chairs or hung in wardrobes, and shoes. What these signs have in common for Calle is suggested when, on her last working day at the hotel, she reflects on the sight of a dented pillow. Before viewing the pillow symbolically as 'un signe d'adieu' (a sign of farwell), she sees in it 'l'empreinte arrondie d'une présence' (p. 36) (the rounded imprint of a presence). In other words, she reads it semiotically as an index, a sign whose relationship with its object is one of causal, sequential or spatial contiguity. Indexicality, of course, has long been recognised and theorised as the most fundamental sign-quality of the photograph insofar as the camera mechanically registers a configured influx of light reflected by the objects placed before it. The pillow, like the bedsheets, and to a lesser extent like the shoes and items of clothing Calle constantly snaps, is a *body-graph*. The body-graph provides another example of Calle not just taking photos, but thinking photographically.

How applicable is the notion of 'experimental experience' to the case of *L'Hôtel*? Calle is obviously once more disguised, and, to the extent that the employee to whom she hands over her responsibilities is described in the text as a '*vraie* femme de chambre' (p. 172) (*real* chambermaid), she admits to having herself been a *false* chambermaid. But does her experience within this experiment draw upon that of a chambermaid? Here, it would seem, the role of chambermaid is basically a pretext, a cover: it's the only way to get into the rooms in the first place. Calle does occasionally advene as other, the most notable example being when, having received a 'nice smile' from a man in the corridor outside Room 30 (one of 'her' rooms), she records her reaction as follows: 'Fabrice en personne? Pour la première fois, j'imagine durant quelques secondes un client se penchant sur mon sort de femme de chambre et me proposant de tout lâcher, de partir avec lui. A Paris peut-être. . .' (p. 109) (Fabrice in the flesh? For the first time, I briefly imagine a patron taking an interest in my plight as a chambermaid and inviting me to drop everything and go away with him. Maybe to Paris. . .). Here, a very conventional romantic script involving knight on horseback and damsel in distress has implanted itself in the subject *as* chambermaid. In most other respects, the experiential dimension seems to build on the opportunity that being a chambermaid has opened up for Calle herself (for the observer rather than the participant). We recognise a similar counterpoint between recording and reacting to that found in the preceding projects, cast here as an alternation of inventory, description and transcription on the one hand, and more personal comments on the other. But in this case the personal comments are mainly expressions of attraction and aversion, of differing reactions to different guests on the basis of the signs they leave around or the stories those signs suggest. This could be, but need not be, the experience of a chambermaid. Thus the notion of an advent of self as other works in a rather different way in *L'Hôtel*.

In this particular project, our image of Calle as both experimenting subject and experiencing subject is at least partly constructed out of a series of parallels or *dédoublements* that align her with the other as absent guest. Indeed, she seems in many ways to share the very 'strangeness' of that other as represented in his or her 'personal effects'. Calle's inventories are reflected in the guests' inventories, her keeping of a diary in their keeping of diaries, her chambermaid mask in their carnival masks. Most of these *dédoublements* seem to point to a shared characteristic of obsessive behaviour. Obsession and mysteriousness combine most pointedly in the final section of the book. This corresponds to the only day, her last, that Calle spent cleaning Room 29 while it was occupied by someone whose few personal effects leave their owner difficult to identify even in terms of gender. (This in a context where the gender of absent guests is usually identified by Calle at a glance.) Having looked around the bathroom, Calle returns to the bedroom, and opens the wardrobe to find no items of clothing, just a quantity of objects, which she proceeds to lay on the bed in order to photograph them. In her diary she makes a list of all the items in question. After the third item, she comes onto a series of articles, 'chacun maniaquement isolé dans un sachet en plastique' (p. 172) (each manically separated in a plastic bag): an SNCF sheet, a sponge, two hairbrushes, and so on. She concludes: 'Tout est ordonné, empaqueté, aseptisé. Ici pas de ménage à faire, ne seraient les dérangements occasionnés par ma propre fouille' (p. 172) (Everything is ordered, wrapped up, sterilised. No tidying up to do here, except to conceal the disruption caused by my own search). Though the notion of sterilising or sanitising has no real echo in Calle's work, those of ordering and packaging do. In this case, for example, her own resort to listing tends not only to record, but in some degree to *repeat*, something of the manic quality she herself identifies in the other.

This guest's obsessive isolation of objects is illustrated in the use of plastic bags, but above all, perhaps, in the image of a box hermetically sealed with Scotch tape. In the original edition of *L'Hôtel*, Calle includes the photo of the box alongside five other photos of equal proportions. The pattern made by the Scotch tape on the visible face of the box appears to reproduce the pattern made by the photos on the page. It is also, of course, a *dédoublement* suggesting a parallel of some kind between the other's mania and Calle's own art. Boxes, grids, rectangles, and right angles do indeed pervade her work, structurally and thematically. However, whereas the other's mania is ultimately figured in an act of binding, sealing and concealing, Calle's art works in virtually the opposite direction. This basic contrast should warn us against pushing the parallels too far. In this respect, it is interesting that, in the new edition of *L'Hôtel* published in 1998 (part of a boxed set, as it happens), Calle chose to extract the photo of the box from its original six-pack and present it on a page of its own (p. 173). The surface of the box no longer doubles the surface of the page, and the manic other (implied to be anal-retentive) no longer doubles the experimental artist. The box now represents something like a full stop, bringing to an end this last section of the book, set on the last day of Calle's period of employment in the Hotel C. Accordingly, I shall use it to bring my own analysis to as full a stop as I can manage.

There is no vanishing point in this photo. The bright glow in the background hints at a sunlit window but is in fact no more than the light from Calle's flashbulb being reflected back by the mirrors on the panels of the wardrobe. Likewise, the eye is drawn towards the focal object, the box, only to be turned back as it meets an unyielding surface head on. The photo locates us in an *entre-deux*: we're inside the walls of the room, but outside the walls of the box. The photo itself has been made possible by another kind of room or chamber or box. We are not trapped so much as poised in this *entre-deux*, for this is the space in which Calle the artist can only work successfully by achieving a balance between *intrusion*, the fact of being in the room, and *discretion*, the fact of being willing to stay outside the box, willing to accept that these lives will ultimately remain 'foreign'. Such discretion belongs to a more general rhetoric, at once behavioural, textual and pictorial, in Calle's work, of *délestage*, or generalised reluctance. Reluctance, for example, to speculate, extrapolate, spell out, or say more than needs to be said (right down to her abbreviations of names: 'Henri B.', the 'Hotel C.'). The photo as repositioned in the 1998 edition of *L'Hôtel* is about suspending operations, about going so far and no further, and about photographic distance as one of the strongest forms of aesthetic tension between 'so far' and 'no further' (this is also the space Christine Angot explored in the 1990s through her evolving series of *autofictions*). The repositioned photo affirms the quality of photography often described by terms like 'cold', 'mechanical', 'minimal', 'merely constative'. What I am calling 'reluctance' proceeds, then, from the thought of photography. Accordingly, few statements may be considered more photographically thoughtful than the very last textual segment of *L'Hôtel*, where Calle, in a conclusion that could hardly be more minimal, writes: '*Le vendredi 6 mars 1981, à 13 heures*, mon service à l'hôtel C. s'achève' (p. 172) (*Friday 6 March 1981, 1:00 p.m.*: my duties at the Hotel C. come to an end).

In engaging with the other on a non-collaborative or intrusive basis, Calle's 1980s projects, as recycled in the late 1990s, raise questions that were once more being strongly echoed at that time. One thinks in the realm of photography of Luc Delahaye's book, *L'Autre*, consisting of photos taken in the Paris Métro using a hidden camera; photos which Delahaye provocatively admits to be 'stolen' insofar as French law states that everyone owns their own image. It comes as no surprise, moreover, that this book should include an afterword by Jean Baudrillard, and that Baudrillard should set Delahaye's photos in a context beyond all 'moral anthropology', beyond all 'forced figuration', defined as 'représentation abusive de ce qui ne veut pas être représenté' (abusive representation of that which does not want to be represented).[11] One thinks also in the literary realm of the work of Christine Angot, whose ongoing project, as embodied in texts like *Les Autres*, *Sujet Angot* and *L'Inceste*, produces complex and controversial intersections of auto–biographical material and fictional techniques. Such intersections are fascinating and unsettling in equal measure, for they leave the works in question, alongside those of Calle and Delahaye, on the edge of the morally, legally and, therefore, aesthetically acceptable. Few works more tellingly measure the extent, and potentially the cost, of the contemporary artist's will to self-implication.

Notes

1   For Calle's self-definition as 'narrative artist', see the text to be found at www.cnp-photographie.com/expo/atelier/archive/sophie/index.html (Anon.).

2   See Celia Lury, *Prosthetic Culture: Photography, Memory and Identity* (London: Routledge, 1998), pp. 23–4.

3   Sophie Calle, *La Filature*, in *A suivre*, book IV of *Doubles-jeux* (Arles: Actes Sud, 1998), p. 116. Translations are either my own or adapted from existing translations.

4   Roland Barthes, *La Chambre claire* (Paris: Cahiers du cinéma/Gallimard/Seuil,

1980), p. 153. Lury (p. 78) discusses this quotation, but in a slightly different context to that operative here.

5 See note 3.

6 Sophie Calle, *Double Game* (London: Violette, 1999).

7 Jean Baudrillard and Marc Guillaume, *Figures de l'altérité* (Paris: Descartes, 1994), p. 148.

8 Whitney Chadwick, 'Three artists/three women: Orlan, Annette Messager and Sophie Calle', *Sites*, 4(1) (2000), 111–17 (113).

9 Sophie Calle, *Suite vénitienne*, Book IV of *Doubles-jeux*, p. 44.

10 Sophie Calle, *L'Hôtel*, Book V of *Doubles-jeux*, p. 9.

11 Jean Baudrillard, 'Transfert poétique de situation', in Luc Delahaye, *L'Autre* (London: Phaidon, 1999), unpaginated.

Christine Angot's *autofictions*: literature and/or reality?

From her very first novel, *Vu du ciel*, which was published in 1990, Christine Angot has established herself firmly as a writer who has made it her mission to explore and expose relentlessly the thin line between reality and fiction.[1] The last quarter of the twentieth century, in French literature, will probably be remembered, among other things, as the period in which a new genre – that of *autofiction* – emerged and flourished. It has become a privileged mode of writing for many writers who have adopted and adapted it to very different and personal poetic visions and approaches to writing. Many literary theorists have long claimed that the meeting point between fiction and autobiography, which so strongly shapes contemporary self-representational aesthetics, is a fundamental area of women's writing. Christine Angot's works, however, have seldom been labelled or viewed in these terms by the French literary establishment. Instead critics have spent much time focusing upon what they see as the very 'poor' and pale use of the imaginary in her texts, often in sharp contrast to the convoluted and complex formal structures of the texts themselves. Indicative of this tendency is the way in which Pierre Marcelle concludes his review of *Sujet Angot* in *Libération*:[2]

> S'il y a quelque chose qui trouble, dans *Sujet Angot*, c'est la complexité de l'élaboration formelle au service d'une 'histoire' si autobiographique. Tant d'imagination au service de si peu d'imagination en quelque sorte.[3]

> (If there is something puzzling about *Sujet Angot*, it is the complexity of the formal elaboration employed for such an autobiographical 'story'. So much imagination serving so little imagination, in a way.)

Complexity of formal elaboration is indeed a trademark of many of Angot's works, and the imaginary counterpart is both schematic and repetitive:

Angot writes about nothing but herself. She repeatedly makes allusions to incest, to the horror of giving birth, and to the difficulties encountered by a character who is a writer, a mother and a lover. Angot's work also consistently reveals the tensions between her public life and her need for privacy: her personal life, it would seem, is made bearable only by being exposed to the public. And yet all these highly personal concerns are presented in her texts as fictional. Angot claims that the Christine we read about is a character and not a real person, and moreover that this character/narrator is prone to telling lies. It is precisely this tension between subject matter that seems to be autobiographical and the element of doubt with which Angot confuses her reader that makes her use of *autofiction* both provocative and enriching. For Angot this is the very function of literature:

> Les écrivains ne devraient jamais cesser d'écrire leur vie en fait. Avec le doute qui plane. Sur la vérité. Que Proust ait créé cette Albertine, c'est génial, car on se demande tout le temps. Prendre le temps de dormir et de revivre. Mais que l'écriture soit vraiment celle de la vie. Paisible, fictive, peut-être, mais qu'elle ne lache jamais ce fil par lequel vous pouvez voir la vie. Venir, vibrer. Même une vie ratée. Le corps en train de vibrer, voilà ce qu'il faudrait raconter. Jusqu'à ce que l'écriture elle-même soit cette vie.[4]

> (Writers should in fact never stop writing about their lives. With a hovering doubt. As to the truth. Proust created Albertine and it is brilliant because one always wonders. Taking time to sleep and to live again. But writing must be the writing of life. Peaceful, fictitious, maybe, but it must never let go of the thread which allows you to see life. Surfacing, vibrating. Even a rotten life. The body living, vibrating, this is what must be told. Until writing itself becomes this life.)

Let us take a detailed look at how, since the early 1990s, Angot has indeed engineered her writing 'to become life itself'. She started writing in the mid 1980s and, after many rejections, published what was to become her first novel, *Vu du ciel*, in 1990. Since then she has published prolifically, and there has been a direct correlation between her increased notoriety and her now disarmingly regular annual output. Angot's corpus also presents a number of intriguing characteristics. First, she establishes a strong sense of continuity between each text. This is most apparent in her treatment of subject matter. All of her texts, with the exception of her second novel, *Not to be* (1991), revolve obsessively around a narrator/writer called Christine Angot.[5] This continuity between texts is temporal also: each focuses on the Christine Angot character at a given time in her life, which corresponds exactly to the temporality of the text itself and to the gaps between texts. The element of continuity is further emphasised by the metatextual dimension of each text and by numerous references made to previously published texts. This is most striking in *Quitter la ville*, which focuses on Angot's life after the publication of *L'Inceste* and offers the writer's response to its reception.[6]

A second characteristic of Angot's work is the way in which it deals with and blurs the notion of established genres. Labels such as 'roman' (novel) or 'théâtre' (theatre) preface some of her texts, but they may disappear in later editions.[7] At times the presence or absence of such labels may seem inappropriate. *Léonore, toujours*, for instance, proclaims itself a 'roman' despite the fact that not only is it presented as a diary but also the textual writer/narrator 'Christine' herself criticises the novelistic genre.[8] *Vu du ciel* and *Not to be* could both be categorised as 'théâtre'; while, from *L'Inceste*, Angot's texts carry no generic appelation at all. Angot's intriguing use of such generic categorisation is clearly significant. In a sense her texts have more in common with one another than with the pragmatics of any of the genres with which she labels them. The theatrical element is present in all of them, through the *mise en scène* (staging) of 'Christine' the protagonist, through the language which is always strongly vocal and through the structure of the texts which is often close to that of a stream of consciousness. Angot's writing displays a directness, a sense of urgency and a corporeal vocality which suggest that it is eminently transferable to the stage. Similarly, although perhaps on more slippery grounds, one could argue that all of her texts do share characteristics that are conventionally attached to the novel. More important than such similarities, however, is that Angot clearly invites us to rethink these categories that are so central to notions of literature.

A third important characteristic of Angot's corpus, which is closely related to the question of genre, is the way in which she makes use of fiction. The fictionality of her first two texts is evident. *Vu du ciel* is a rather curious text which juxtaposes segments narrated by 'Christine' (who is not yet a writer but a law student in Reims) and others narrated by Severine Nivet, a child who, in real life, was raped and murdered in Reims and who, in Angot's novel, becomes a guardian angel. *Not to be*, the only text from which 'Christine' is totally absent, is the delirious first-person monologue of a man lying prostrate on a hospital bed. Angot's third 'novel', *Léonore, toujours*, is a key text which marks a step away from the type of fictional writing employed thus far. This text is the diary of 'Christine', a writer who says she can no longer write since giving birth to her baby daughter Léonore. The banal but horrifically sudden death of Léonore at the end of *Léonore, toujours* (the baby falls off a chair) defies belief, and shocks, given the apparently autobiographical nature of this text. Subsequently, the death is affirmed to be fiction as future texts make reference to Léonore growing up. From this point on, we cannot tell whether 'Christine', the protagonist, of Angot's texts is a fictional or 'real life' entity.

After *Léonore, toujours*, Angot's texts could be described as *autofictions* in which the insistence on the fictional element is purely metatextual and by means of which she cultivates a diffuse element of doubt around the apparently autobiographical events narrated. Indeed, the distinction between literature and life is one which Angot repeatedly sets out to undermine. Her texts are resolutely set against a backdrop of media activity from which writing cannot be sheltered.[9] One of the great merits of Angot's works is the way they question, albeit indirectly, the nature of literature in an age in which intimacy, privacy and personal histories are so relentlessly mediatised and exploited, and real lives are packaged, performed and televised for a mass audience.

In order to do justice to Angot's works, and to appreciate the web she weaves between life, truth and literature, it is important not to overlook the particular modalities of a textual production that is an autobiographical quest and, at the same time, plays with fiction. Referring to Angot's texts as *autofiction* is problematic, however, and the author herself would strongly refute such a label. My reason for describing her works in this generic way is that this permits a discussion of her disruption of, and formal literary experimentation with, the autobiographical pact as defined by Philippe Lejeune, as well as enabling her literary production to be addressed from the perspective of remodelling self-representational aesthetics.[10] But what exactly is *autofiction*? What is at stake behind this term and how does it illuminate Angot's work?

The term *autofiction* first appeared in 1977 on the back cover of *Fils* by Serge Doubrovsky. It is no coincidence that this occurred around the time when Lejeune's theories of autobiography were in full bloom and beginning to be disseminated. *Autofiction*, for Doubrovsky, is a form of writing in which autobiographical and fictional elements are intertwined in a creative activity linked to psychoanalytical experience. *Autofiction* is now often used to refer to texts which, like Angot's works, hover somewhere between autobiography and fiction, although the definition of the term remains critically problematic. Interestingly, the issues at stake are precisely those which form the core of Angot's literary production; that is, the parameters of the relationship between life, truth and fiction within literature.

The debate around the term *autofiction* has arisen primarily because the parameters within which it operates are articulated around the antithetical opposition of reality–truth versus fiction on the one hand, and yet, on the other, are extratextual. To define *autofiction* as either a fictional autobiography or as the first-person narration of events belonging to the fictional life of an author/character who shares a name with the author, clearly leads to difficulties. Doubrovsky's definition is a common starting point, yet it would seem to imply, then, that almost all first-person narratives are *autofictions*, including Proust's *A la recherche du temps perdu*, Camus's *L'Etranger* and even Dante's *Divine Comedy*. Attempts to clarify the term according to the relative fictionality of the text are unhelpful, and efforts to define the truthfulness of *autofictions* in relation to autobiography, or their fictionality in relation to first-person narratives, are bound to produce convenient results or redundant conclusions. As Michael Riffaterre has shown in *Fictional Truth*, notions of truth and fictionality in literature are extremely complex and at times highly paradoxical.[11] Riffaterre underlines how in many narratives the notion of truth – that is, verisimilitude, which is nothing but a linguistic perception – is in fact produced by the very mechanisms of fictionality. Paul John Eakin also reminds us that, when talking about autobiography, what we call fact and fiction are 'rather slippery variables in an intricate process of self discovery'.[12] The main problem with many definitions of *autofiction* is that they dispense with the literary process in their efforts to define a genre on the basis of the truthfulness of biographical information which lies outside the text. This is precisely a mode of reading which Angot's use of *autofiction* teases and ridicules.

If it is to be considered a genre, *autofiction* must rely on formal distinctions found within the text or have a grammar of its own which determines the particular modalities of its reading. While much of the argument among critics revolves around which of these two alternatives is most appropriate, many seem to have forgotten the difficulty with which previous generations of critics arrived at a distinction between autobiography and first-person narrative. Thus the definition of *autofiction* which strikes me as most promising is that put forward by the author Marie Darrieussecq, who makes a pragmatic distinction between first-person narrative, third-person narrative and autobiography. In an essay ironically entitled 'L'*autofiction*, un genre pas sérieux', Darrieussecq comes to the conclusion that, unlike third-person narrative which represents a double act of illocution – one being an assertion of the type 'I decree fictionally that. . .', and the other being a request of the type 'imagine that. . .' – and unlike first-person narratives which are simple acts of illocution in which the assertion is not accompanied by any request – first-person narratives do not in anyway attempt to declare or disguise their fictionality – and again unlike autobiographies, which are double acts of illocution differing from third-person narratives in that the request that they entail could be formulated as 'believe me when I say that' (here we find the notion of the 'autobiographical pact' formulated by Lejeune), *autofictions* present a double act of illocution which is itself double. It is a double request which could be formulated as both 'believe me when I say. . .' *and*, at the same time, 'don't believe me when I say. . .'.[13] *Autofiction* is fundamentally and willingly ambiguous in that it borrows discursive strategies from first-person narrative and autobiography at the same time.

Autofictions never allow the reader to identify the real from the fictional at the level of enunciation. Angot makes extensive use of this impossibility in her writing: the reader can never really know whether the incest story that weaves through her œuvre is true, or whether Leonore really does exist and, if she does, whether she lives or dies. The advantage of Darrieussecq's definition is that it allows a distinction between *autofiction* as a hybrid and in-between genre, and, on the one hand, autobiographies containing elements of fiction and, on the other hand, first-person narratives containing autobiographical elements. Thus *autofiction* acquires an autonomous status which is free from any convoluted process of verification with external facts and which does clearly indicate a specific – uncertain – mode of reading.

The definition of *autofiction* in terms of willed ambiguity is useful as a means of designating a corpus of texts, and it is most suited to Angot's works, but are we in fact dealing with a genre as such? *Autofictions* are perhaps more of a mode than a genre, in the way and for reasons that are not dissimilar to those that led Todorov, and many others in his wake, to make use of the term in relation to the fantastic.[14] In both cases the defining element is pragmatic: in the fantastic it has to do with hesitation as a mode of reading; in the case of *autofiction* it also has to do, as we have seen, with a degree of undecidability. Both the fantastic and *autofiction* function as border or frontier genres which borrow elements from other related genres, and *autofictions* are not necessarily limited to borrowings from autobiography. Indeed, other confessional and intimate modes of writing may equally be employed, as is the case in Angot's works: diaries, letters, monologues, streams of consciousness. *Autofictions* are also potentially subversive in a similar way to fantastic literature, as Rosemary Jackson identifies.[15] Darrieussecq outlines an important feature of this subversive element: 'L'important est de constater à quel point l'*autofiction* met en cause la pratique "naïve" de l'autobiographie, en avertissant que l'écriture factuelle à la première personne ne saurait se garder de la fiction' (p. 379) (The important thing to note here is that *autofiction* undermines a 'naïve' practice of autobiography as it reminds us that factual first-person writing cannot do away with fiction). It is in this sense that to define *autofiction* and to identify texts as such can be legitimate and useful. Whether or not auto-fictional texts should be categorised as '*autofiction*' or as 'novel' is of little consequence. What is important is that, by not being labelled autobiographies and yet resembling them, they play upon and disrupt the 'autobiographical pact'.

Of course, the disruption of autobiography's pact with the reader is not new. It rests upon an established tradition both within autobiographical writing and within the philosophical and critical sphere, a fact which has been brought to the fore and analysed by many critics and which has been the focal point of much of the debate surrounding autobiography after Lejeune. As Paul John Eakin notes in *Fictions in Autobiography*: 'the self that is at the centre of all autobiographical narrative is necessarily a fictive structure' (p. 25). Indeed, the genealogy of *autofiction* is broad and well documented: from the crisis of the notion of selfhood in modern times, to notions of the death of the subject and the author, to postmodern claims of absence and privation – all of which are paralleled by the loss of confidence in the referential power of language to tell the crumbling reality of the self in a text.

Whichever way one chooses to trace the fact that writing an autobiography can no longer be a naïve practice, it is undeniable that *autofiction* has grown in reaction to this and as a resilient attempt to deal with notions of self and subjectivity in writing in an age of multiple crisis. There is, however, one genealogical approach to *autofiction* which calls for a more detailed analysis here, since it is highly relevant to the works of Angot: namely the feminist claim that women's writings, along with the writings of other previously silenced minority groups, have been greatly influential in breaking down and reshaping the practice of writing autobiography. In her introductory essay to *Redefining Autobiography in Twentieth-Century Women's Fiction*, Janice Morgan argues that the notion of the death of the subject/author, which has condemned autobiography to a short life, is the product of the arrogance of the white, male, 'happy few' and that it has been seriously challenged by the reshaping of the body politic through discourses of civil rights, feminism and post-colonialism which have reclaimed the importance of the question 'who am I?'.[16] What is more, many of the features of contemporary self-representational poetics – fragmentation, discontinuity, duality and self-conscious textuality – have been a recurrent feature of women's autobiographical writings for quite some time. Here both the postulation of female selfhood as fundamentally relational – 'concerned with various levels and intensities of connection *to* rather than separation *from*' (p. 15) – and the sense of the woman writer as plural – wife, mother, writer, divided by a conflict between private and public roles – are of particular importance in determining an entry into discourse which 'bears the peculiar, conflicting stresses of this dual experience' (p. 15). Many of these elements are fundamental to contemporary French *autofictions* and, in particular, to the way in which Angot makes use of the zone between autobiography and fiction. They also account for the potential of the intricate mechanisms at work within *autofictions*, as Angot constantly plays with, challenges, tests and wilfully confuses the reader with her insistence on the notion of fictionality.

Angot's *L'Inceste* and *Quitter la ville* deal with recognisable elements from the life and work of the author in a far more direct manner than her earlier work. It is as though she has become the protagonist of a TV show of her daily life. The early use of fiction seems to have been a necessary step towards a more freely autobiographical discourse and more liberated use of the first-person pronoun, as the incest narrative has proliferated. The wall between fiction and reality is then perhaps more of an artist's looking glass than a formal opaque division – a looking-glass which may be necessary as a means of finding a voice in the face of trauma.

The publication of *Normalement* followed by *La Peur du lendemain* in 2001 as the text following *Quitter la ville* in itself is not indicative of a new direction in Angot's writing, since both texts were written and previously published before *Quitter la ville*. Rather, they must be considered as indicative of a publishing decision. However, although they undeniably disrupt the autofictional corpus that had come to a climax with *Quitter la ville*, they may not signal the end of it as such. *Normalement* is a fragmented and poetic expression of pain and anger with strong echoes of Marguerite Duras. It was written originally for the theatre under the title *Arrête, arrêtons, arrêtez*. The performance Angot has so relentlessly constructed throughout her œuvre comes to an abrupt end as she evokes time and again 'la souffrance de ne pas être entendu' (p. 11) (the pain of not being heard (or understood)). She seems to be withdrawing from the game:

> Pardon? J'ai bien entendu? J'ai cru entendre pourquoi. J'ai cru entendre 'c'est autobiographique ou quoi?' Si on te demande, tu diras que tu sais pas. Qu'est-ce que c'est que cette manie? Il en va d'un artiste et de sa vie privée comme d'une accouchée et de son enfant. Le lien entre les deux est secret. Vous pouvez regarder l'enfant, mais ne soulevez pas la chemise de sa mère pour voir si elle est tachée de sang. Qu'est-ce qu'on peut imaginer de plus indélicat? Qu'est-ce que c'est que ça? (pp. 31–2)

> (Excuse me? Have I heard correctly? I thought I heard why. I thought I heard 'is it autobiographical or what?'. If they ask you, you'll say you don't know. What is this obsession? An artist and her private life are like a woman and her newly born child. The link between them is secret. You can look at the child, but don't lift the mother's gown to see if she is blood-stained. Could you imagine anything more offensive? What is this?)

Normalement evokes a theme which is already present in many of Angot's texts and which, given their nature, can seem highly paradoxical: the need for privacy, the need for intimacy. This writer who relentlessly exposes herself to her reader – revealing the most intimate details of her life, teasing the reader with her crudest fantasies – is also a writer who repeatedly asks to be left alone and not to be judged while claiming not to be understood and not wanting to be understood. Angot is constantly flaunting her secrets while endeavouring to protect them, at once inviting and forbidding the reader to lift the gown and see the blood. This dynamic is most striking in a text such as *Interview* which juxtaposes a harrowing interrogation by a journalist who is voraciously curious about the most gruesome details of the writer's private life with pages narrating the birth of Léonore. The text skilfully places the reader in the awkward position of a voyeur who shares the journalist's craving for intimate revelations. This phenomenon is also at work on an intertextual level between *L'Inceste* and *Quitter la ville*: the latter text reclaims a need for privacy which had been endangered by revelations made in the former. Although the need for privacy is frequently expressed in Angot's texts, *Normalement* is the first text in which it triumphs over the ambiguous mechanism present in earlier works: there are no revelations here about the author's life.

In contrast, *La Peur du lendemain* is more familiar in style and immediacy yet it may actually redefine Angot's subject matter. If *Normalement* can be seen as a text which interrupts a dynamic process that had long been established in Angot's writing, this second text may initiate a new approach to writing, one which is still, at the time of going to press, to be defined. If *Normalement* marks an end, as the original title of the play strongly suggests (*Arrête, arrêtons, arrêtez* (Stop, let us stop, stop)), *La Peur du lendemain* (Fear of the next day) looks somewhat apprehensively ahead. 'Christine', the character, narrator or writer, appears to adopt a new stance: 'Je ne cherche pas à me connaître et je ne vois pas l'importance' (p. 71) (I'm not interested in self-knowledge and I don't see that it matters). There is a shift away from narrating or even the simple, spare 'marking' of *Léonore, toujours*, towards a more inquisitive form of writing. Instead of being about her life, her role as a writer, or as a mother or lover, it questions the very subject matter of her writing. It is in this sense that *La Peur du lendemain* seems to mark a turning point. The Angot who was once so determined about the function and nature of what writing should be about (becoming life) now appears to be calling the whole enterprise into question. It is ironical to read Angot interrogating herself about her subject when the 'subject' of so many of her texts is herself. But perhaps *La Peur du lendemain* is not after all so much a turning point as a text which offers new light on the nature of Angot's literary endeavours, and the denial of the quest for self-knowledge represents yet another attempt to reclaim ownership of her work.

While Angot apparently lays bare her writing or working tools, the reader is implicitly invited to reflect upon the themes of her work and, at the same time, to call into question the mechanisms of her *autofictions*. Ultimately we might ask whether the closing words of *La Peur du lendemain* in fact characterise *autofictions* of the 1990s in general: 'Car ce qui est positif un jour peut être négatif le lendemain. Ce qu'on croit un jour peut être une tromperie le lendemain, les pièges sont posés' (p. 113) (For what is positive one day may be negative the next. What you believe (in) one day may prove to be an illusion the next, the traps have been set).

Notes

1 Christine Angot, *Vu du ciel* (Paris: L'Arpenteur Gallimard, 1990).

2 Christine Angot, *Sujet Angot* (Paris: Fayard, 1998).

3 Pierre Marcelle, 'Je, faute de mieux', *Libération* (26 August 1998).

4 Christine Angot, *Interview* (Paris: Fayard, 1995), p. 24.

5 Christine Angot, *Not to be* (Paris: L'Arpenteur Gallimard, 1991).

6 Christine Angot, *Quitter la ville* (Paris: Stock, 2000); *L'Inceste* (Paris: Stock, 1999).

7 *L'Usage de la vie* (Paris: Fayard, 1998) is described as 'théâtre', but no longer designated as such in the 1999 reprint by Mille et une Nuits; *La Peur du lendemain* was first published by *Elle* in 2000 as a 'nouvelle' (short story), but is no longer referred to as such in the edition, *Normalement* followed by *La Peur du lendemain* (Paris: Stock, 2001).

8 Christine Angot, *Léonore, toujours* (Paris: L'Arpenteur Gallimard, 1994).

9 The importance of the media is made explicit in texts such as *Interview* or through Angot's regular references to the press and to television within her work. Its influence is also evident in the ways she herself uses the media, be it through her appearance on TV shows such as 'Bouillon de Culture', or in newspapers such as *Libération* where she published her father's obituary.

10 Philippe Lejeune, *Je est un autre: l'autobiographie, de la littérature aux médias* (Paris: Seuil, 1980).

11 Michael Riffaterre, *Fictional Truth* (Baltimore and London: Johns Hopkins University Press, 1990).

12 Paul John Eakin, *Fictions in Autobiography: Studies in the Art of Self-Invention* (Princeton: Princeton University Press, 1985), p. 15.

13 Marie Darrieussecq, 'L'autofiction, un genre pas sérieux', in *Poétique*, 107 (1996), 369–80.

14 Tzvetan Todorov, *Introduction à la littérature fantastique* (Paris: Seuil, 1970).

15 Rosemary Jackson, *Fantasy: The Literature of Subversion* (London: Methuen, 1981).

16 Janice Morgan and Colette T. Hall (eds), *Redefining Autobiography in Twentieth-Century Women's Fiction* (New York and London: Garland Publishing, 1991).

'Il n'y a pas de troisième voie' (There is no third way): Sylvie Germain and the generic problems of the Christian novel

Sylvie Germain (1954–) is an unusual phenomenon on the French literary scene. Having studied philosophy at the Sorbonne, she entered the audio-visual section of the Ministère de la culture in 1981, securing immediate literary success four years later with her first novel, *Le Livre des nuits* (1985).[1] Establishment recognition was soon to be consolidated by the award of the prix Fémina for her third novel, *Jours de colère* (1989).[2] Since then she has produced a steady output of texts: novels (set principally in either the French provinces or Prague, where she taught philosophy at the Ecole française from 1986, before returning to France in 1992); shorter fictional works; explorations of religious faith articulated around striking commentaries based on both mystical and literary texts; works on Vermeer and on Holocaust diarist Etty Hillesum; and a venture into children's writing. Germain's work is characterised by a combination of powerful lyricism and a lush proliferation of imagery, the deployment of an eclectic range of written and visual intertexts, all set into taut crystalline structures. These are texts which cross boundaries, integrating myth and fable, incursions into the fantastic and an acute realism, a minute attention to visual detail.

What singles Germain out as a contemporary female writer, however, is the fact that her work is informed by Christianity. More specifically, it reflects a self-confessed preoccupation with the existence of human suffering and evil (*le mal*) and their effect upon the waxing and waning of religious faith. As she states: 'Chez presque tous les créateurs, la vie ne tourne qu'autour d'un thème. Chez moi finalement, il me semble que c'est le mal' (For nearly all creators, life revolves around a single theme, and in my case I'd say that theme is suffering/evil).[3] Germain's engagement with Christianity is unusual in a French female author; she follows in a predominantly male tradition of novelists, most notably Mauriac and Bernanos (though one could cite, among others, Barbey d'Aurevilly, Huysmans in his later work, Léon Bloy and Julien Green). Inasmuch as Germain could be said to have female precursors these are to be found not in the genre of the novel, but in the field of devotional and mystical literature, often autobiographical in form, which flourished in France especially in the seventeenth century (represented by, for example, Madame Acarie, Marie Guyard, Marguerite-Marie Alacoque and Madame Guyon). Notable later figures include Thérèse de Lisieux (1873–97) and Simone Weil (1909–43), with both of whose work Germain engages in her *Les Echos du silence* (1996).[4]

Many of the above figures departed, often quite radically, from Catholic orthodoxy, a fact which raises questions about the label 'Catholic' or 'Christian writer'. My intention, however, is not to analyse the problematic definition of genre, but to consider a specific issue relating to Germain's work, that of monologism and closure. The above title – 'Il n'y a pas de troisième voie' (There is no third way) – refers to the words of Prokop, principal character of Germain's *Immensités* (1993), as he ponders his perceived need to settle the question of the existence of God: one either believes or one does not; there can be no middle ground.[5] Is Germain's Christian novel, like the nature of faith as articulated by Prokop, a case of all or nothing? Does the author present her potentially recalcitrant readership with a closed, 'epic' text, or an open, polyphonic form? Germain's novels are undeniably highly engaging texts, but they are also highly engaged texts. Is the author's artistic integrity compromised by the Christian ideology which informs her work? Can the Christian faith be represented – in both senses of the word – in literary form, without threatening the aesthetic viability of the text?

The following analysis focuses upon four key elements, the first of which is *genre*. In his *The Struggle for the Soul of the French Novel*, Malcolm Scott identifies a conflict between the realist novel and the Catholic novel, a conflict based on two opposed visions of 'the real'. For the realist novelist, 'reality' is visible, material; for the Catholic (and we might extend this to the Christian) novelist, 'reality' includes an invisible, non-material dimension.[6] The writer wishing to impart a Christian message – a writer whose potential audience includes non-believers – is placed in an invidious position: she has to create a fictional universe wherein the invisible, non-material dimension is somehow rendered acceptable to that audience.

One of the ways in which this may be achieved is by exploiting the reader's genre expectations, specifically, by drawing upon the genre of the literary fantastic, whereby readerly conventions include a belief (or suspension of disbelief) in the non-material dimension:

> A characteristic strategy links Barbey, via Huysmans and Bloy, to Green and Bernanos: the loosening of the reader's expectation of a fictional world perceptible to the senses, the suggestion of an unseen but no less real dimension, and finally the reintegration of this supernatural plane into the world of flesh-and-blood characters, whose moral and psychological drama are intelligible in terms of the beliefs taught by the Church. (Scott, *The Struggle*, pp. 268–9)

Following on from this insight, it might be suggested that the Christian novelist wishing to maximise her chances of 'success' (from the point of view of the non-believer) may benefit from the adoption of a non-realist genre into which the Christian 'message' can be introduced.

The second factor to be considered is that of *point of view*, initially in the sense of the ideologies or thought-systems inscribed within the text. Ideally, again drawing on Scott, the Christian novel should represent the relativity of the modern world: 'The Catholic novelist, working in the genre which above all others mirrors the moral relativism of the age, is in a position of extreme difficulty: the clear victory of one point of view over another, which we seldom encounter in life, spells the death of his art . . . Whatever the Catholic novel is, it is not propaganda' (Scott, *The Struggle*, p. 71). As we will see, *point of view* must also be understood in the sense of the author's choice of narrative focalisation: the deployment of a first- or third-person narrator; the use of free indirect discourse.

Third, and this point is implicit in Scott's phrases 'and *finally* the reintegration of this supernatural plane into the world of flesh-and-blood characters', and 'the *clear victory* of one point of view over another' (above, my emphases), our analysis must include the *structure* and especially the *endings* of texts. Are we, as readers, invited to engage in further interpretation, or does the heavy hand of the author–creator slam the book shut thanks to an all too visible teleological principle? Finally, an examination of closure and monologism must turn to the role played by intertextual material: does such material introduce dialogism into the text, or does it rather reinforce the singular voice of the author?

Le Livre des nuits, the opening volume of Germain's diptych, traces the ebb and flow of faith within the Péniel family, centring on the principal character, Victor-Flandrin, and the suffering he endures. Germain weaves into her fictional universe historical events drawn from our own 'reality':

generations of the Péniel family are caught up in the Franco-Prussian War, and the First and Second World Wars. Two observations must be made here: first, Germain is not writing in the realist genre, and second, she does not restrict her text to a representation or promotion of Christianity. Alongside representations of 'real' historical events, and running parallel to the thematic exploration of the Christian faith, we find a series of fantastical events permeating the everyday world of the characters; occurrences and events drawn from a thought system which might be broadly categorised as popular European myth, folklore or superstition. Thus, to name but a few of the curious phenomena which occur: a shooting star crosses the skies at the moment of Victor-Flandrin's birth and his mother's death;[7] mirrors cloud into opacity when Victor-Flandrin looks in them; dubbed 'Nuit-d'Or-Gueule-de-Loup', Victor-Flandrin can tame wolves; the death of his first wife Mélanie is heralded by a sparrow flying into her room;[8] his fourth wife Ruth wears a green dress on the day she meets him, and subsequently on the day she is deported to a concentration camp.[9]

Given the presence of such phenomena, we might categorise *Le Livre des nuits* as an example of the 'marvellous': the reader is invited to suspend disbelief and accept the supernatural phenomena as a part of everyday life.[10] Narrative point of view is key here. Neither the characters, nor, crucially, the narrator, express astonishment in the face of these bizarre events. Equally appropriate might be the generic term 'magic(al) realism': true to the genre, *Le Livre des nuits* draws on a culture, or sub-culture, which is unlikely to be that of the reader (superstition, folklore), as well as on the Christian faith.[11] The disruption of the realist code is mirrored by a disruption of cultural codes. This is a text which invites a reassessment of boundaries and hierarchies: between Christianity and so-called 'superstition'; Christianity and myth; myth and history.

Returning to the problems of the Christian novel, it can be suggested that the Christian aspects of this text 'pass', are aesthetically acceptable, first, because the reader is 'softened up' to accept the non-material dimension; second, because more than one thought system 'compete' within the text; and finally, because there is no 'clear victory' of one thought system over another by the close of the novel. However, with *Nuit-d'Ambre* (1987), the second volume of the diptych, the situation changes: the elements drawn from the thought system 'European superstition, folklore, or myth' gradually fade out; Victor-Flandrin dies uttering the name of God, and the eponymous Nuit-d'Ambre finds absolution and peace when he wrestles with a stranger in the woods.[12] The text, in other words, closes with the reinstatement of hierarchies, with Christianity placed firmly at the top. Furthermore, Nuit-d'Ambre's struggle with the stranger retrospectively imposes a closed, teleological structure upon both volumes of the diptych. The choice of the family name 'Péniel', emphasised at the very start of *Le Livre des nuits*, becomes clear: Péniel was the name given by Jacob to the place where he wrestled with the angel and came face to face with God.[13]

Unlike *Le Livre des nuits*, *L'Enfant Méduse* (1991), which centres on the child sexual abuse of the protagonist, Lucie, 'flirts' with the idea of a non-realist genre and with the existence of non-Christian supernatural phenomena, but it does not fall into the category of the 'marvellous' or 'magic realism'.[14] It does not 'soften up' its reader to accept an 'invisible' dimension. Consequently when, towards end of text, the non-material, or 'invisible' does appear, and is specifically Christian in nature, and is furthermore promoted by the narrator, the Christian 'message' simply does not 'pass' aesthetically.

To grasp what is meant here by 'flirting' with non-realism and the introduction of alternative thought systems into the text, we need to consider narrative point of view. Two principal narrative modes are deployed. First, we find examples of the narrator *telling* the reader about the characters' belief in fables, legend and folklore. Thus, for example, we learn of Lucie's syncretic imagination, her capacity to view local legends, fairy tales and the Christian faith on an equal footing: 'Alors Lucie a fini par intégrer le mystère de la mort d'Anne-Lise à son imaginaire pétri de fables et de légendes, et de récits de la vie de Jésus et des saints' (p. 62) (So Lucie ended up integrating the mystery of Anne-Lise's death into her imaginary world steeped in fables and legends, and the stories of the life of Christ and the saints). The validity of this syncretic capacity, the ontological status of fable and legend as 'real' is, however, never corroborated by narrator; we, as readers, are not invited to suspend *our* disbelief. This is a far cry from the realm of tamed wolves, bad omens and opaque mirrors.

Furthermore, although certain events in the text could be read as belonging to a non-realist (non-material, 'invisible') dimension, such events are consistently filtered through the point of view of the characters, thereby allowing the reader to dismiss a non-realist interpretation and view potentially fantastical events as the delusions of individual characters. Thus, to cite just one example, the suggestion that Victor, husband to Aloïse, Lucie's mother, haunts her son Ferdinand (Lucie's abusing stepbrother) reads as little more than a whimsical notion: 'Ce soupçon grandit en Aloïse; les preuves lui semblent de plus en plus nombreuses, et accablantes. Victor est un mort mal mort. La précocité et la violence de sa mort sont la première cause du tourment qui a dû saisir son âme' (p. 167) (This suspicion begins to grow in Aloïse's mind; the evidence seems ever-increasing and ever more overwhelming to her. Victor is a dead man who has not found rest in death. The premature and violent nature of his death are the main causes of the torment which must have gripped his soul). The second incident which has the potential to disrupt the realist code, Lucie's striking down of Ferdinand by the sheer power of her gaze (hence the title's allusion to the mythical Medusa), is again never corroborated by the narrator, who merely states that Lucie believed herself to be responsible for her stepbrother's catatonic state and eventual death. This again leaves room for a realist interpretation: Ferdinand, who fell heavily while climbing in Lucie's bedroom window, suffered, we assume, severe physical trauma.

As we have seen, the narrative point of view in *L'Enfant Méduse* shifts between an 'inside' and an 'outside' perspective on the characters; to employ Genette's terminology, the text has a 'focalisation variable' (variable point of view).[15] Alongside the 'inside' perspective, we find an omniscient narrator repeatedly alluding to future events outwith the characters' ken, and uttering gnomic truths about the human condition: 'Elle [Lucie] ne sait pas non plus que cette voix qui aura retenti si souvent dans ses soirées d'enfance résonnera plus tard . . . Elle ignore que la mémoire s'empare, pour accomplir son œuvre clandestine, de tous les matériaux qu'elle trouve sur son chemin' (p. 71) (She [Lucie] is also unaware that this voice which will have resounded so often during the evenings of her childhood will resonate once again in the future . . . She is unaware that memory, in order to carry out its secret work, seizes upon all the materials which it comes across along the way). The presence of the omniscient narrator effectively renders null and void the 'freedom' of the characters. As Sartre indicated in his famous diatribe against François Mauriac, in the novel there can be no 'third way' with respect to narrative point of view: 'Les êtres romanesques ont leurs lois, dont voici la plus rigoureuse: le romancier peut être leur témoin ou leur complice, mais jamais les deux à la fois. Dehors ou dedans. Faute d'avoir pris garde à ces lois, M. Mauriac assassine la conscience des personnages'[16] (Fictional characters are subject to certain laws, of which the most important is this: the author can be their witness or their accomplice, but never both at once. Outside or inside. Because he has failed to obey these laws, Mr Mauriac murders the consciousness of his characters).

Genette may have defended the use of 'focalisation variable' – 'c'est là un parti narratif parfaitement défendable . . . et qui prendrait aujourd'hui au sérieux les remonstrances de Sartre à Mauriac?' (*Figures*, p. 211) (this is a perfectly justifiable narrative mode to adopt . . . and who would take Sartre's objections to Mauriac seriously these days?) – but in this particular case, and irrespective of the perhaps dated nature of the debate, there is little doubt that the presence of the omniscient narrator is such that *L'Enfant Méduse* suffers from aesthetic incoherence. On a thematic level, the text insists throughout that human beings should not play God, must not judge their fellow creatures. Lucie, we learn, will only find peace when and if she forgives her abuser; judgement should be God's, and God's alone. But Germain preaches one law for her characters then flouts that law in her role of author as God, for the omniscient narrator repeatedly judges the characters' moral stance. To give just one example, which is especially jarring in the context of child sexual abuse:

> Le petit soldat Lucie veut bouter l'ennemi hors de tout pardon, l'expédier au fin fond de l'enfer. Le jeu est grave. Lucie le joue à la folie avec le plus parfait sérieux. Lucie y joue la vie et l'âme de son frère. Sans se douter . . . que le mal est à présent dans son camp plus encore que dans celui du frère déjà vaincu. Déjà châtié. (p. 202)

> (Lucie the brave little soldier wants to drive the enemy away from all chance of forgiveness, wants to send him to the furthest reaches of hell. This is a serious game. Lucie plays it to the point of distraction, and with the utmost gravity. At stake are the life and the soul of her brother. She does not realise that evil is now in her camp even more than it is in that of her brother, who is already vanquished. Already punished.)

So far the focus has been on point of view and genre, and it has been suggested that both of these contribute to a closed, monologic text, but what of the structure and the intertextual material? *L'Enfant Méduse* is divided into five chapters or sections ('Enfance', 'Lumière', 'Vigiles', 'Appels' and 'Patience'). Each of the first four of these chapters is further subdivided into six subsections, three of which take their titles from visual arts mediums ('Enluminures', 'Sanguines', 'Sépias', 'Fusains'), and three entitled 'Légende'. The 'légendes' are in roman type; the visual arts sections in italics. The last of the five chapters ('Patience') breaks the pattern, with just two subsections, the first of which is entitled 'Fresque', and comprises a description of Taddeo Gaddi's 'Annunciation to the Shepherds', part of a fresco of the *Life of the Virgin* decorating the Baroncelli Chapel in Santa Croce, executed in the late 1320s to early 1330s. The movement from 'Enluminures' through to Gaddi's fresco panel appears to signal a shift from the Medieval tradition – the 'enluminures' are perhaps especially associated with illuminated manuscripts of the lives of the saints – towards the humanism of the Renaissance. Gaddi, Giotto's greatest pupil, was renowned for his development of his master's experiments with light and perspective. His work represented a move away from the Byzantine tradition of the iconic and two-dimensional to the representation of three-dimensional, individualised figures. In many respects, we might say that Gaddi, in the night scene of his 'Annunciation to the Shepherds', in which the hillside is lit up by a dazzling light, aimed specifically to negotiate that difficult third way between the material and the non-material, the natural and the supernatural: 'Taddeo Gaddi's adventures into the problem of depicting light were motivated by the need to evoke not simply the splendour of natural light, but the mystery of the supernatural light of heaven'.[17]

Ironically, however, the presence of the intertextual material, which prompts a comparison between the visual and the written mediums, serves to show up the latter's limitations. Germain's characters remain as two-dimensional as the iconic figures from which Gaddi's art sought to distance itself. More than this, the Gaddi intertext foregrounds the teleological nature of the novel's structure. *L'Enfant Méduse* opens with a solar eclipse witnessed by the young Lucie and her friend Louis-Félix. At the start of the final section 'Patience', we learn that thirty years have passed, and that Lucie, having travelled the world, lacks joy. When she receives a postcard from her old school-friend Louis-Félix, depicting Gaddi's 'Annunciation', everything changes. The symbolic light eclipsed in her childhood returns, bringing with it that missing ingredient: joy. And in case the reader is left in any doubt as to the symbolic reading of the text, the precise nature of that joy is made explicitly clear in a particularly heavy-handed move: 'La joie que Lucie attend désormais est autre, elle est légère . . . Une joie pure de toute colère et de toute violence, qui lui viendrait d'ailleurs, et autrement. Une paix qui descendrait soudain éclairer la pénombre où elle sommeille encore, comme l'ange de l'Annonciation aux bergers' (p. 273) (Henceforth the joy which Lucie awaits is different, it is gentle . . . A joy purified of all anger and all violence, which would come to her from elsewhere, and in another way. A peace which would descend suddenly and illuminate the half-light in which she still slumbers, like the angel of the Annunciation to the Shepherds).

As was the case with the second volume of Germain's diptych, where Jacob's struggle with the angel emerged as the structural principle behind

both *Le Livre des nuits* and *Nuit-d'Ambre*, so the Gaddi fresco is foregrounded here as the teleological key to the whole text. From loss of light
to return of light: the authorial presence could not be clearer. Furthermore,
the closing moments of the text introduce, for the first time, an unequivocal
shift to the non-material dimension for which the reader is ill-prepared.
The device of the postcard as trigger for Lucie's epiphany is, to say the
least, intrusive, and to make matters worse, the final words of the text foreground the Christian message of 'tidings of great joy' via the omniscient
narrator, with the central character reduced to a mere cypher: 'Là-bas, ici,
une enfance nouvellement née luit dans la paille blonde. Il faut s'en
occuper. Lucie lui donne asile dans son regard. Dans son regard couleur
de nuit, toujours. Mais, désormais, nuit de Nativité' (p. 281) (There, here,
a newborn childhood shines forth amid the pale straw. It must be heeded.
Lucie offers it sanctuary within her gaze. In her gaze which is the colour of
night, still. But, henceforth, the night of the Nativity).

   If the textual presence of Taddeo Gaddi's fresco panel contributes to
a closed, monologic text, then the same can be said of another intertext,
George du Maurier's *Peter Ibbetson*, a work cited by Germain on three
occasions.[18] In du Maurier's novel the principal characters, Ibbetson and
Lady Towers, overcome spatial boundaries, and ultimately death itself,
when they come together via the bizarre phenomenon of 'dreaming-true'.
Sharing the same dreams, they travel through both space and time to their
childhood past, and indeed to the very beginnings of human history. Lady
Towers, communicating from beyond the grave, speaks of heightened sensations and extraordinary mysteries. 'Dreaming-true' reveals that 'the
whole cosmos is in a man's brain' (p. 72), that 'there exists in the human
brain hidden capacities, dormant potentialities of bliss' (p. 73).

   In *L'Enfant Méduse* it is Aloïse who seeks to contact her comatose son,
Ferdinand, via the same process of 'rêver-vrai' (dreaming-true), but in her
case the outcome is less fruitful. Germain's narrator emphasises the potential for 'rêver-vrai' to overcome suffering: 'legs miraculeux que le vieil
homme avait fait à sa fille pour l'aider à supporter et surmonter tous les cha-
grins, toutes les douleurs' (p. 152) (A miraculous legacy which the old man
had bestowed upon his daughter to help her endure and overcome all
suffering). However, this particular *mal* (illness/evil) will not be cured by
such unorthodox measures. Ibbetson, after all, informs us in du Maurier's
text that he is 'a born "infidel"', 'a congenital agnostic' (p. 110), adding:
'every argument that has ever been advanced against Christianity (and I
think I know them all by this time) had risen spontaneously and

unprompted within me, and they have all seemed to me unanswerable, and indeed, as yet, unanswered' (p. 112). The potential for an alternative thought system to be validated in *L'Enfant Méduse* is firmly quashed when Aloïse, far from contacting her son, is overcome by unbearable lust as she dreams of her dead husband Victor. Aloïse believes that she can conquer eternity – 'Elle s'était crue ... plus puissante que la mort' (p. 215) (She had believed herself to be stronger than death itself) – but she is punished for her pride and lack of true faith:[19] 'C'est ici et maintenant qu'elle veut voir reparaître son fils, et Victor également. Si Dieu lui ramène son fils, alors elle croira en Lui' (p. 220) (It's here and now that she wants to see her son reappear, and Victor as well. If God restores her son to her, then she will believe in Him). Germain's narrator describes the art of 'rêver-vrai' as a 'pâtre-magicien' (p. 152) (shepherd-magician), but, in fact, it seems that the only shepherd who can deliver eternal life in this literary world is Christ.

According to the parameters set here, *L'Enfant Méduse* is not a great success as a Christian novel. With *Immensités*, however, Germain's approach changes, as she progresses to a more open, and, crucially, self-conscious text. First, in terms of narrative point of view, the explicitly Christian elements are largely removed from the omniscient third-person narrative, to be located instead in a number of intercalated secondary narratives. Thus, for example, a rather saccharine tale concerning the trials and tribulations of a cross is recounted in the first-person by the protagonist Prokop, who writes the 'conte' (tale) in an attempt to comfort his suicidal daughter.

Second, the structure of *Immensités* is no longer so unrelentingly teleological. Prokop's apparent discovery of faith and his tale of the cross is, for example, succeeded by a deflatory indictment of Christianity – 'Non seulement rien ne valait tripette et Dieu n'était qu'un ballon de baudruche qui venait de faire clac, mais en plus son foutu lumbago récidivait' (p. 238) (Not only was the whole thing a dead loss and God just an inflated balloon which had just gone pop, but what's more his bloody lumbago was playing up again) – and though the text does subsequently move away once more from an outright negation of God, the final words of the text strike a more humanist note: 'Prokop se sentait pleinement le frère de cette enfant à tête folle, au cœur volage et aux pas trébuchants, – l'humanité, sa sœur prodigue' (p. 256) (Prokop felt that he was truly the brother of this crazy child of flighty heart and stumbling steps, – humanity, his prodigal sister). Given the previous fluctuations of Prokop's belief, the way for further developments seems to be open.

The most striking change, however, consists in the introduction of a degree of self-consciousness or reflexivity into the novel. Prokop, now a publisher, is given a story written by his neighbour M. Slavik. The untitled autobiographical tale explains how M. Slavik came to realise that his dog was an angel sent by God to watch over him. In a reflexive gesture, the response to Prokop's reading of this unlikely narrative raises the issue of the relative conceptions of the nature of reality: 'S'il n'avait pas connu monsieur Slavik, il aurait lu cette histoire comme une fiction' (If he hadn't known M. Slavik he would have read this story as a work of fiction), we are told, but M. Slavik 'n'avait écrit que pour relater des faits qu'il jugeait réels' (p. 170) (had written only to relate facts which he judged to be true). The ontological status of 'reality' is itself in question; one man's 'reality' is another's fantastic. Furthermore, M. Slavik's words to Prokop explicitly raise the problematic issue of reception: 'Vous comprenez qu'il y aurait une grande impudeur à publier ces lignes qui ne pourraient que paraître ridicules à la plupart des lecteurs' (p. 169) (You understand that it would be very unwise to publish these lines which could only appear ridiculous to most readers).

As a Christian novelist, it may be that Germain faces an impossible task. The Christian point of view should ideally be seen to prevail, yet it must do so without alienating the non-believer, without the author's presenting us with an open and closed case. As she herself points out in *Les Echos du silence*, stasis and closure are the marks of closed minds: 'Tout intégrisme hait le mouvement' (p. 36) (All fundamentalism abhors movement). The Christ of the resurrection, Germain states, could only be represented by means of dynamic, open forms: 'toute peinture où la force prime la forme, où le mouvement brise les lignes, où vibre la lumière, où la vitesse transfigure le visible' (p. 45) (any painting in which force is more important than form, in which movement shatters line, in which light vibrates, in which speed transfigures the visible). By openly acknowledging the twin issues of both reception and relative world-views by means of reflexive gestures to the reader, Germain certainly does go some way towards opening up her texts, but it may be that another, more intractable problem remains: how can one describe the ineffable?

Statements which appear in her later novels acknowledge this dilemma too. In *Immensités*, commenting on the state of mind of those who succumb to despair, is a statement which ultimately seems to question the capacity of any art form to represent Christianity: 'Ils avaient cru, ces deux êtres aux cœurs trop épris d'absolu, que la beauté, que le salut résidaient dans le jeu, dans l'art, dans les amours humaines. Mais la vraie vie se jouait encore ailleurs, et autrement. Elle était un drame hors mesure et *hors texte*' (p. 192, my emphasis) (These two individuals whose hearts were too enamoured of the absolute had believed that beauty, that salvation, resided in the game, in art, in human love. But real life was unfolding in another place, and in another way. It was a drama beyond any measure, and *beyond any text*).

It would appear that the answer, if there can be an answer, ultimately lies beyond the will of the author, and perhaps the reader. Might it be that a Christian novel may ultimately be a Christian novel in spite of its author or indeed reader? Just as the individual cannot will or solicit the grace of God, so the Christian novelist cannot set out to write a Christian novel. Grace, as Lucie discovers in *L'Enfant Méduse*, may be conferred at any time, and by any means. As the narrator of *La Pleurante des rues de Prague* (1992) suggests, the spark of recognition may be flamed by any text (plastic or written) and at any time:[20] 'Or les textes aussi sont des lieux, – ils le sont même par excellence. Ils sont des lieux où tout peut advenir, – l'éblouissement et les ténèbres, et jusqu'à la Parole de Dieu' (pp. 85–6) (But texts are also places – indeed they are places par excellence. They are places where anything can transpire – dazzling light and darkness, and even the Word of God).

Notes

1 Sylvie Germain, *Le Livre des nuits* (Paris: Gallimard, 1985) was awarded le prix Grévisse, le prix Hermès, le prix du Lion's Club International, le prix du Livre insolite, le prix de la Ville du Mans and le prix Passion.

2 Sylvie Germain, *Jours de colère* (Paris: Gallimard, 1989).

3 Cited in P. Tison, 'Sylvie Germain: l'obsession du mal', *Magazine Littéraire*, 286 (1991), 64–6 (65). Translations are mine throughout.

4 Sylvie Germain, *Les Echos du silence* (Paris: Desclée de Brower, 1996).

5 Sylvie Germain, *Immensités* (Paris: Folio, 1995), p. 134. First published: Gallimard, 1993. All quotations are from the Folio edition.

6 Malcolm Scott, *The Struggle for the Soul of the French Novel* (Basingstoke: Macmillan, 1989), pp. 5, 44, 50.

7 Shooting stars are identified as portents of death in Jean Chevalier and Alain Gheerbrant (eds), *Dictionnaire des symboles* (Paris: Robert Laffont/Jupiter, 1982), p. 417; Iona Opie and Moira Tatem (eds), *A Dictionary of Superstitions* (Oxford: Oxford University Press, 1990), p. 376; Stith Thompson, *The Folktale* (New York: Holt, Rinehart & Winston, 1964), p. 258; Philippa Waring, *A Dictionary of Omens and Superstitions* (London: Souvenir Press, 1978), pp. 209 and 218.

8 The flight of a bird through an open window as an omen of death is noted in Chevalier and Gheerbrant, *Dictionnaire*, pp. 695–9; Opie and Tatem, *Dictionary of Superstitions*, pp. 25–6; Thompson, *Folktale*, p. 258; Waring, *Dictionary of Omens*, pp. 32–3.

9 Both Opie and Tatem (*Dictionary of Superstitions*, pp. 181–2) and Waring (*Dictionary of Omens*, p. 229) identify the colour green as an unlucky colour, especially for a bride-to-be.

10 See Neil Cornwell, *The Literary Fantastic* (New York and London: Harvester Wheatsheaf, 1990), pp. 40–1.

11 Cornwell, in fact, includes magic realism within his category of the 'marvellous' (p. 40).

12 Sylvie Germain, *Nuit-d'Ambre* (Paris: Gallimard, 1987).

13 Genesis 32.30: 'And Jacob called the name of the place Peniel, for, said he, I have seen God face to face, and my life is preserved.'

14 Sylvie Germain, *L'Enfant Méduse* (Paris: Gallimard, 1991). All quotations are taken from the 1993 Folio edition.

15 Gérard Genette, *Figures III* (Paris: Seuil, 1972), p. 211.

16 Jean-Paul Sartre, *Situations I* (Paris: Gallimard, 1947), p. 48.

17 Alastair Smart, *The Dawn of Italian Painting 1250–1400* (Oxford: Phaidon, 1978), p. 79. For a detailed discussion of the portrayal of light in the Baroncelli Chapel fresco sequence, see Paul Hills, *The Light of Early Italian Painting* (New Haven and London: Yale University Press, 1987), pp. 75–93.

18 George du Maurier, *Peter Ibbetson* (London: James R. Osgood. McIlvaine & Co., 1894). Extracts are cited on the following pages: (*L'Enfant* p. 153, *Ibbetson* p. 190); (*L'Enfant* pp. 157–8, *Ibbetson* p. 250); (*L'Enfant* p. 158, *Ibbetson* p. 206).

19 Just as Aloïse is, apparently, punished for her pride, so, according to his adviser Fra Simone, was Taddeo Gaddi's sight damaged (and his faith weakened) when he watched a solar eclipse, specifically because he manifested a wilful desire to seek out mysteries. In the word of Fra Simone in a letter to Gaddi: 'Your eyes are weakened because you looked surmisingly into the heavens; yea, they are affected and darkened because you lifted your face with pride towards the heights, not towards your Creator and not to praise His majesty or the wonders He has made, but so that you might understand those things which there is no usefulness in knowing' (cited in Alastair Smart, 'Taddeo Gaddi, Orcagna and Eclipses', in Irving Lavin and John Plumber (eds), *Studies in Late Medieval and Renaissance Painting* (New York: New York University Press, 1977), p. 405).

20 Sylvie Germain, *La Pleurante des rues de Prague* (Paris: Gallimard, 1992). The quotation is taken from the Folio 1994 edition.

The subversion of the gaze: Shérazade and other women in the work of Leïla Sebbar

Of mixed Franco-Algerian parentage, Leïla Sebbar spans a variety of genres in her writing, including short stories, journalism, essays, children's writing and contributions to collaborative works, including collections of visual material. She also has a number of major novels to her credit. In its thematic content, Sebbar's work straddles the Mediterranean, focusing attention on the dynamics between the generations. She is not engaged in any mission of nostalgia for lost youth, however. Her writing is resolutely orientated towards the youth of today. This focus is evident not only in her characters, but also in the young audience that she targets. Her recent work, such as *Soldats*, is marked by a preoccupation with war and the images used to represent conflicts, wherever they may be.[1] In her earlier work, she concentrated on the problems of second-generation immigrant families – uprooted to France, often through violent conflict – as they explored new strategies to enable them to come to terms with their situation.

At the same time, Sebbar's œuvre has also been preoccupied with the link with the past. In some respects, her role could be compared with the traditional role of Maghrebian women as custodians of memory through the oral storytelling tradition. Her efforts to transmit knowledge of the Algerian War to the younger generation, particularly regarding the October 1961 killings of Algerians in Paris in *La Seine était rouge*, could be seen in this light.[2] Sometimes her characters become active participants in retelling the past themselves. However, as for Sebbar herself, it is often through writing that the record is kept. This is not a static relationship with the past, where storytelling serves to preserve the identity of the group; rather her work tackles the dynamics of interaction with the other. In this project, the visual relation is of paramount importance, expressing as it does the fundamental relation which has operated between coloniser and colonised other. Yet she injects fundamentally new meanings into this relation through the dynamics of subversive interaction with the powers which, whether in the colonial period or in the present day, define her characters as others.

The gaze, or *le regard*, is thus one of Sebbar's most important themes, but also one which is given a highly complex, multifaceted treatment. This chapter will concentrate on the gaze and its subversion, as it affects some of her female characters. These characters cannot be isolated in any particular text, for it is a feature of much of Sebbar's work that it constitutes an integrated fictional universe in which the texts are interrelated, with numerous cross-references to characters and events. In many cases, the women have no particular names of their own, but reappear from one text to another as almost archetypal figures – the Mother, the Daughter, the Old Woman. As this intertextuality also applies to the visual references which concern us, I shall refer to texts from the whole corpus.

My starting point is the role which the gaze has played in the theorisation of the other, for which much is owed to the analyses of Jean-Paul Sartre, who not only developed this notion generally in respect of relations between the self and the other, but also specifically with regard to the relationship between coloniser and colonised other. Sartre developed the Hegelian master–slave dialectic to include the colonial relation in which the colonised is determined by the colonising gaze and transformed by absolute negation into the object of that gaze. However, the relationship to the gazed-upon other always implies the possibility, indeed the necessity, of the object returning the gaze to look upon the subject in his turn. Just as the master cannot exist without the slave's acknowledgement of him as master, so this acknowledgement in itself not only transforms the master into an object in a reversal of the gaze, but also contains the implicit recognition of the slave as subject. The possibility of the colonised other becoming the subject of the gaze and overturning the relation is implicitly contained within it, as the seed of its own destruction, as Sartre eloquently describes in 'Orphée Noir' and Fanon will develop further.[3]

This theorisation of the gaze provides useful insights into the role which it plays in Sebbar's work. However, the problematical status of the relation to the other in the gaze is compounded by the complication that the other is not simply the absolute negation or enemy, but can be also, and often at the same time, the object of desire. Furthermore, there are problematics deriving from the Maghrebian cultural context, which also come into play. These relate to the gaze as it specifically affects women and popular beliefs attached to the evil eye and measures to avert it, for instance, the use of Fatima's hand and other types of amulet.[4] It also relates to the role of the visual in Islam. In Sebbar's short piece 'Père et fils, mère et fils', father and son are killed because the son is an artist who has depicted human figures.[5] Sebbar's treatment of the gaze is thus rich and complex. It is addressed not only in a direct, unmediated form – with her characters engaged in the act of looking – but also in a variety of mediated forms, in which it is focused on an *image*. In the latter case, a number of visual media forms appear as a recurrent feature in the texts, including painting, cinema, *objets d'art*, artefacts, advertising and pornography. However, it is the photograph that has pride of place in her visual universe.

Sebbar often uses the unmediated gaze to convey something about a particular moment in a personal relationship. These relations may be those of friendship as well as, at least potentially, sexual, but very often concern problematical relationships between different generations of the same family. In relationships which involve sexual desire, it is the power of the gaze which is highlighted; indeed, 'seeing' women can sum up the whole relation.[6] The eyes become the most important feature and are frequently the only physical characteristic noted to describe the beauty, and power, of the woman concerned.[7] Eye colour is especially significant. Shérazade's green eyes signal her out and also provide the basis for identification with one of Delacroix's *Femmes d'Alger*. Roland thinks of ways to save Lise 'with the blue eyes' from prison, because of her 'regard' (*J. H. cherche*, pp. 202–3). Blue eyes are sometimes associated with the French and, as such, can portend ill, as when they are seen as the eyes of the devil, particularly by a mother who warns her son against marriage to a blue-eyed woman (*Parle mon fils*, p. 42). Yet they may also be the object of desire. Indeed, this mother will later try to interest her son in marrying his cousin with eyes which are coloured blue like the sea (*Parle mon fils*, p. 79).

Chance encounters usually start with the gaze, often with the object unaware that he or she is being looked at. Whether the relationship develops or remains at the voyeuristic stage depends on successfully negotiating the stage of reciprocal eye contact, as when Eve first sees the boy known as 'Le Chinois' peering into her bookshop window (*Le Chinois*, p. 205), or when Jaffar has the following encounter:

> Il sent le regard de la femme sur lui, elle a tourné la tête en s'éloignant de la vitre . . . Il la regarde, elle non. Pourtant, il est sûr qu'elle sourit, elle lui

sourit sans chercher son regard, à qui elle sourirait, personne ne l'a remar-
quée au bout de la banquette, pressée contre la vitre. Elle ne sourit plus.
Elle a posé sa main contre son front comme pour dormir en cachant son
visage. Jaffar renverse la tête contre le dossier haut et ferme les yeux. (*J.
H. cherche*, pp. 163-4)

(He felt the woman's gaze upon him, she turned her head as she moved
away from the window . . . He looked at her, but she did not look at him.
Yet he was sure that she was smiling, she was smiling at him without trying
to catch his eye, who might she be smiling at, no one was paying any attention to her at the end of the bench, face pressed against the glass. She
stopped smiling. She had covered her forehead with her hand as if she was
hiding her face to sleep. Jaffar threw his head back against the high back
of his seat and closed his eyes.)

In other relations, the gaze may express a move towards knowledge or
understanding. Indeed, seeing things with one's own eyes is stressed as the
only reliable source of knowledge, although in fact other channels, including the traditional transmission of knowledge through the generations, can
also have their role (*Parle mon fils*, p. 47). The mother explicitly links her
knowledge with her seeing:

Je sais tout, je ne ferme jamais les yeux . . . je ne sors pas beaucoup, mais
je vois tout, j'écoute tout, je sais sur la vie peut-être plus que toi et ceux
qui sont allés très loin pour voir les autres. (*Parle mon fils*, pp. 72-3)

(I know everything, I never close my eyes . . . I don't go out much, but I
see everything, I listen to everything, it may be I know more about life than
you do, as well as those people who have travelled a long way to look at
others.)

A passage from *Le Chinois vert d'Afrique* reinforces this. Lounès says that
he *saw* a neighbour rinse her mouth out with disinfectant after she was told
that she had unwittingly eaten pork; his whole credibility rests on whether
he was an eyewitness, whether he had actually seen the label on the bottle,
with his own eyes (*Le Chinois*, pp. 23-4).

The gaze may also be a vehicle for an implicit judgement of its object.
Where this is a positive judgement, it can lead to pride on the part of the
object. However, another reaction is to avert the eyes. This refusal to reciprocate the gaze can be explained, in Sartrean terms, through the notion of
shame at being the object of the other's defining, judgmental gaze. Gazing
at oneself in a real or imaginary mirror can also lead to self-knowledge and
self-assessment. This typically happens when prisoners visit the barber's

shop (*J. H. cherche*, pp. 157-9), where viewing themselves in the mirror leads to confession, shame, tears or pride in their newly smart appearance. In Sebbar's situations, this is no abstract philosophical notion. The interaction of the gaze and the aversion of the eyes often arise in a situation of tension between different values and lifestyles, resulting from cultural conflict between different generations of a migrant family. Thus, while theoretically possible that the character will accept this judgement and the ensuing shame, the typical response is a refusal, though rarely articulated as a direct challenge; indeed the object of the gaze attempts evasion by not returning the gaze.

This turning away represents an unwillingness to become drawn into complicity with the subject of the gaze. It is a refusal to accept the perceptions and values of the subject of the gaze through a gesture of abdication rather than through confrontation, which would involve the positive assertion of freedom on the part of the character concerned, as in the chance encounter between 'le Chinois' and his mother (*Le Chinois,* pp. 103-4). Turning away from the gaze can also be a means of maintaining a secret, private life – cutting off the possibility of knowledge, as in another visual duel, where the mother tries to force her son to look at her. He resists, eyes firmly fixed on the floor, for he knows that with one look his mother will know everything about him (*Parle mon fils*, pp. 9-10). Later, he eats, still not looking at his mother, although he feels her black, khôl-framed eyes keenly piercing him with their gaze (*Parle mon fils*, p. 14).

The knowledge acquired through the gaze does not just apply to personal relationships; it extends to the wider world. When no one bothers about the killings of Arabs in the suburbs, the mother accuses her son of closing his eyes and seeing nothing (*Parle mon fils*, p. 17). Opening one's eyes, looking at the world, is the first step to knowledge and opportunity (*Parle mon fils*, p. 20). She complains that no photographs of the Marche des beurs have appeared in the media; they are invisible (*Parle mon fils*, p. 26).

The refusal to reciprocate the gaze is often carried to the next stage where it involves removing one's entire physical presence. Thus the mother stops herself from looking at her son, as this would provoke him to leave (*Parle mon fils*, p. 57). This is what the teenage runaways, like Shérazade herself do, even though this can lead to a more extreme deprivation of their liberty, through confinement in prison, or as a hostage.

It is important to note that the reciprocal gaze, as the articulation of relations of friendship, love or family ties, is rarely encountered in Sebbar's work. One notable example is, however, contained in the first sentence of the second volume of the Shérazade trilogy, *Les Carnets de Shérazade*: 'Il la regarda et la trouva belle, jeune, intrépide. Elle le regarda et le trouva jeune, pas vraiment, beau pas vraiment. . .' (He looked at her and found her beautiful, young, fearless. She looked at him and found him not exactly young and not exactly handsome. . .).[8] The encounter between Shérazade and the lorry driver, Gilles, starts with his gaze and obvious attraction to her. This is quickly deflated, however, by the judgement of her gaze. In fact the mutual looking-over is the prelude to what will turn out to be a real friendship and companionship during the journey through France.

Of even greater significance to Sebbar's work is the multiplicity of examples of the gaze mediated through images. By its very nature, the mediated gaze implies a one-way, unreciprocated process. Although the *voyeur* can also operate directly in this way – by observing the object of the gaze without being seen and without the object's knowledge – this type of *voyeurism* is inscribed as a characteristic feature of the way the viewer relates to the mediatised visual image. The fundamental inequality and lack of reciprocity in the relation of the viewer to the object viewed can, of course, lead to an exploitative use of such imagery, though this is only one possibility. What is most interesting is the process whereby this relation is subverted and transcended, leading to a reappropriation of the image within a new set of meanings.

Images constitute a rich thematic seam running through all of Sebbar's books, where they feature in different ways. They may be official markers, for identification purposes, as with the hostages in *Le Fou de Shérazade*.[9] Shérazade, herself, is first presented to us as a missing person – *Shérazade, 17 ans, brune, frisée, les yeux verts* (*Shérazade, 17 years old, brunette, curly hair, green eyes*).[10] This is her description for the police files, her identity photograph. Yet, as I shall show, photographs are used for more complex reasons than simply fixing an official identity. They may serve as visual aids to fix memory and preserve history and tradition, for instance with family photographs (*J. H. cherche*, pp. 19, 67), or, in the case of war photojournalism – a recurrent theme in Sebbar's work – they may fulfil a number of ideological and propaganda functions (*Le Fou*, pp. 128–32). They also figure as a stimulus to sexual desire: ranging from images used as aids for matchmaking and pen-pal correspondence with prisoners, to the outright pornographic (*J. H. cherche*, pp. 17–18). In addition to contributing to the construction of an imaginary universe, photographs play an important role in reinforcing or challenging the relations of power.

Sebbar's visual universe is filled with family photographs, whether as wedding pictures, family groups, school photographs or simple snapshots capturing a moment of family life. Unlike the simple identity photograph used for official purposes, these images have a particular role to play as vehicles for the preservation of the family's memory. They function not so much as reminders of particular events in the family's past, but as safeguards of the family's continuity across the generations. This can be achieved through the visual representation of previous generations. Alternatively, when parents give pride of place to their children's pictures on the sideboard, it affirms their confidence in their children as investments in the family's future. When there is a rupture between the generations, however, the photograph of the delinquent child acquires a special significance. The photograph of a young person who has run away from home assumes a new function: it acts at some level as a substitute for the missing child. Thus when Shérazade's mother sees a blown–up portrait of her daughter on the filmset from which she has absented herself, she responds by equating the picture with Shérazade herself and wants a small copy to keep with her. As far as she is concerned, the photograph is not just an image; it is her missing daughter (*Le Fou*, p. 31).

This is in marked contrast to the fathers' typical response. In *Parle mon fils*, the father of another runaway puts a sticker over his daughter's image to signify the severing of all relations with the actual person (p. 30). The mother does not accept that the rupture is definitive and removes the photograph, so as not to allow the blanking out of the daughter's image to become the permanent repudiation of the daughter's existence in reality. Despite their differing reactions, it is clear that, for both parents, the daughter's image is more than a mere picture: it represents a real continuity both with them and with the rest of the family.

On a more general social level, images created and disseminated by media of various types are also highly significant in Sebbar's work. On the one hand, she brings out the all-pervasiveness of media imagery in determining the way in which the world is interpreted. The influence of the media, particularly the cinema, is ever present, acting as a grid for the interpretation of the viewer's own experience. Shérazade, like her friend Julien, is forever imagining herself as a film character (*Le Fou*, p. 73, pp. 87–8). On the other hand, it can take the form of a critique of the ways in which the media, and particularly journalism, manipulate images – deliberately or otherwise – in order to present particular versions of reality to the public. Essentially, this is the critique which the Lebanese militiamen make of foreign journalists who come to spy on them and present an erroneous view of them to the outside world (*Le Fou*, p. 19). The critique concentrates on the photograph itself, which is far from being a representation of reality seized in a flash of truth. Not only does the transparency of the lens not guarantee objectivity of representation; interpretation and manipulation of meaning intervene as well at all stages of the process of taking and viewing the photographed image. Algerian War photographs, which frequently reappear in the Shérazade trilogy, and in other texts, are a particular case in point. Sebbar uses them to show how the same images can be the object of very different interpretations. The photograph of the funeral procession which plays such an important role in *Le Chinois vert d'Afrique*, for instance, appears fleetingly in *Le Fou de Shérazade* (p. 17), where it merely reminds Shérazade of her uncle's funeral in Mascara. 'Le Chinois', however, with the benefit of different narratives, invests the picture with a wholly different significance.

Sometimes photographs are intentionally used for the purposes of deception, as is clearly the case when Shérazade's captors plan to use her photograph to convince the press that she is still alive once they have killed her (*Le Fou*, p. 71). The motives of the photographers themselves can seem almost gratuitously manipulative. One such photographer, Michel, delights in pasting the walls of Beirut with pictures of Shérazade with the sole purpose of giving rise to speculation as to who she might be – a hostage, or a terrorist who has been using a photographer to engage in an elaborate deception (*Le Fou*, pp. 158–9). When Julien sees the pictures, he can think of nothing better to do than to photograph the photographs (*Le Fou*, p. 142).

The imaging of Shérazade by others is a crucial element in the novels and it is here that Sebbar really comes into her own by isolating the particular images of the other with which her various characters are confronted and by exploring the way they deal with their own self-image in consequence. Shérazade is constantly coming up against image-makers who want to reproduce her image as the stereotypical other, the archetypal exotic woman. There are instances where photographers attempt to capture her as a Moorish dancer (*Shérazade*, p. 124), or where she is hired along with friends to be portrayed as jungle guerrillas in a pornographic film (pp. 152–6). In both cases, she counters by refusing the imaging process and the photographer's gaze. In the first instance, she simply breaks the photographer's camera, putting an end to his activity in the same way as she tears up the pictures which Julien had taken of her (pp. 158–9).

In the second encounter, her friends take control of the script, refusing to perform as directed and leaving with the fee, but no images for the pornographer. Later, she agrees to be filmed by Julien's friend, but runs away again, when she finds she cannot relate to the screen image he is creating of her (p. 219).

There is one further important category of the gaze to consider – that of the forbidden gaze. The notion of the forbidden is crucial to Sebbar's treatment of some of the war photographs mentioned earlier. The photograph of the Algerian funeral procession, for instance, is considered by 'le Chinois' to be off-limits to French eyes (*Le Chinois*, pp. 207–10). The forbidden nature of photography is especially applicable to photographs of women taken against their will or in voyeuristic situations.[11] Perhaps the most striking example of this is seen in the case of the women who were photographed for identity purposes by the French army photographer Marc Garanger during the Algerian War. Sebbar uses these pictures in her story 'La Photographie' as well as elsewhere.[12] The story concentrates on one of the women photographed unveiled against her will in a context in which the taking of such photographs was expressly forbidden. In some ways there are parallels here with Delacroix's painting, *Femmes d'Alger*. The painter was allowed to enter the forbidden space of the harem in the recently conquered Algiers of 1832, whereas the photographer in Sebbar's text is backed up by the full weight of the French army. In both instances, 'un regard interdit' (a forbidden gaze) results from the visit.[13]

The recurrent notion of the forbidden image or gaze in Sebbar's work is often linked with violence or war. For instance, when Shérazade is forced to burn her books, the ritualistic act is described as an execution which may be witnessed only by those who are authorised to watch – all other eyes being banished (*Le Fou*, p. 34). In 'La Photographie', the forcible unveiling of the women is treated as an act of violence perpetrated by the colonising power against the colonised. The transgression of a religious taboo is not at issue. Elsewhere, however, Sebbar has written critically of religious attitudes to the veiling of the female body: for instance, in her open letter to Taslima Nasreen she talks of the perceived need by clerics to control the 'scandal' of the female body by veiling what might offend the 'pure gaze guided by faith'.[14] Here, the prohibition against photography relates to the political context of the Algerian War, rather than to a religious ban on the representation of the human figure; it is social and political in its significance. The family concerned has had family portraits taken before ('La

Photographie', p. 110), but these were for the family's eyes only. What is problematic is the intrusion of the gaze of the French male outsider and the threat of violence it carries. As such, this incident is paralleled by the efforts of Maghrebian women in the Paris suburbs to prevent the police from entering their homes when they are alone (*Le Chinois*, p. 138).

Refusing, or blocking the gaze is but a first step in the process of regaining control over one's self-image and setting the parameters of one's own conditions of existence. We have seen Shérazade deny the photographer his picture, by one means or another. The Algerian women of the identity photographs are powerless to refuse the picture-taking, but none the less manage to stare their defiance into the camera, thus reversing the gaze and thereby asserting that they are subjects in their own right. One of the women's daughters transforms the photograph into a commemorative icon and invests it with political meanings which allow her to come to terms with the incident. The woman's granddaughter, however, marks a further stage in self-determination: she tears the picture to pieces as a way of asserting that she will not be defined by this image in the future.

Shérazade develops further strategies for dealing with the gaze. She discovers that there is more to her identity than the images with which she has hitherto been presented, as she becomes entranced with the images of women in Orientalist paintings and tries to identify with their innermost thoughts (*Le Fou*, p. 27). Although, on the one hand, these paintings reflect a stereotypical image of the Oriental woman – object of the gaze and desires of the European man – Shérazade is able to go beyond the gaze of the painter, to reach the women themselves, and in so doing to restore their subjectivity to them. As Winifred Woodhull has pointed out, what is at stake is her control over the image-making process itself.[15] In the end, Shérazade does achieve a measure of success. The film director is forced to concede that she is not merely a stereotypical figure: no replacement can be found for her when she goes missing – only she will do (*Le Fou*, p. 30). Her young neighbours from the housing estate share in this subversive process, transforming her portrait into a fully-fledged icon over which they mount guard, while the other pictures of naked odalisques are attacked (*Le Fou*, pp. 47–51). It is now the filmmaker's turn to see this as sacrilegious by claiming that the transformation of Shérazade into what amounts to a replica of the Virgin Mary is forbidden (*Le Fou*, pp. 51–2). For the women of the estate, however, it is the images of the naked women themselves which are forbidden. Their response is to bring out their veils (unused except in Algeria) to cover them up. To the film crew, who do not comprehend the way that the women are taking control over the images, the veils appear as shrouds (*Le Fou*, p. 52).

I have shown that Shérazade cannot identify with her own screen image, yet she has no such difficulty in identifying with Algerian women depicted in a book of photographs she comes across. The pictures move her to tears because she knows that these were women who all spoke the same language – the language of her mother (*Shérazade*, p. 220). Thus it is that photographs of the forbidden acquire a quite different significance for Shérazade. They provide the key to a new form of solidarity with other women and, in particular, open onto the eventual possibility of looking into the eyes of her own mother. Shérazade has been engaged in a quest to come to terms with the conflicts both within herself and in her relations with others. This does not mean a simple return to the past; it has involved a whole process of reappropriation of the imagery through which she and others like her have been defined as others. It has also involved the use of other strategies, which have helped her clear the ground for a new self-definition, in a personalised symbolic universe to which she can relate.

In addition to appropriating the gaze, Shérazade also has recourse to writing. Throughout her wanderings, she has filled countless notebooks with her jottings. The strategy of writing is one which Sebbar attributes to many other characters who are grappling with similar problems. In her narratives, she is not the only writer. The written word is a powerful means for her characters to challenge the interpretations and definitions of others, as well as a way to create their own imaginary selves, whether this be through telling stories, retelling history, or writing letters and poems. The subversion of the gaze is just one stage in the process of self-determination, but none the less a crucial part of Sebbar's complicated textual universe.

Notes

1　Leïla Sebbar, *Soldats* (Paris: Seuil, 1999).

2　Leïla Sebbar, *La Seine était rouge* (Paris: Thierry Magnier, 1999).

3　Jean-Paul Sartre, 'Orphée noir', preface to Léopold Sédar Senghor, *Anthologie de la nouvelle poésie nègre et malgache* (Paris: PUF, 1948).

4　Leïla Sebbar, *Le Chinois vert d'Afrique* (Paris: Stock, 1984), pp. 38–45, 148–50, 160, 175.

5　Leïla Sebbar, 'Père et fils, mère et fils', in *2000 ans d'Algérie* (Paris: Séguier, 1998), pp. 159–62.

6　Leïla Sebbar, *Parle mon fils, parle à ta mère* (Paris: Stock, 1984), p. 72.

7　Leïla Sebbar, *J. H. cherche âme sœur* (Paris: Stock, 1987), pp. 34, 63.

8 Leïla Sebbar, *Les Carnets de Shérazade* (Paris: Stock, 1985), p. 7.

9 Leïla Sebbar, *Le Fou de Shérazade* (Paris: Stock, 1991), p. 71.

10 Leïla Sebbar, *Shérazade, 17 ans, brune, frisée, les yeux verts* (Paris: Stock, 1982).

11 Regrettably, space does not permit a discussion here of the particular significance of photographs taken of children.

12 Leïla Sebbar, 'La Photographie', in Daniel Zimmermann (ed.), *Trente ans après, nouvelles de la guerre d'Algérie* (Paris: Le Monde Editions/Nouvelles Nouvelles, 1992); the photographs were published with text by Leïla Sebbar, in Marc Garanger and Leïla Sebbar, *Femmes des Haut-Plateaux, Algérie 1960* (Paris: La Boîte à Documents, 1990). The story is discussed in Margaret A. Majumdar, 'A travers le miroir: le regard de l'Autre sur l'Autre', *Bulletin of Francophone Africa*, 3(5) (spring 1994), 12–27.

13 On the Delacroix painting, see Assia Djebar, 'Regard interdit, son coupé', in *Femmes d'Alger dans leur appartement* (Paris: Des Femmes, 1980), pp. 167–93.

14 Leïla Sebbar, *Chère Taslima Nasreen* (Paris: Stock, 'Reporters sans Frontières', 1994), pp. 46–7.

15 See Winifred Woodhull, 'Exile', in Françoise Lionnet and Ronnie Scharfman (eds) 'Post/colonial conditions: exiles, migrations and nomadisms', *Yale French Studies*, 82 (1993), 7–24 (20).

Unnatural women and uncomfortable readers? Clotilde Escalle's tales of transgression

Described by critics variously as one of the 'new barbarians' of French writing,[1] as one of the cruel 'Barbarellas' who seek only to depict the disarray of contemporary French society,[2] and as one of the new breed of women writers who hold a violent and deep-seated grudge against the gaze of men,[3] Clotilde Escalle is remarkable among new writers for the dispassionate way in which she presents violent sexual and familial dramas.

Escalle was born in 1958 in Fez, Morocco, where she lived for many years. When she came to France, it was to join the Théâtre-Laboratoire and work with Ludwik Flaszen, the Polish critic, writer and theorist who had co-founded that radical theatrical enterprise with Jerzy Grotowski. With the publication in 1993 of her first novel, *Un long baiser*, she immediately established herself as a novelist who presents unpalatable scenes and confronts disagreeable truths about interpersonal relationships, notably within families and couples. Each one of her four novels, *Un long baiser*, *Pulsion* (1996), *Herbert jouit* (1999) and *Où est-il cet amour* (2001), challenges the reader to bear with her as she relentlessly anatomises the lives of women who have lost their way, both figuratively and literally. Escalle's women rage against their families and especially against their loveless mothers, who have emotionally mutilated them. They give themselves sexually to any man who will take and abuse them, yet they are not sacrificial victims: that would be to glorify and romanticise their acts of driven wantonness. They very occasionally seek and take revenge on those who have hurt them, but they resort to violence as a means not of salvation, but of survival. Furthermore, the violence is directed much more often against themselves than against others.

These novels are tales of oppression, of violence and abuse, of masochism, of cruelty and despair, of lancinating indifference, and ultimately of transgression. They portray a world in which love is strikingly absent, if none the less sometimes – nostalgically rather than prospectively – yearned for. They present sex brutally and almost pornographically. They tear the soul, they can repel the senses, they offer little hope. So why read Escalle? Is she just part of the ephemeral literary phenomenon that is the 'new barbarism' of post-feminism? Or is there a point in reading her which takes us beyond voyeurism and beyond the satisfaction of reading and living in the security of a world that is safer and more comfortable than the hellish limbos of Escalle's imagination? What, if anything, in her work makes her worth reading and rereading – and rereading again? What do her novels *do* that they both demand and merit sustained attention? The answers to these questions are neither single nor simple, but they are worth seeking, because they draw readers into an interrogation of post-feminist sexualities that questions many of the shibboleths of both feminist and masculinist/patriarchal ideologies.

It is axiomatic that one of the defining features of the late twentieth century and early twentieth-first century is the sexual liberation of women. While less fully and less universally realised than some would have us believe, this social, political and personal liberation has enabled among women writers an explosion of exploratory ways of saying sexuality (or, rather, sexualities) and of telling tales of selfdom. Hélène Cixous has argued that what she calls *écriture féminine* (feminine writing) 'means embarking on "the passage toward more than the self, toward another than the self, toward the other"'.[4] Elsewhere, she affirms that feminine writing is a 'fidelity to what exists. To everything that exists. And fidelity is equal respect for what *seems* beautiful to us and what *seems* ugly to us'.[5] Cixous's theoretical position is clear and seductive, but it does rely on a notion of subjectivity that is perhaps questionable. Above all, it assumes that there can be – even temporarily – a sense of certainty in selfness that allows us to know what seems beautiful or ugly to us. On the one hand, Cixous's arguments might lead us to see in Escalle's work a manifestation of a (feminine) writing that gives equal place and weight to the pure and the putrid, to the marvellous and the maimed. On the other hand, in the actual promotion of a writing that articulates and embodies a passage 'toward the other', Cixous's definitions of feminine writing problematically presuppose a self that is grounded – or grounded enough to know what is self and what is other.

Since the feminist debates of the 1980s, our hold on gender identity has become ever less firm and less unitary, as the full force of representation as construction has been recognised. Identity has increasingly been understood to be made rather than given, to be a (shifting) product of psycho-social and cultural processes. In 'Women's time', Julia Kristeva poses the crucial question: 'what can "identity", even "sexual identity", mean in a new theoretical and scientific space where the very notion of identity is challenged?'.[6] Other theorists maintain the concept in their thinking, but refuse the presupposition of any fixity or permanence in any given identity. For example, Judith Butler, in her contestatory analysis of both the politics of sexuality and representational politics, argues for a situation in which it is possible to 'affirm identities that are alternately instituted and relinquished according to the purposes at hand'.[7] If identities are to be adopted only within the contingency of individual intentions and needs or particular situations, this brings admirable freedom for psychic movement, but it does pose problems for any stable theory of personal development and social incorporation. Indeed, in one of the most pro-actively interesting recent analyses of how feminine and masculine identities can be defined and developed, Nancy J. Chodorow argues for the importance of women to recognise that woman as subject can expand into woman as subject–object as 'she becomes object to her own subjectivity as she internally relates to and identifies with or against another internally experienced woman', and she insists that '(w)oman as subject or as subject–object contrasts with woman as object in the masculine psyche'.[8] Chodorow persuasively challenges the founding premise and, implicitly, the historicity of Freud's differentiation of masculine and feminine according to an axis of active and passive, which is actually based on 'the distinction between phallically endowed and castrated: women, basically, are castrated men' (p. 28). According to Chodorow:

> gender makes a difference but does so in particular ways [. . .] What becomes important to an individual is not just femaleness or maleness but the psychologically and culturally *specific* meanings that gender holds *for that individual.*
>
> The problem, then, is how to consider gendered subjectivity without turning such a consideration into objective claims about gender difference [. . .]
>
> [The] sense of gendered self is itself individually created and particular, a unique fusion of cultural meaning with a personal emotional meaning that is tied to the individual psycho-biographical history of any individual. (pp. 90–1)

Although Chodorow does not frame her arguments explicitly in terms of identity and identification (except to have a pertinent side-swipe at Freud's construal of gender identity and personality almost exclusively as issues of sexuality (see p. 99, note 4)), her conception of subjectivity as grounded in the lived and gendered experiences of the individual subject is a productive way of approaching an understanding of how senses of the self can be established through looking inwards as well as outwards – and finding plurality in both cases.

As the concept of identity has been shown to be inadequate as a way of accurately defining our means of psycho-social engagement and development, it is gradually being replaced by the more appropriate concept of identification, which has the merit of fusing the psychoanalytical and the political and of addressing the issues of both the individual subject and the group. Yet even identification poses problems, in that a subject may identify with women and/or her mother, yet in a misplaced or even deluded way, since she may see no other alternatives for identification. In Escalle's work, the women protagonists invariably identify with the mother, even if this identificatory process is usually aggressive. The men chosen (or found) as sexual partners are abusers (and not infrequently grubby and unwashed), and the fathers weak, emotionally and familially ineffectual, simultaneously sexually inadequate for their wives and unfaithful to them. The father is therefore an impossible source and target of identification – and yet psychoanalysis, from Freud through to Kristeva, tells us that the first identification is with the father-as-phallus, even if, as Kristeva herself points out, that father is no more than a question mark over the mother's lack of a phallus.[9] In Escalle's desolate world where rough promiscuous sex and the quest for violence seem to be the only substitutes for the lack of love and affection, identification takes the form of an aggressive anti-identification with the mother. The full implications of this in the context of masochism will be explored later, but for now I want to insist on the importance in these novels of a generalised sense of loss which haunts the characters and permeates Escalle's discourse: the term '*abandon*' (abandonment), for instance, occurs time and again in her novels like a leitmotif.

The four novels tell of anger, bitterness, uncertainty, violence, promiscuity and above all the loss – or, more precisely, the absence – of self-knowledge and sense of self-worth. They tell tales that reveal families and societies riven by misunderstandings, silences and cruelties, and seamed through with indifferences that drive the characters to sudden passions and extreme acts of violence. They portray social units in disarray and in the process of disintegrating, and thereby cause anxiety in the reader, but they are not driven by any moral or political purpose. Rather, these narratives –

all written in the third person, although they often contain reported streams of fantasy-consciousness – unveil, probe and expose what it is to be a woman in an environment in which there is no space for growth and no knowledge of how to grow and separate from one's roots. Significantly, Escalle's protagonists are not always young women and the objects of their erotic attentions can also be not merely older men, but positively decrepit, senile men.

In *Un long baiser*, a disillusioned, lonely old woman returns, after a long absence, to the house in which she grew up in an unnamed town in a hot, unspecified North African country. The house is filled with memories of her past life and of the abuse she suffered at the hands of her mother. Childhood fears and a sense of powerlessness haunt the old woman still, so that when two male intruders break into her house and stalk her, she can do nothing to resist their desires. The older, Gribouille, is grey-haired, bearded, with dirty clothes, like a tramp, and seems to be fleeing the misery of poverty and 'la vie triste' (p. 44) (the sadness of life), whereas the younger, Virgile, is black-haired, with a bruised face, and initially seems to want to flee her anger at their attempted break-in. Both are defined as fleeing (*en fuite*); both, like the old woman, have 'ce goût de poussière dans la bouche, le goût de l'amertume, de la désillusion' (p. 44) (that taste of ashes in the mouth, that taste of bitterness and disillusionment). Gribouille caresses her, slipping a finger into her mouth to see how many teeth she has left, and then slides a hand under her dress, initially to the disgust of his younger friend who none the less joins in the coarse fondling of this aged body of a woman who has 'passé l'âge de l'amour' (p. 46) (passed the age of love). He takes her time and again, in acts of joyless and mindless sex that she accepts only by remembering her lover. Virgile then decides to make her suck him as she is being penetrated brutally by Gribouille. The sex acts become increasingly violent until she is finally kicked and beaten to death. Virgile commits suicide out of despair and disgust, and Gribouille starves alongside their two bodies. All that remains is ugliness and pathos (p. 72).

Pulsion recounts the story of Pauline, who is in her early twenties, the older daughter of French parents living in Morocco. Her father is a respected doctor, her mother an unstable and deeply dissatisfied woman with only one desire – to leave the country to live in France. This fervent wish is not shared by the family – and especially not by Pauline – but the mother's will prevails. The novel follows Pauline's attempts to lessen the pain of the enforced departure through indiscriminate and increasingly violent sex with Arab boys and men. Wild with jealousy, her boyfriend,

François, takes her away to an isolated hotel where, in scenes demonically evocative of Cocteau's *Les Enfants terribles*, he locks both her and himself in a room, which they gradually destroy. But even here, Pauline initiates sex – with the hotel manager, whom she entices into the room and into sex with her. Jealousy drives François to attack him, and the manager is wounded by a bullet from his own gun. Instead of treating the wound properly, François – with growing cooperation from Pauline – resorts to torture. Eventually, the pain from his partially severed, gangrenous foot grows so extreme that the manager rips it off himself. The two decide to leave, abandoning the manager to be rescued by an ambulance crew, but Pauline remains haunted by 'la magie de la chambre' (p. 80) (the magic of the bedroom). She and her parents finally board the ferry for France, and the fissures between mother and father, and between mother and daughter, widen further.

In *Herbert jouit*, Escalle returns to the virtually taboo subject of the sexuality of the elderly, this time portraying a decrepit old man whose sexuality is revived by a somewhat younger woman. The protagonist, who finally gives her name as Renée, is haunted by violent dreams involving her (now dead) mother. She has carried throughout her life the sense of disgust that her mother felt and expressed about her daughter and her daughter's body. However, in a social club for old people, 'Renée' meets Herbert. By overcoming her own sense of disgust at the aspect and behaviour of Herbert's aged and somewhat dirty body, she rediscovers pleasure in her own body and, in nurturing her geriatric lover like a newborn baby (p. 80), she learns gradually to come to terms with her own childhood rejection. In the end, her sexual satisfaction is as great as his. Both have succeeded in – and enjoyed – cheating death for a while.

Escalle's most recent novel, *Où est-il cet amour*, is her most ambitious and complex work. It tells the story of the perverse sexuality of an abusive, incestuous, secretive and mendacious family. Told from the point of view of the daughter, Anne, who in vain craves affection from her parents, the novel follows Anne's attempts to make sense of the difference between the love shown to her by her nanny, Khadija, the humiliation that her father and grandfather inflict on their respective wives, her father's love of prostitutes and his necrophiliac passion for his dead patients (some of whom were former mistresses), and the masochistic sex that she undergoes with her boyfriend, Léonard. Anne's mother, herself abused as a child by the (much older) man who was to become her husband, is frigid in every sense of the word. She is incapable of loving herself or her children. While she endures and ignores her husband's liaisons with prostitutes and women patients from his abortion clinic, she does not know the crucial fact that he has also had a passionate affair with her own mother, an affair that was witnessed – from the wardrobe in which she was often kept locked as a small child – by Anne, who gazed on as her father penetrated her grandmother. Tormented by this family secret, Anne in the end finds grim satisfaction in exacting violent and triumphant revenge on all of her family by murdering her ailing grandmother in a way that can never be traced.

What marks these harrowing novels is their *depth*, a depth which comes from the complexity of emotions and impulses that lurk beneath – and that underpin and, indeed, generate – these simple, spare, direct accounts of 'perverse' desire and sex. Since Aristotle, it has been accepted in the West that sexual pleasure, while desirable, subverts rationality. In the eighteenth century, when so many modern points of reference were determined, reason and rationality were instituted as the foundations of personal freedom – which was true freedom only if it led to and entailed self-discipline and moderation. Furthermore, rationality was considered to be the mark of masculinity, in contra-distinction to feminine intuition and, ultimately, hysteria. However, as Vic Seidler has argued, the identification of masculinity with reason and the consequent manipulation of language by men pose problems for modern men, perhaps most insidiously because 'men can learn to use language to distance and hold in check their experience [. . .] we can learn to use language instrumentally to conceal ourselves'.[10] For men, then, language becomes less a means of communicating or expressing than a defence against self-exposure, a means of distancing themselves from their emotions. While there are other deeply embedded institutional and social reasons for the problems that individual men experience in speaking of themselves, the cultural heritage of enforced silence or, at least, reticence has come to form part of the psychic make-up of modern Western man. Women have not been subject to such silencings, at least not directly, but they have been denied access to language as subjects, being rather maintained, as Luce Irigaray has powerfully argued, in the position of the object of language.[11] Indeed, it is widely recognised that the relationship between women and language is bound up with the degree of consciousness they have been permitted to have within patriarchy (the historical prominence given to hysteria as a 'feminine' condition testifies powerfully to the way in which men have oppressed and maintained women inside a language that they define and control).

In many ways, Escalle's work takes issue with the notion that women are silenced through oppression by men. She does not operate a simplistic reversal of oppressive relationships nor does she conceive of or present women's language as some outpouring of intuition or subjectivity. Rather, in her world, women can simply have and use language. This possession of language often frightens those around them, as in *Pulsion*, where Pauline's mother is terrified by her daughter's 'pouvoir de dire' (p. 60) (ability to say), which Pauline herself can see is – for others – a monstrous thing. When she chooses to have rapid, wordless sex with a grubby, middle-aged man who has picked her up when she is hitch-hiking, she offers to have sex with him again, even though she does not find him at all attractive, as long as she can then re-enter the world of language:

> Elle soulève sa robe, pose la main de l'homme contre son sexe.
> 'Nous pourrions recommencer. . . si je peux parler ensuite.'
> L'homme la pénètre de ses doigts. Il dit:
> 'Si vous arrivez à parler ainsi, pourquoi pas? Alors vous vouliez parler?'
> Jamais elle n'aurait imaginé avoir autant de plaisir. (p. 13)

> (She hitches up her dress, puts the man's hand on her vagina.
> 'We can do it again. . . if I can talk afterwards.'
> The man penetrates her with his fingers. He says:
> 'If that helps you to talk, then why not? So, you wanted to talk?'
> She had never imagined that she could experience such pleasure.)

It is evident throughout the novel that Pauline sees no need to explain her desire for unknown men or for violence to be inflicted on her (p. 46); rather, her attitude towards language and violence is bound up with a preoccupation with the giving of form and shape. For her, saying is not explaining; it consists of giving names and thereby ordering the chaos around her (cf. p. 89).

The question of consciousness is, of course, at the heart of all attitudes towards existence, whether one is a man or a woman. However, as the French feminist anthropologist, Nicole-Claude Mathieu has shown, society has contrived to make it difficult for women to have access to the information necessary to make informed choices, notably in the realm of sexuality and violence.[12] Women have traditionally been considered by male theorists such as Freud and Krafft-Ebing as 'essentially' masochistic, and for this reason focused on the 'perversion' of masochism in men. However, underpinning their thinking lies the view rehearsed later and most forcefully by Bataille in *Eroticism*: while women are the privileged objects of desire, they are inherently no more desirable than men, 'but they lay themselves open to be desired. They put themselves forward as objects for the aggressive desire of men. Not every woman is a potential prostitute, but prostitution is the logical consequence of the feminine [i.e. passive] attitude'.[13]

Bataille's reading of feminine sexuality seems particularly appropriate when reading Escalle's work, since many of her characters are highly promiscuous, having easy sex with many men and putting themselves in the role of passive recipient of male desire, violence and abuse. On the other hand, much feminist thinking has considered masochism to be self-hatred and consequently something from which women should try to free themselves, since masochistic women are perceived not only as being oppressed, but also as colluding in their own oppression. However, Mathieu problematises this, first by questioning whether women can in fact consent to their subordination if they are not fully aware of what their subordination entails and then why it has come about and by arguing that in situations of (domestic, sexual) violence, women are always oppressed before the violence takes place – by the forces of social order – and cannot collude because they are not fully conscious, never mind autonomous (p. 225).

Yet is consciousness always possible – or even desirable? Furthermore, is the insistence on the value of consciousness – even in this context – not simply a reinforcing of the eighteenth-century privileging of reason and rationality and therefore of masculinity?

While based on some premises that feminism would necessarily want to challenge, Bataille's analysis of eroticism none the less offers a useful perspective on how one lives an intense sexuality. For him, eroticism is 'the disequilibrium in which the being consciously calls his own existence in question . . . the deliberate loss of self in eroticism is manifest; no one can question it' (p. 31). A lived sexuality binds life in and towards death: 'Eroticism, it may be said, is assenting to life up to the point of death', and 'Desire is really the desire to die' (pp. 11 and 141). A key point here is that there is deliberate, willed loss of self when engaged in erotic sexuality. Bataille's thinking is useful, because it foregrounds the importance of the notion of the relationship with the self without falling into a narrow 'conscious vs. unconscious dichotomy'. There is a conscious choice to lose balance, sense of self and adherence to normative sexuality, yet this is effected in order to be oneself more fully and to avoid what he conceives of as the danger of sexual exuberance being reduced to a mere thing (pp. 155–8). The fundamental paradox for Bataille is that:

> Sexuality, thought of as filthy or beastly, is still the greatest barrier to the reduction of man to the level of the thing [. . .]
> *Animal nature*, or sexual exuberance, is that which prevents us from being reduced to mere things.
> *Human nature*, on the contrary, geared to specific ends in work, tends to make things of us at the expense of our sexual exuberance. (p. 158)

Bataille's work undermines the hegemony of reason by triangulating willed loss of sense of self, the animal(istic) and the human (the social). He also challenges the principles underpinning both self-discipline and societal discipline and organisation, showing how the controlling of sexuality by laws, customs and taboos infects sex with hypocrisy, guilt, exploitation, anxiety and notions of 'perversion'. For Bataille, it is essential to recognise the necessity of transgression, particularly with regard to the place of violence, which can lead to the liberation of the instincts: he notes that there is a 'complementary relationship uniting taboos which reject violence with acts of transgression which set it free' (p. 49). Without a sense of transgression, he suggests, 'we no longer have the feeling of freedom that the full accomplishment of the sexual act demands, – so much so that a scabrous situation is sometimes necessary to a blasé individual for him to reach the peak of enjoyment' (p. 107).

Most of Escalle's women yearn to leave their homes, both physically and mentally: they are profoundly dissatisfied, unwanted, unloved and lost, seemingly congenitally useless and at a loose end, their lives deadened by ennui. The only domain in which they can exercise choice is that of sexuality, where they choose to be victims in order to experience some sort of intensity and also to find some sort of comfort (cf. *Où est-il cet amour*, pp. 107 and 114). For instance, in *Où est-il cet amour*, after Léo has penetrated Anne with a crude dildo he has made himself from a block of wood, he decides to sodomise her with his fingers, his face becoming ever more distorted as he ploughs deeper into her. She accepts this mutely and muses:

> C'est cela l'amour? songe-t-elle.
> Il se fait plus violent.
> Son corps meurtri n'existe plus. Elle n'en finit pas de frissonner. (p. 68)

> (So is this what love is, she wonders.
> He penetrates her more and more violently.
> Her bruised body no longer exists. She trembles over and over and over again.)

Gayle Rubin shows how contemporary sexual norms differentiate between
'good sex' which is broadly heterosexual, marital, monogamous and reproductive and 'bad sex', which is the sex of the unmarried, gay or lesbian, promiscuous, non-procreative and those who engage in casual and/or
sado-masochistic sex.[14] According to these norms, Escalle's women are all
clearly practitioners of 'bad sex' and deviant with regard to the espoused
and lived norms of most of her readers. However, while on reading the
novels, one cannot but be shocked by the violence and the humiliation the
women undergo, one also accepts their treatment, first, because it is presented so directly, without either comment or hyperbolic language, and
secondly, because the women so clearly choose a sexuality that is abusive
for their own internal reasons.

The feminist philosopher, Linda LeMoncheck, argues that sexuality
should not be divided into 'good' and 'bad' or 'normal' and 'perverse', but
should be rethought as 'a differentiated category of nonstigmatized sexual
variation'.[15] She further argues that from such a perspective:

> both normal and perverse sex become forms of sexual difference. Within
> this framework, no sexual preference is advantaged by being 'normal' . . .
> understanding both the normal and the perverse as two types of sexual
> difference from the 'view from somewhere different' has the added benefit
> of revealing the ways in which normative judgements about sex may
> involve pragmatics *and* aesthetics *and* ethics. (p. 108)

The potential triangulation of aesthetics and pragmatics with ethics is a
radical step, but a creatively enabling one – one which helps us to view
Escalle's women and their choices more positively, since their decisions
often avoid or bypass the ethical (which none the less remains as a backdrop), as they opt for particular situations for pragmatic, self-protecting
and self-furthering reasons (and occasionally, in an almost Augustinian
way, as with Pauline in *Pulsion*, so that language and expression can give
shape to their lives).

Escalle's women undoubtedly make masochistic choices. Yet does this
make them perverse? In *A Defence of Masochism*, Anita Phillips argues that:
'We are all masochists – at least some of the time, in some form or other,
because in an important way, the sense of a self depends on it'.[16] She highlights the fact that post-feminist women can consciously choose masochism, but that this means that 'masochism, once the province of the man
who wanted to enjoy the feeling of being placed in an inferior position, can
now be seen as a problem for women, who have repudiated secondary

status and striven for equality' (pp. 48–9). Crucially, her reading of this so-called perversion argues that masochism 'is not so much about bringing pleasure to an existing suffering but about bringing sensation to a state of unfeeling' (p. 63). Escalle's women do not seek to understand or justify; they simply seek to escape from unfeeling by following their instincts – which may seem abnormal, unnatural or perverted to some readers. In many ways, her novels are challenges to, even attacks on, the power of the normal. It is, however, important to remember that the normal is not, and should not be, equated with the natural, but that it is the normal which holds sway in society. Furthermore, we should remember that even the natural is a category that is suspect and invariably context-dependent.

As Phillips argues, in psychoanalytic terms, when a woman chooses masochism in a relationship, sado-masochism can be seen as representing masculine domination and feminine submission in a pure form, with the masochist being 'a woman with a problem: she cannot separate from her mother . . . she has difficulties in becoming *psychologically* autonomous' (p. 52). In this scenario, the woman has an image of a good, powerful mother and protects this fantasy from destruction by 'inhibiting her own aggression, which leads her to identify with a sadist instead to get a vicarious sense of power and freedom' (p. 52). Escalle's novels are striking for their depictions of violent and abusive sex, but it is important to note that the relationships that her women have with men and sex are all bound up with their relationships with their (abusive and cruel) mothers. Maternal love is to be found only in surrogate mothers: for instance, the sole affection and innocent, playful tenderness Anne ever experiences in *Où est-il cet amour* comes from Fatima, the mother of Jilali, the gardener (p. 79).

Each of the novels begins with an evocation of the ways in which the protagonists have been mistreated by their mothers. In *Un long baiser*, the old woman remembers how she was tortured by her mother, who tied her up until she cried and then simply watched her struggling, telling her imperiously to be silent. However, as she recalls these scenes, her attitude changes: 'A présent elle est cet enfant qui veut bouger et cette femme qui l'en empêche' (p. 13) (Right now she is both the child who wants to move about and the woman who stops her from doing so). The aggressive anti-identification with the mother is now doubled by an identification with herself as mother, which makes her both victim and oppressor – of herself. In *Pulsion*, Pauline's mother feels a 'visceral hatred' for her eldest daughter, whom she says, she could happily see die without feeling the slightest regret (pp. 16–17). *Herbert jouit* begins with 'an atrocious nightmare' in which Renée's mother is torturing her by disembowelling her with a knife, an experience which the child experiences as an almost sexual 'ecstasy' (p. 7). Renée returns to this scene later, when she 'offers' her ageing body to her dead mother and muses in chillingly eucharistic overtones: 'Tu cherches dans le sang et le corps de ta fille l'idée que tu te faisais de l'amour, de l'enfance, de la maternité' (p. 137) (You seek in the blood and the body of your daughter your idea of what love, childhood and maternity should be). In *Où est-il cet amour*, Anne is often locked in a wardrobe for long periods of time – according to her mother, for 'educational' purposes, so that she learns about 'the vicissitudes of life' (p. 10). Her mother hurts her physically when punishing her, yet it is in the wardrobe, cramped and howling that Anne has her first erotic experiences (pp. 10–11).

The novels suggest clearly that the 'perverse' and self-abusive sexualities of the women characters are formed in childhood, notably in relationship to (and against) cruel mothers who withhold love. However, one must avoid the temptation of thinking simplistically that Escalle's mothers are responsible – and blamed – for their daughters' adult perversities. As Bataille has affirmed, eroticism 'is the problematic part of ourselves' (p. 273). Much more than her men, who conform to stereotypical norms of dominant male heterosexual behaviour, Escalle's women live out unconventional and challenging sexualised lives – because that is how they are. Psychoanalytical and psychological theories and models can aid us to understand the context in which they live and submit, but they are not sufficient, since we are dealing here with fictions, which have meaning on their own terms, rather than as narrations of psychodramas.

Foucault has persuasively argued that in Sade, 'sex is without any norm or intrinsic rule that might be formulated from its own nature'.[17] I would not argue that Escalle is a Sadean woman in any simplistic way, in that her expository scrutiny of 'perverse' sexual practices and sexualities has more to do with the (inner and social) politics of identity than with the philosophy of being. However, it is undeniable that she is a transgressive writer in the sense that she chooses to write about subjects that are surrounded by taboos and moral interdictions. Her novels involve complex personal relationships between people who are emotionally damaged, psychologically unstable and sexually disturbed. At least, that is how we may initially judge them. Yet the reader is drawn into these fictional worlds as if they are quite normal – and certainly the novels present them as such. Escalle deals with the very real problems of abuse, exploitation, emotional inadequacy, violence and 'perverse' sexuality. However, in reality, these issues are all too often marginalised, relegated to specialised discourses or simply not discussed at all, or, at worst, criminalised.

Escalle's work confronts the oppressive power of the normal by saying – simply, directly – that another world, another way of living, is (also) normal, one in which the marginal, the silenced and the occulted become mainstream and are posited as the 'norm'. As a creator of fictions, Escalle can and does establish her universe with authority, in a prose which is clear, confident and focused. These novels do not request understanding; they *state* and so compel acceptance, even if only at the time of their reading. The media have been unjust to Escalle in over-rapidly compartmentalising her as one of the 'new barbarians'. Her work is best seen as belonging in the long tradition of exploration of the erotic and of the self's relationship with it that in France is associated especially with such names as Sade and Bataille. However, as her discourse itself reveals, explicitly or intertextually, the engagement is also with psychoanalysis, with Christianity, and with the problematics of post-colonialism. These works are very modern; they also speak of issues which are in us all, but which society silences for its own reasons of control. To read Escalle is not a pleasurable experience, that is certain. However, both intellectually and emotionally, it is immensely challenging and enriching to read her novels which successfully dare to give voice to the silenced and to open the horizons of the blinkered.

Notes

1 See Didier Jacob, 'Les nouveaux barbares', in *Le Nouvel Observateur*, 1816 (26 August 1999), http://archives.nouvelobs.com/.

2 See Isabelle Falconnier, *L'Hébdo*, 35 (2 September 1999), www.webdo.ch/hebdo/hebdo_1999/hebdo_35/culture2_35.html.

3 See Damien Le Guay, 'Rentrée féminine?', *France Catholique*, 2714 (12 November 1999), pp. 22–3.

4 Hélène Cixous, *Readings: The Poetics of Blanchot Joyce, Kafka, Kleist, Lispector, and Tsvetayeva*, ed., trans. and introd. Verena Andermatt Conley (New York and London: Harvester Wheatsheaf, 1992), p. 112.

5 Hélène Cixous, 'The last painting or the portrait of God', in *'Coming to Writing' and Other Essays*, introd. Susan Rubin Suleiman, ed. Deborah Jenson, trans. Sarah Cornell, Deborah Jenson *et al.* (Cambridge, MA and London; Harvard University Press, 1991), p. 119.

6 Julia Kristeva, 'Women's time', trans. Alice Jardine and Harry Blake, in Toril Moi (ed.) *The Kristeva Reader* (Oxford: Basil Blackwell, 1986), pp. 187–213 (p. 209).

7 Judith Butler, *Gender Trouble: Feminism and the Subversion of Identity* (New York: Routledge, 1990), p. 5.

8 Nancy J. Chodorow, *Femininities, Masculinities, Sexualities: Freud and Beyond* (London: Free Association Books, 1994), p. 3.

9 See Julia Kristeva, 'Freud and love: treatment and its discontents', trans. Léon S. Roudiez, in Toril Moi (ed.) *The Kristeva Reader* (Oxford: Basil Blackwell, 1986), pp. 238–71 (pp. 256–7).

10 Victor J. Seidler, *Rediscovering Masculinity: Reason, Language and Sexuality* (London and New York: Routledge, 1989), pp. 123–4.

11 See, for instance, Luce Irigaray, *Ce sexe qui n'en est pas un* (Paris: Minuit, 1977), pp. 122 and 133; *This Sex Which is Not One*, trans. Catherine Porter with Carolyn Burke (Ithaca, NY: Cornell University Press, 1985).

12 Nicole-Claude Mathieu, *L'Arraisonnement des femmes: essais en anthropologie des sexes* (Paris: Editions de l'école des hautes études en sciences sociales, 1985), pp. 169–245.

13 Georges Bataille, *Eroticism*, trans. Mary Dalwood (London and New York: Marion Boyars, 1987), p. 131.

14 See Gayle Rubin, 'Thinking sex: notes for a radical theory of the politics of sexuality', in Carole Vance (ed.), *Pleasure and Danger: Exploring Female Sexuality* (London: Pandora Press, 1989), pp. 267–319, especially pp. 280–4.

15 Linda LeMoncheck, *Loose Women, Lecherous Men: A Feminist Philosophy of Sex* (New York and Oxford: Oxford University Press, 1997), p. 108.

16 Anita Phillips, *A Defence of Masochism* (London: Faber & Faber, 1998), p. 5.

17 Michel Foucault, *The History of Sexuality 1: An Introduction*, trans. Robert Hurley (London: Penguin, 1990), p. 149.

Conclusion

One of the major features of this book is its focus on various aspects of the subject and identity as they are conceived and represented in contemporary women's writing in France. The contributors to this volume have overwhelmingly read the works of our chosen writers as tales of, quests for, explorations of, and crises in the self. It should be noted that this self is actually plural and that the selves in question are not necessarily those of the writers (either within or outside the text). Rather, as fictions, they exemplify the kaleidoscopic proliferation of selves that we are as individuals. When we are traumatised and damaged by unspeakable loss, our psychical selves work to protect us; this work consists, as with Louise Lambrichs's Hannah, in a shoring up of our psychical defences until we are sufficiently strong to begin the reparative and creative process of mourning. Art and literature are themselves part of that reparative, healing process. Indeed, we would go further and argue that loss is an intrinsic part of artistic creation. It can take the form of sublimation, or, as in the case of Chantal Chawaf, contamination. Alternatively, loss can take the form of a more conscious attempt to convey its effects and be traceable in the aesthetics of a text, surfacing in motifs, in metaphors, or in form, as for example, in the works of Paule Constant or Sibylle Lacan.

   Our internal selves are also manifest in other ways. Fears and fantasies are given material reality in Marie Darrieussecq's novels of women in crisis, in the literalisation of metaphors pertaining to women's bodies, in the undercurrents of presence and absence, in the void at the heart of emotional relationships. The place of the body in literature and thought is a complex one, since the body can only ever be signified or suggested in literature; it cannot be produced by it. On the other hand, the literary body plays an important part in articulating and shaping the physical body as it is understood and experienced by individuals and by groups. Indeed, as Judith Butler and Elisabeth Bronfen have argued, one might even question whether the body exists outside language and whether our knowledge of it is not always necessarily determined by our precise socio-cultural and historical contexts.[1] The body is one of the most important objects of representation for writers, as is witnessed by Régine Detambel's experiments with textual dissection or by Clotilde Escalle's insistent detailing of the movement of hands or the droolings of an ageing mouth.

The body is also an object of negotiation (between society and the individual, between men and women, between parents and children) – and a central locus of that negotiation. This is particularly true of women's bodies, which are more publicly shared and made visible than men's. While the project of many contemporary women writers is to retrieve their bodies from public gaze, definition and consumption and to speak more directly and personally about their bodies and how they inhabit them, by writing, they also re-enter the public realm. The transposition of our private and personal selves into the public sphere is, as has been shown in this volume, a risky endeavour. Part of the reason why Christine Angot's work is so controversial is because she puts into writing the intimate feelings, secret and unacceptable thoughts, and images that flash through her/her narrator's mind: images such as a baby daughter grown in a flash to an actively sexual woman in *Léonore, toujours*, fantasies, daydreams, the day's conversations turned over, worked over, returning in fragments and out of context. Similarly, Escalle's private worlds of sex and violence, whose transgressions are, actually, part of real lives, shock precisely because they are brought into the public sphere, expressed in and through writing.

If our inner selves are multifaceted, our external, social and embodied selves are even more plural – and fragmented. Our relations with others are themselves multiple, as we are constantly oscillating between our working lives and personas and our private lives and personas, and as we interact with colleagues, teachers, students, with casual acquaintances, with friends, lovers, partners, children and so on. Moreover, the social self is not only multiple but constantly challenged as we navigate relations with others and exist in the tension between the way we see or present ourselves and the way others perceive and judge and react to us. In this context, Agnès Desarthe's protagonists are of particular interest, caught as they are in a web of misunderstanding and exemplifying the gap between self and others even as they reach out and strive to breach that gap. The hybrid

bi-cultural selves of the *beur* narrators and protagonists in the novels by
Farida Belghoul, Ferrudja Kessas and Soraya Nini testify to the complexities of racial and sexual politics in the lives of the children of Algerian
immigrants, while Leïla Sebbar's Shérazade struggles against and flees
from the images that others produce of her. Perhaps the most 'civilised'
thing we can do at the start of the new post-feminist, post-colonial, postmodern millennium is to recognise that we are implicated on both sides of
the identity equation. If the way in which others see us sometimes seems
far removed from the ways in which we see ourselves, we must not forget
that our perspectives on and judgements of others do not fit any more
readily with their own frameworks of self-perception. We are all 'selves in
process' in the modern world.

The modern trend for self-referentiality in literature means that the
writing self is also clearly manifest and, indeed, foregrounded in the work
of a significant number of the contemporary French women writers discussed in this volume. The authorial self as narrator or protagonist is
subject to the same tensions and negotiations as other aspects of the self –
above all, in relation to her readers. Sophie Calle's experiments with
her/self both challenge and implicate the reader in an ethical relation to the
text, in which respect for the other and the self is precisely at stake. In
Detambel's *L'Ecrivaillon*, the writing self is embodied, only to be carefully
and lovingly dissected. In a different way, Sylvie Germain's novels engage
the reader in a politics of reading in which the author's self invades the text
in the form of her religious belief to the extent of closing off freedom of
interpretation.

As the last chapter identifies, a recurrent theme in Escalle's novels is
the difficult relationships her female protagonists have with their mothers,
and it is striking how frequently variations on the mother–daughter theme
have appeared throughout this volume. However one considers it, the
mother–daughter relationship is important, influential – and also charged
with emotion, with ambivalence, with the sorrow of loss, or, more rarely in
literature, with pleasure. Angot as an example of the latter may surprise, but
she is one of the few writers here (along with Louise Lambrichs) who treat
the theme from the perspective of the mother.[2] The prevalence of problematic mother–daughter relations does not simply point to – or reinforce –
the blaming of mothers for the state in which the daughters find themselves. Rather, it acknowledges that for both mothers and daughters, the
relationship is formative – a key player in women's sense of self, even if, as
Christiane Baroche seems to suggest, alternative maternal relationships

(with 'surrogate' mothers) may supplement it. For their part, Marie Redonnet's motherless characters attempt, with varying degrees of success, to create memory texts in their quest for the grounding and self-representation they lack. Sebbar's Shérazade reconnects with her mother through identification with a book of photographs of Algerian women, and as such is able to begin to assume an identity of her own.

The work of Leïla Sebbar is now well known and fairly widely commentated, but the majority of the chapters in this volume are a starting point on the authors and the works they discuss. They are among the first sustained analyses to be published on these writers and texts, and they attest to the richness of the writing that has been produced by women in France since the beginning of the 1990s. They also attest to the breadth of approaches that scholars are taking to contemporary women's writing. All the contributors engage closely with the individual works, carrying out close readings of the aesthetics, the form and the workings of the text. A remarkable feature is that these very close readings lead the various critics to draw on a range of different theoretical and interpretative frameworks from within literary criticism and, importantly, beyond – from psychoanalysis to linguistics, through trauma and post-colonial studies and performance art. The critical discourse generated by these interdisciplinary forays produces fruitful and thought-provoking analyses of contemporary writing and confirms its relevance to contemporary issues. However, this new literature does not simply offer a reflection of current issues at stake for women – or womanness. Indeed, it is not one 'new literature', and even less a coherent body of work. Rather, in all their diversity, the texts discussed in this volume offer spaces for working through, for exploring and for speculating on the freedoms and limitations, the pleasures and pains of being – and constantly renewing what it is to be – a woman, as we, both women and men, advance – and read ourselves – into the twenty-first century.

Notes

1 See Judith Butler, *Gender Trouble: Feminism and the Subversion of Identity* (New York and London: Routledge, 1990); *Bodies that Matter: On the Discursive Limits of Sex* (New York and London: Routledge, 1993); Elisabeth Bronfen, 'The body and its discontents', in Avril Horner and Angela Keane (eds) *Body Matters: Feminism, Textuality, Corporeality* (Manchester and New York: Manchester University Press, 2000), pp. 109–23.

2 The rarity of the mother's perspective in a wider breadth of literature is confirmed in Marianne Hirsch, *The Mother–Daughter Plot: Narrative, Psychoanalysis, Feminism* (Bloomington and Indianapolis: Indiana University Press, 1989).

INDIVIDUAL AUTHOR BIBLIOGRAPHY

Christine Angot

WORKS

Vu du ciel (Paris: L'Arpenteur Gallimard, 1990).

Not to be (Paris: L'Arptenteur Gallimard, 1991).

Léonore, toujours (Paris: L'Arpenteur Gallimard, 1994; Fayard, 1997).

Interview (Paris: Fayard, 1995).

Les Autres (Paris: Fayard, 1997).

L'Usage de la vie (Paris: Fayard, 1998).

Sujet Angot (Paris: Fayard, 1998).

L'Inceste (Paris: Stock, 1999).

'La Page noire', *Libération* (6 November 1999).

'Sujet: l'amour', *L'Infini*, 68 (1999).

'Ecrire n'est pas une vie', *Sites*, 3(2) (autumn 1999), 267–72.

Quitter la ville (Paris: Stock, 2000).

Normalement followed by *La Peur du lendemain* (Paris: Stock, 2001).

Pourqui le Brésil? (Paris: Stock, 2002)

INTERVIEWS

Guichard, Thierry, '"En littérature, la morale n'existe pas"', *Le Matricule des Anges*, 21 (November–December 1997), www.lmda.net/mat/MAT02127.html.

SELECTED SECONDARY CRITICISM

Cornelius, Nathalie G., 'Christine Angot, *Quitter la ville*', *French Review*, 75(2) (December 2001), 380–1.

Guichard, Thierry, 'Christine Angot, la bâtarde libre', *Le Matricule des Anges*, 21 (November–December 1997), www.lmda.net/mat/MAT02125.html.

Hughes, Alex, '"Moi qui ai connu l'inceste, je m'appelle Christine" [I have had an incestuous relationship and my name is Christine]: writing and subjectivity in Christine Angot's incest narratives', *Journal of Romance Studies*, 2(1) (spring 2002), 65–77

Le Matricule des Anges, special issue on Angot, 21 (November–December 1997).

Lindon, M., 'Trois, deux, un … Angot', *Libération* (26 August 1999).

An extensive, regularly up-dated website devoted to Angot, with information, reviews and links to interviews and articles, can be found at: http://eva.domeneghini.free.fr.

Christiane Baroche

WORKS

Les Feux du large (Paris: Gallimard, 1975).

L'Ecorce indéchiffrable (Marseille: Sud, 1975).

Chambres, avec vue sur le passé (Paris: Gallimard, 1978).

Pas d'autre intempérie que la solitude (Paris: Gallimard, 1980).

. . .Perdre le souffle (Paris: Gallimard, 1983).

Un soir, j'inventerai le soir (Paradou: Actes Sud, 1983).

Plaisirs amers (Paradou: Actes Sud, 1984).

Les Rimes intérieures, I: du vertige et du vent (Marseille: Sud, 1984).

L'Hiver de beauté (Paris: Gallimard, 1987; extended *folio* edition, 1990).

. . .Et il ventait devant ma porte (Paris: Gallimard, 1989).

'Si j'étais l'Homme que tu dis. . .', in *Maupassant, Baroche, Marsan*, Triolet 3 (Paris: Nouvelles Nouvelles, 1989), pp. 53–73.

Giocoso, ma non. . . (Paris: Presses de la Renaissance, 1990).

Le Boudou (Paris: Grasset, 1991).

Le Collier, illustrations Frédéric Clément (Paris: Ipomée-Albin Michel, 1992).

'Le Recensement de Noé, ou la fausse légende d'un monde du deuxième type', *Brèves*, 39 (1992), 22–31.

Les Ports du silence (Paris: Grasset, 1992).

Bonjour, gens heureux. . . (Paris: Julliard, 1993).

Rimes intérieures II: à la tour abolie, special issue, *Sud*, 105 (1993).

La Rage au bois dormant (Paris: Grasset, 1995).

Les Petits Bonheurs d'Héloïse (Paris: Grasset, 1996).

Ailleurs, sous un ciel pâle. . . (Bordeaux: Le Castor Astral, 1997).

'La nouvelle, don de parole à l'instant', in Johnnie Gratton and Jean-Philippe Imbert (eds), *La Nouvelle hier et aujourd'hui* (Paris: L'Harmattan, 1997), pp. 179–85.

'Alchimie de la lecture', *L'Ecole des Lettres* II, 89(14) (July 1998), 111–17.

Petit traité de mauvaises manières (Paris: Grasset, 1998).

La Petite Sorcière de l'hôpital (Illkirch: Le Verger, 1999).

'L'homme de ma vie', *Lettres Internationales*, 14 (June 1999), 112–15.

L'Homme de cendres (Paris: Grasset, 2001).

ENGLISH TRANSLATIONS

'My birthplace' ('Mon pais Arlaten') and 'The God' ('Le Dieu'), trans. Katherine Massam and Gill Rye, *Interstice*, 2 (spring/summer 1997), 40–3; 45–7 (from *Les Rimes intérieurs*).

Bio-bibliography and a selection of poems by Baroche, in Martin Sorrell (ed. and trans.), *Elles: A Bilingual Anthology of Modern French Poetry by Women* (Exeter: University of Exeter Press, 1995), pp. 25–37.

'Do you remember the rue d'Orchampt?' ('Tu te souviens de la rue d'Orchampt?', trans. Elizabeth Fallaize, in Elizabeth Fallaize (ed.), *The Oxford Book of French Short Stories* (Oxford and New York: Oxford University Press, 2002, pp. 295–310) (short story from *Chambres avec vue sur le passé*).

INTERVIEWS

'L'abîme et après' (Entretien avec G.-O. Châteaureynaud et François Coupry), *Roman*, 18 (March 1987), 67–77.

'Conversation avec Christiane Rolland Hasler', *Brèves*, 39 (1992), 3–21.

'Entretien avec Christiane Baroche' (Denise le Dantec), *L'Ecole des Lettres* II, 84(12) (15 May 1993), 79–83.

'Passions' (Interview with Françoise Colpin), *Regards*, 7 (November 1995), 48.

SELECTED SECONDARY CRITICISM

Constant, Paule, 'Regards intérieurs' (review of *Le Boudou*), *Revue des Deux Mondes* (June 1991), 158–9.

Delorme, Marie-Laure, 'De souvenirs en souvenirs' (review of *La Rage au bois dormant*), *Magazine Littéraire* (September 1995), 75.

Harris, Nadia, 'Elle a vécu, Helga, la jeune Berlinoise' (with Christiane Baroche, 'Une mort suffisante' (from . . . *Et il ventait devant ma porte*), pp. 273–82), in Madeleine Cottenet-Hage and Jean-Philippe Imbert (eds), *Parallèles: anthologie de la nouvelle féminine de langue française* (Quebec: L'Instant même, 1996), pp. 283–91.

Lovichi, Jacques, '*L'Hiver de beauté*', *Sud*, 17(73/74) (1987), 275–7.

—— '*Le Boudou*', *Sud*, 99 (1992), 200–2.

Rye, Gill, 'Reading identities with Kristeva and Cixous in Christiane Baroche's *L'Hiver de beauté*', *Paragraph*, 19 (July 1996), 98–113.

—— 'La ré-écriture mythologique: tradition, originalité et identité dans *Un soir, j'inventerai le soir* de Christiane Baroche', in Johnnie Gratton and Jean-Philippe Imbert (eds), *La Nouvelle hier et aujourd'hui* (Paris: L'Harmattan, 1997), pp. 159–65.

—— 'Weaving the reader into the text: the authority and generosity of modern women writers', *Women in French Studies* (1997), 161–72.

—— 'Lire: se lire ou lire les autres?', *L'Ecole des Lettres*, II, 89(14) (July 1998), 89–93.

—— 'Time for change: re(con)figuring maternity in contemporary French literature (Baroche, Cixous, Constant, Redonnet)', *Paragraph*, 21 (November 1998), 54–75.

—— 'Textual genealogies and the legacy of Mme. de Merteuil: reading relations in Christiane Baroche's *L'Hiver de beauté*', *French Forum*, 24 (January 1999), 67–81.

—— 'Women's writing', in Abigail Gregory and Ursula Tidd (eds), *Women in Contemporary France* (Oxford and New York: Berg, 2000), pp. 133–51.

—— *Reading for Change: Interactions between Text and Identity in Contemporary French Women's Writing (Baroche, Cixous, Constant)* (Bern: Peter Lang, 2001).

Tixier, Jean-Max, 'Des *Liaisons dangereuses* à *L'Hiver de beauté* de Christiane Baroche', *L'Ecole des Lettres* II, 83(5) (1991–2), 18–22.

Worton, Michael, 'Le chant de la sirène: les romans de Christiane Baroche', *Sud*, 105 (1993), 73–85.

—— 'The author, the reader, and the text', in Jill Forbes and Michael Kelly (eds), *French Cultural Studies: An Introduction* (Oxford: Oxford University Press, 1995), pp. 191–212.

Farida Belghoul

WORKS

Georgette! (Paris: Bernard Barrault, 1986).

SELECTED SECONDARY CRITICISM

Bacholle, Michele, 'Pushing the limits of autobiography: schizophrenia in the works of Farida Belghoul, Agota Kristof and Milcho Manchevski', *RLA: Romance Languages Annual*, 10(1) (1998), 5–11.

—— *Un passé contraignant: double bind et transculturation* (Amsterdam and Atlanta GA: Rodopi, 2000).

Delvaux, Martine, 'L'ironie du sort: le Tiers Espace de la littérature beure', *French Review*, 68(4) (1995), 681–93.

Durmelat, Sylvie, 'L'apprentissage de l'écriture dans *Georgette!*', in Michel Laronde (ed.), *L'Ecriture décentrée: la langue de l'autre dans le roman contemporain* (Paris: L'Harmattan, 1996), pp. 33–54.

Hargreaves, Alec G., 'Sexualité et ethnicité dans le roman beur', *Revue Celfan/Celfan Review*, 7(1–2) (1987–88), 18–20.

—— 'Resistance and identity in *beur* narratives', *Modern Fiction Studies*, 35 (1989), 87–102.

—— 'Language and identity in beur culture', *French Cultural Studies*, 1 (1990), 47–58.

—— 'History, gender and ethnicity in writing by women authors of Maghrebian origin in France', *L'Esprit Créateur*, 33(2) (1993), 23–34.

Holmes, Diana, *French Women's Writing 1848–1994* (London: Athlone, 1996).

Mainil, Jean, '*Le Baiser de la femme speakerine*: télévision et romans beurs', *Sites*, 1(1) (1997), 125–40.

Preckshot, Judith, '"L'éducation obligatoire" et les voix minoritaires dans les écrits francophones', *French Review*, 74(4) (2001), 660–72.

Rosello, Mireille, '*Georgette!* de Farida Belghoul: télévision et départenance', *L'Esprit Créateur*, 33(2) (1993), 35–46.

Ryan, Angie, 'The construction of the female subject: Belghoul and Colette', in Diana Knight and Judith Still (eds) *Women and Representation* (Nottingham: WIF Publications, 1995), 92–105.

Talahite, Anissa, 'Constructing spaces of transition: "beur" women writers and questions of representation', in Jane Freedman and Carrie Tarr (eds) *Women, Immigration and Identities in France* (Oxford and New York: Berg, 2000), pp. 103–19.

Woodhull, Winifred, 'Ethnicity on the French frontier', in Gisela Brinker-Gabler and Sidonie Smith (eds) *Writing New Identities: Gender, Nation and Immigration in Contemporary Europe* (Minneapolis: University of Minnesota Press, 1997), pp. 31–61.

Sophie Calle

WORKS

Suite vénitienne (Paris: l'Etoile, 1983).

L'Hôtel (Paris: l'Etoile, 1984).

Des histoires vraies (Arles: Actes Sud, 1994).

L'Erouv de Jérusalem (Arles: Actes Sud, 1996).

Doubles-jeux (Paris: Actes Sud, 1998), 7 vols, Book 1: *De l'obéissance* (incl. *Le Régime chromatique* and *Des journées entières sous le signe du B, du C, du W*). Book 2: *Le Rituel d'anniversaire*. Book 3: *Les Panoplies* (incl. *La Garde-robe* and *Le Strip-tease*). Book 4: *A suivre* (incl. *Préambule, Suite vénitienne*, and *La Filature*). Book 5: *L'Hôtel*. Book 6: *Le Carnet d'adresses*. Book 7: *Gotham handbook: New York, mode d'emploi*.

Souvenirs de Berlin-Est (Arles: Actes Sud, 1999).

Disparitions (Arles: Actes Sud, 2000).

Fantômes (Arles: Actes Sud, 2000).

Les Dormeurs, 2 vols (Arles: Actes Sud, 2000).

ENGLISH TRANSLATIONS

Double Game (*Doubles-jeux*) (London: Violette, 1999).

The Detachment/Die Entfernung (translations of *Souvenirs de Berlin-Est*) (G+B Arts International, Arndt & Partner Gallery, no date or place of publication given).

INTERVIEWS

Leith, William, 'A quick Calle', *Observer Life Magazine* (17 January 1999), pp. 17–20.

SELECTED SECONDARY CRITICISM

Baudrillard, Jean, 'Please follow me', in Sophie Calle, *Suite vénitienne* (Paris: l'Etoile, 1983), pp. 83–93.

Bois, Yves-Alain, 'Character study', *Artforum* (April 2000), 126–31.

Chadwick, Whitney, 'Three artists/three women: Orlan, Annette Messager and Sophie Calle', *Sites*, 4(1) (2000), 111–17.

Gratton, Johnnie, 'Degrees of irony in Sophie Calle's *Des histoires vraies*', in Alex Hughes and Andrea Noble (eds), *Phototextualities* (Albuquerque: University of New Mexico Press, 2002).

Grundberg, Andy, 'Photography's dark side: the work of Sophie Calle', in *Crisis of the Real* (New York: Aperture, 1999), pp. 250–3.

Guibert, Hervé, '"Suite vénitienne" de Sophie Calle: le chichi de Sophie', in *La Photo, inéluctablement: recueil d'articles sur la photographie 1977–1985* (Paris: Gallimard, 1999), pp. 377–8.

——'Deux livres de Sophie Calle: les tribulations de Sophie en enfance', in *La Photo, inéluctablement*, pp. 423–8

Kuchler, Susanne, 'The art of ethnography: the case of Sophie Calle', in Alex Coles (ed.), *Site-Specificity: The Ethnographic Turn, de-, dis-, ex-.*, vol. 4 (London: Black Dog, no date given).

Robin, Régine, 'Etre sans trace: Sophie Calle', in *Le Golem de l'écriture: de l'autofiction au Cybersoi* (Montréal: XYZ, 1997), pp. 217–30.

An extensive bibliography of work by and on Calle from 1985 to 1999, including reviews of her exhibitions, is available at www.crousel.com/calle/bib-sc.html (accessed February 2002).

Chantal Chawaf

WORKS

Retable/la rêverie (Paris: Des Femmes, 1974).

Cercoeur (Paris: Mercure de France, 1975).

Blé de semences (Paris: Mercure de France, 1976).

Chair chaude, l'écriture: théâtre (Paris: Mercure de France, 1976).

'La chair linguistique', *Les Nouvelles littéraires* (26 May 1976), p. 18.

Le Soleil et la terre (Paris: Pauvert, 1977).

Rougeâtre (Paris: Pauvert, 1978).

'De *Retable* à *Rougeâtre*', *Des Femmes en Mouvements*, 6 (1978), 86–8.

'Chantal Chawaf, écrivain', *Marie-Claire* (March 1979), p. 30.

Maternité (Paris: Stock, 1979).

Landes (Paris: Stock, 1980).

Crépusculaires (Paris: Ramsay, 1981).

'Des femmes et leurs œuvres', *Magazine Litteraire*, 180 (1982), 36.

Les Surfaces de l'orage (Paris: Ramsay, 1982).

'Aujourd'hui', *Roman*, 5 (1983), 135–40.

'Portrait: écrire à partir du corps vivant', *Lendemains*, 30 (1983), 119–25.

La Vallée incarnate (Paris: Flammarion, 1984).

Elwina, le roman-fée (Paris: Flammarion, 1985).

'Contre la fiction', *Roman*, 18 (1987), 47–64.

L'Intérieur des heures (Paris: Des femmes, 1987).

Fées de toujours (Paris: Plon, 1988).

'La Peur du féminin dans le langage', *Roman*, 25 (1988), 34–45.

'Donner aux émotions leur écriture', *La Quinzaine Littéraire*, 532 (1989), 10.

Rédemption (Paris: Flammarion, 1989).

L'Eclaircie (Paris: Flammarion, 1990).

Le Corps et le verbe – la langue en sens inverse (Paris: Presses de la Renaissance, 1992).

Vers la lumière (Paris: Des femmes, 1993).

Le Manteau noir (Paris: Flammarion, 1998).

Issa (Paris: Flammarion, 1999).

ENGLISH TRANSLATIONS

Mother Love, Mother Earth (*Maternité*), trans. Monique Nadem (London and New York: Garland, 1992).

Redemption (*Rédemption*), trans. Monique Nadem (Normal, IL: Dalkey Archive Press, 1992).

INTERVIEWS

Accad, Evelyne, 'Interview avec Chantal Chawaf', *Présence Francophone*, 17 (1978), 151–61.

Jardine, Alice and Anne Menke (eds), 'Chantal Chawaf', in *Shifting Scenes: Interviews on Women, Writing and Politics in Post-68 France* (New York: Columbia University Press, 1991), pp. 17–31.

SELECTED SECONDARY CRITICISM

Bosshard, Marianne, 'Chantal Chawaf: le magma maternel', *Revue francophone*, 9(1) (spring 1994), 27–38.

—— 'Marie Redonnet et Chantal Chawaf: divergences et convergences dans deux écritures engagées', in Michael Bishop (ed.), *Thirty Voices in the Feminine* (Rodopi: Amsterdam, 1996), pp. 174–81.

—— 'Chantal Chawaf: de l'eu-topie champêtre, intrautérine et féerique à l'uchronie linguistique', in Joëlle Cauville and Metka Zupančič (eds), *Réécriture des mythes: l'utopie au féminin* (Amsterdam: Rodopi, 1997), pp. 75–82.

—— *Chantal Chawaf* (Amsterdam: Rodopi, 1999).

Fallaize, Elizabeth, *French Women's Writing: Recent Fiction* (Basingstoke: Macmillan, 1993).

Hannagan, Valerie, 'Reading as a daughter: Chantal Chawaf revisited', in Margaret Atack and Phil Powrie (eds), *Contemporary French Fiction by Women: Feminist Perspectives* (Manchester: Manchester University Press, 1990), pp. 177–91.

Haxell, Nichola Anne, 'Woman as lacemaker: the development of a literary stereotype in texts by Charlotte Bronte, Nerval, Laine and Chawaf', *Modern Language Review*, 89(3) (July 1994), 540–60.

Ionescu, Mariana, 'La dimension mytho-poétique dans *Vers la lumière* de Chantal Chawaf', *Women in French Studies*, 6 (1998), 56–64.

Powrie, Phil, 'A womb of one's own: the metaphor of the womb-room as a reading-effect in texts by contemporary French women writers', *Paragraph*, 12 (1989), 197–213.

—— 'Myth, allegory and the problematisation of narrative in Chantal Chawaf's *Le Soleil et la terre*', in Helen Wilcox *et al.* (eds), *The Body and the Text: Hélène Cixous, Reading and Teaching* (Brighton: Harvester Press, 1990), pp. 78–86.

Raffy, Sabine, 'L'écriture contre de Chantal Chawaf', *Dalhousie French Studies*, 13 (autumn–winter 1987), 129–34.

Saigal, Monique, 'Comment peut-on créer un nouveau langage feminine aujourd'hui?', in Michael Bishop (ed.), *Thirty Voices in the Feminine* (Amsterdam: Rodopi, 1996), pp. 65–76.

Zupančič, Metka, 'Eurydice et Persephone: paradigmes revisités par Cixous et Chawaf', *Women in French Studies*, 3 (1995), 82–9.

—— 'Chantal Chawaf: la quête de la lumière, entre Demeter, Persephone et Hecate', *Etudes Francophones*, 12(2) (autumn 1997), 165–75.

Paule Constant

WORKS

Ouregano (Paris: Gallimard, 1980).

Propriété privée (Paris: Gallimard, 1981).

Balta (Paris: Gallimard, 1983).

Un monde à l'usage des demoiselles (Paris: Gallimard, 1987).

White spirit (Paris: Gallimard, 1989).

Le Grand Ghâpal (Paris: Gallimard, 1991).

'L'exil des éducatrices', *Papers on French Seventeenth-Century Literature*, 21(41) (1994), 375–9.

La Fille du Gobernator (Paris: Gallimard, 1994).

Confidence pour confidence (Paris: Gallimard, 1998).

ENGLISH TRANSLATIONS

The Governor's Daughter (*La Fille du Gobernator*), trans. Betsy Wing (Lincoln: University of Nebraska Press, 1998).

Trading Secrets (*Confidence pour confidence*), trans. Betsy Wing (Lincoln: University of Nebraska Press, 2001).

INTERVIEWS

'L'entretien par Catherine Argand', *Lire* (April 1998), 36–41.

Grondein, Danielle, 'Rencontre: Paule Constant, "On passe notre vie à remonter vers la source"', *Encres Vagabondes*, 19 (2000), 2–7.

'Interview', *L'Officiel d'Afrique*, 10 (December 1983–January 1984), 34–5.

SELECTED SECONDARY CRITICISM

Almira, J., 'Alice au pays des horreurs' (*La Fille du Gobernator*), *Revue des Deux Mondes* (October 1994), 186–9.

Baroche, Christiane, '*Un monde à l'usage des demoiselles*', *Roman*, 19 (June 1987), 185–9.

Cappelletti, Mireille Revol, '*White Spirit* ou les arcanes de la sublimation', in Monique Streiff-Moretti, Mireille Revol Cappelletti and Odile Martinez (eds), *Il senso del nonsenso: scritti in memoria di Lynn Salkin Sbiroli* (Naples: Edizioni Scientifiche Italiane, 1994), pp. 677–710.

Chandernagar, Françoise, 'Femmes entre elles' (*Confidence pour confidence*), *Revue des Deux Mondes* (July–August 1998), 152–6.

Duffy, Patricia, 'Of White Spirit and other cleaning substances', *New Zealand Journal of French Studies*, 14(2) (1993), 38–54.

—— 'Laye versus Constant: a child's perspective of Africa, *Journal of the Australasian Universities Modern Language Association* (AUMLA), 81 (May 1994), 65–79.

Fisher, Claudine, 'Topographie de la maison dans *Propriété privée* de Paule Constant', in Ginette Adamson and Eunice Myers (eds), *Continental, Latin-American and Francophone Women Writers, III* (Lanham and New York: University Press of America, 1997), pp. 163–9.

Martinoir, Francine de, '*Propriété privée*', *La Nouvelle Revue Française*, 347 (1 December 1981), 117–20.

Miller, Margaret Porter, 'In search of shelter: a psychological reading of Paule Constant's fiction' (unpublished PhD thesis, University of Maryland, 2001).

Miller, Margot, 'Introduction', in Paule Constant, *Trading Secrets*, trans. Betsy Wing (Lincoln: University of Nebraska Press, 2001), pp. v–xii.

Rye, Gill, 'Weaving the reader into the text: the authority and generosity of modern women writers', *Women in French Studies*, 5 (1997), 161–72.

—— 'Time for change: re(con)figuring maternity in contemporary French literature (Baroche, Cixous, Constant, Redonnet)', *Paragraph*, 21 (November 1998), 354–75.

—— 'Re(dis)covering one/self: Julia Kristeva's *expérience littéraire* and Paule Constant's little girls', *Journal of the Institute of Romance Studies*, 7 (1999), 303–12.

—— 'The (im)possible ethics of reading: identity, difference, violence and responsibility (Paule Constant's *White spirit*)', *French Studies*, 54 (July 2000), 327–37.

—— 'Women's writing', in Abigail Gregory and Ursula Tidd (eds), *Women in Contemporary France* (Oxford and New York: Berg, 2000), pp. 133–51.

—— *Reading for Change: Interactions between Text and Identity in Contemporary Women's Writing (Baroche, Cixous, Constant)* (Bern: Peter Lang, 2001).

—— 'The name's the thing: Paule Constant's *comédie humaine*', *Nottingham French Studies*, 41(1) (spring 2002), 70–9.

Steadman, Victoria, 'L'intertextualité dans (la) *Propriété privée* de Paule Constant', in Ginette Adamson and Eunice Myers (eds.), *Continental, Latin-American and Francophone Women Writers, IV* (Lanham and New York: University Presses of America, 1987), pp. 193–9.

Vaquin, Agnès, 'L'enfant aux yeux trop pointus' (*Propriété privée*), *La Quinzaine Littéraire* (1 November 1981), 7.

Marie Darrieussecq

WORKS

'La notion de leurre chez Hervé Guibert: décryptage d'un roman-leurre, *L'Incognito*', *Nottingham French Studies*, 34(1) (spring 1995), 82–8.

'L'autofiction, un genre pas sérieux', *Poétique*, 107 (September 1996), 369–80.

Truismes (Paris: POL, 1996).

'Quand je me sens très fatiguée le soir', *L'Infini*, 58 (Summer 1997), 26–8.

Naissance des fantômes (Paris: POL, 1998).

'Marie Redonnet et l'écriture de la mémoire', in Dominique Viart (ed.) *Ecritures contemporaines 1: mémoires du récit* (Paris and Caen: Lettres Modernes Minard, 1998), pp. 177–94.

'Isabel', *L'Infini*, 62 (summer 1998), 16–19.

Le Mal de mer (Paris: POL, 1999).

Précisions sur les vagues (Paris: POL, 1999).

Claire dans la forêt, previously unpublished short story sold with *Elle*, 2848 (31 July 2000).

'Lamarche-Vadel immanquablement', *L'Infini*, 70 (summer 2000), 57–64.

Bref séjour chez les vivants (Paris: POL, 2001).

Le Bébe (Paris: POL, 2002).

ENGLISH TRANSLATIONS

Pig Tales (*Truismes*), trans. Linda Coverdale (London: Faber & Faber, 1997).

My Phantom Husband (*Naissance des fantômes*), trans. Helen Stevenson (London: Faber & Faber, 1999).

Breathing Underwater (*Le Mal de mer*), trans. Linda Coverdale (London: Faber & Faber, 2001).

Undercurrents: A Novel (*Le Mal de mer*), trans. Linda Coverdale (New York: The New Press, 2001).

INTERVIEWS

Baudet, M., 'Marie Darrieussecq, auteur à haute résolution', *Libre Culture* (19 May 1999), p. 21.

Bourcier, Jean-Pierre, 'Marie Darrieussecq: "européenne, féministe et athée"', *La Tribune* (13 November 1996), p. 20.

Garcin, Jérôme, 'Marie Darrieussecq: l'après-*Truismes*', *Le Nouvel Observateur*, 1684 (19–25 February 1998), pp. 88–90.

Gaudemar, Antoine de, 'Darrieussecq, du cochon au volatil', *Libération (Livres)* (26 February 1998), pp. I–III.

Henley, J., 'Parables of Panic', *Guardian* (G2) (16 June 1999), p. 16.

Le Fol, Sébastien, 'Marie Darrieussecq: "Je veux changer la langue!"', *Le Figaro* (11 March 1999), p. 79.

Vantroys, Carole and Catherine Argand, 'Ils publient leur premier roman', *Lire* (September 1996), pp. 34–5.

Weitzmann, M., 'Sup normal', *Les Inrockuptibles* (18 February 1998), pp. 16–18.

Wrobel, Catherine, 'Cochonne rose et humour noir', *France Soir* (4 September 1996), p. 11.

SELECTED SECONDARY CRITICISM

Baron, Anne-Marie, '*Truismes* de Marie Darrieussecq: une expérience pédagogique en classe de seconde', *L'École des Lettres* II, 8 (1997–8), 3–9.

Favre, Isabelle, 'Marie Darrieussecq ou lard de la calorie vide', *Women in French Studies*, 8 (2000), 164–76.

McAllister, N., 'Woolf at the shore', *Observer Review* (13 May 2001), p. 15.

Michel, Christian, '"Le réel dort aussi": un panorama du jeune roman français', *Esprit*, 225 (October 1996), 43–67.

Nettelbeck, Colin W., 'Novelists and their engagement with history: some contemporary French cases', *Australian Journal of French Studies*, 35(2) (May–August 1998), 243–57.

Phillips, John, '*Truismes* by Marie Darrieussecq', in John Phillips, *Forbidden Fictions, Pornography and Censorship in Twentieth Century French Literature* (London: Pluto Press, 1999), pp. 182–92.

Rodgers, Catherine, 'Aucune évidence: les truismes de Marie Darrieussecq', *Romance Studies*, 18(1) (June 2000), 69–81.

Rye, Gill, 'Women's writing', in Abigail Gregory and Ursula Tidd (eds), *Women in Contemporary France* (Oxford and New York: Berg, 2000), pp. 133–51.

Sadoux, Marion, 'Le corps au fantastique: métamorphoses de Marie Darrieussecq', *La Chouette*, 29 (1998), 15–25.

—— 'Marie Darrieussecq's *Truismes*: hesitating between fantasy and truth', *Journal of the Institute of Romance Studies*, 7 (1999), 197–203.

Samoyault, Tiphaine, 'Mer cannibale', *Les Inrockuptibles* (17 March 1999), pp. 58–9.

Agnès Desarthe

Not included here are Desarthe's numerous children's books and her translations (notably of the works by the American writer Alice Thomas Ellis).

WORKS

Quelques minutes de bonheur absolu (Paris: Seuil, 1993).

Un secret sans importance (Paris: Olivier/Seuil, 1996).

Cinq photos de ma femme (Paris: Olivier/Seuil, 1998).

Les Bonnes Intentions (Paris: Olivier/Seuil, 2000).

Preface to *Paris Romance* (Paris: Parigramme, 2000) (a collection of photos).

ENGLISH TRANSLATIONS

'Transient Bliss' (excerpt from *Quelques minutes de bonheur absolu* (pp. 71–83)), trans. Ros Schwartz, in Georgia de Chamberet (ed.), *Xcités: the Flamingo Book of New French Writing* (London: Flamingo, 1999 (1st edn); 2000 (2nd edn)), pp. 69–82.

Five Photos of my Wife (*Cinq photos de ma femme*), trans. Adriana Hunter (London: Flamingo, 2001).

Régine Detambel

WORKS

L'Amputation (Paris: Julliard, 1990).

L'Orchestre et la semeuse (Paris: Julliard, 1990).

La Modéliste (Paris: Julliard, 1990).

Le Long Séjour (Paris: Julliard, 1991).

La Quatrième Orange (Paris: Julliard, 1992).

Les Ecarts majeurs (Paris: Julliard, 1993).

Le Vélin (Paris: Julliard, 1993).

Graveurs d'enfance (Paris: Christian Bourgois, 1993).

La Lune dans le rectangle du patio (Paris: Gallimard, 1994).

Le Jardin clos (Paris: Gallimard, 1994).

Le Ventilateur (Paris: Gallimard, 1995).

Album (Paris: Calmann-Lévy, 1995).

Blasons d'un corps masculin (Montpellier: Via Voltaire, 1996).

La Verrière (Paris: Gallimard, 1996).

Colette. Comme une flore, comme un zoo. Un répertoire des images du corps (Paris: Stock, 1997).

Solos (Paris: Gallimard Jeunesse, 1997).

La Comédie des mots (Paris: Gallimard Jeunesse, 1997).

Les Massachusetts prennent la plume (Paris: Gallimard, Folio Junior, 1997).

L'Arbre à palabres (Paris: Flammarion, Castor poche, 1997).

L'Avarice (Paris: Centre Pompidou, 1998).

Le Prince aux pinces d'or (Paris: Flammarion, Faim de loup, 1998).

Ernest Poustoufle danse la javanaise (Paris: Flammarion, Castor poche, 1998).

Ernest Poustoufle cavale après M. Cruciphore (Paris: Flammarion, Castor poche, 1998).

Le Poème indigo (Paris: Gallimard Jeunesse, 1998).

Le Valet de carreau (Paris: Gallimard Jeunesse, 1998).

Le Mystère de la dame de fer (Paris: Gallimard Jeunesse, 1998).

Elle ferait battre les montagnes (Paris: Gallimard, 1998).

L'Ecrivaillon ou l'enfance de l'écriture (Paris: Gallimard, 1998).

Les Contes d'apothicaire (Paris: Gallimard, 1998).

Le Rêve de Tanger (Paris: Thierry Magnier, 1998).

La Ligne âpre (Paris: Julliard, 1998).

La Nouvelle comédie des mots (Paris: Gallimard Jeunesse, 1999).

La Patience sauvage (Paris: Gallimard, 1999).

Icônes (Seyssel: Champ Vallon, 1999).

Premier Galop (Paris: Gallimard Jeunesse, 1999).

Ernest Poustoufle fait son numéro (Paris: Flammarion, Castor poche, 1999).

Le Mémo des gens merveilleux (Paris: Hachette Jeunesse, 1999).

La Fille mosaïque (Paris: Gallimard Jeunesse, 1999).

Blasons d'un corps enfantin (Montpellier: Fata Morgana, 2000).

La Chambre d'écho (Paris: Gallimard, 2001).

SELECTED SECONDARY CRITICISM

'Régine Detambel' (author feature), *Le Matricule des Anges*, 17 (September–October 1996), see www.lmda.net.

Allera, Emilie and Elisabeth Beaumont, *Gammes en mots majeurs: autour de Régine Detambel* (Montpellier: SUFCO Université Paul Valéry, D.U. Réalisations audiovisuelles).

Houppermans, Sjef, 'Le jardin clos de Régine Detambel', in Michael Bishop (ed.), *Thirty Voices in the Feminine* (Amsterdam and Atlanta, GA: Rodopi, 1996), pp. 151–65.

Lebrun, Jean-Claude, 'Régine Detambel ne nous épargne rien: le tranchant d'une prose', Cultures, *L'Humanité* (22 November 1996), www.humanite.presse.fr /journal/1996.

—— 'Régine Detambel: "Meurs et deviens"', Cultures, *L'Humanité* (9 September 1999), www.humanite.presse.fr/journal/1999.

Naudin, Marie, 'Review of *La Patience sauvage*', *The French Review*, 74(3) (February 2001), 597–9.

Clotilde Escalle

WORKS

Un long baiser (Paris: Manya, 1993).

Pulsion (Paris: Zulma, 1996).

'Un cadeau de la mer', *Nouvelle Revue Française*, 526 (November 1996), pp. 105–7.

Herbert jouit (Paris: Calmann-Lévy, 1999).

Où est-il cet amour (Paris: Calmann-Lévy, 2001).

SELECTED SECONDARY CRITICISM

Rye, Gill, 'Women's writing' in Abigail Gregory and Ursula Tidd (eds), *Women in Contemporary France* (Oxford and New York: Berg, 2000), pp. 133–51.

—— 'New women's writing in France', *Modern and Contemporary France*, 10(2) (May 2002), 165–75.

Worton, Michael, 'Looking for kicks: promiscuity and violence in contemporary French fiction', *Nottingham French Studies*, 37(1) (spring 1998), special issue, 'French erotic fiction: ideologies of desire', ed. Jean Mainil, pp. 89–105.

Sylvie Germain

WORKS

Le Livre des nuits (Paris: Gallimard, 1985)

Nuit-d'Ambre (Paris: Gallimard, 1987).

Jours de colère (Paris: Gallimard, 1989).

Opéra muet (Paris: Maren Sell, 1989).

L'Enfant Méduse (Paris: Gallimard, 1991).

La Pleurante des rues de Prague (Paris: Gallimard, 1992).

Immensités (Paris: Gallimard, 1993).

Patience et songe de lumière : Vermeer (Charenton: Flohic, 1993).

Les Echos du silence (Paris: Desclée de Brouwer, 1996).

Eclats de sel (Paris: Gallimard, 1996).

Céphalophores (Paris: Gallimard, 1997).

L'Encre du poulpe (Paris: Gallimard, 1998).

Bohuslav Reynek à Petrkov: un nomade en sa demeure (Paris: Christian Pirot, 1998).

Tobie des marais (Paris: Gallimard, 1998).

Etty Hillseum (Paris: Pygmalion, 1999).

Cracovie à vol d'oiseau (Monaco: Rocher, 2000).

Grande nuit de Toussaint (with Jean-Michel Fauquet) (Cognac: Le Temps qu'il fait, 2000).

Célébration de la paternité: regards sur saint Joseph (co-authored with Eliane Gondinet-Wallstein) (Paris: Albin Michel, 2001).

ENGLISH TRANSLATIONS

The Book of Nights (*Le Livre des nuits*), trans. Christine Donougher (Sawtry: Dedalus, 1992).

The Book of Nights (*Le Livre des nuits*), trans. Christine Donougher (Boston, MA: D. R. Godine, 1993).

Night of Amber (*Nuit-d'Ambre*), trans. Christine Donougher (Sawtry: Dedalus, 1995).

Night of Amber (*Nuit-d'Ambre*) trans. Christine Donougher (Boston, MA: D. R. Godine, 1999).

Days of Anger (*Jours de colère*), trans. Christine Donougher (Sawtry: Dedalus, 1993).

The Medusa Child (*L'Enfant Méduse*), trans. Liz Nash (Sawtry: Dedalus, 1994).

The Weeping Woman on the Streets of Prague (*La Pleurante des rues de Prague*), trans. Judith Landry, with an interview by Elizabeth Young and introduction by Emma Wilson (Sawtry: Dedalus, 1993).

Infinite Possibilities (*Immensités*), trans. Liz Nash (Sawtry: Dedalus, 1998).

The Book of Tobias (*Tobie des marais*), trans. Christine Donougher (Sawtry: Dedalus, 2000).

INTERVIEWS

Carbone, Bruno, Jean-Pierre Foullonneau *et al.*, (Poitiers: Office du livre de Poitou-Charentes, 1994), http://perso.wanadoo.fr/office.du.livre/Pages/residents/germain.html.

Le Dantec, Denise, 'Entretien avec Sylvie Germain', *Ecole des Lettres II*, 1 (1994–5), 57–60.

Magill, Michèle, 'Entretien avec Sylvie Germain', *French Review*, 73(2) (1999–2000), 334–40.

Nicolas, Alain, 'Sylvie Germain et les anges', *L'Humanité* (18 October 1996), www.humanite.presse.fr/journal/96/96-10/96-10-18/96-10-18-080.html.

Schwarze, Waltraud, 'Gespräch mit Germain', *Sinn und Form* 44 (1992), 231–42.

Tison, P., 'Sylvie Germain: l'obsession du mal' (Germain discusses *L'Enfant Méduse*), *Magazine Littéraire* 286 (1991), 64–6.

SELECTED SECONDARY CRITICISM

Bacholle, Michèle, '*L'Enfant Méduse* de Sylvie Germain, ou Eurydice entre deux éclipses', *Religiologiques*, 15 (spring 1997), www.unites.uquam.ca/religiologiques/no15/bacholle.html.

Begue, Sylvain, '*Le Livre des nuits* de Germain: rôle du double et thème de l'initiation dans l'œuvre', *Recherches sur l'Imaginaire*, 20 (1990), 13–25.

Berthet, Jocelyne, 'Pour une métaphysique du déchet chez Sylvie Germain', *Iris*, 19 (2000), 93–102.

Bishop, Michael, 'Modes de conscience: Germain, N'Diaye, Lépront et Sallenave, *La Revue des Lettres Modernes*, 1425–30 (1999), 99–114.

Blanckeman, Bruno, 'Les mondes parallèles: Antoine Volodine, *Le Port intérieur*, Sylvie Germain, *Eclats de sel*', *Prétexte*, 11 (autumn 1996), 69–73.

Boblet-Viart, Marie-Hélène, 'From epic writing to prophetic speech: *Le Livre des nuits* and *Nuit-d'Ambre*', *Esprit Créateur*, 40(2) (2000), 86–96.

Fisher, Claudine Guégan, 'Germain, la falseuse de mythes', *Revue Francophone*, 7(2) (1992), 131–43.

Kwaschin, J., 'Noires clartés de Germain', *La Revue Nouvelle*, 95(1) (1992), 92–7.

Lucas, Françoise, 'Quand voir c'est faire: l'énonciation performative et le trou de la serrure', *Etudes Littéraires*, 28(3) (1996), 29–42.

Montoro-Araque, Mercedes, 'Sarra, Anna, Deborah... Du féminin dans le merveilleux de Sylvie Germain', *Cahiers du Gerf*, 6 (1999), 135–50; also available at www.u-grenoble3.fr/gerf/articles/Montoro-araque.html.

——'L'esthétique du "corps-déchet" de cette fin de siècle: Virginie Despentes et Sylvie Germain', *Iris*, 19 (2000), 103–14.

Schaffner, A., 'L'Europe centrale dans les derniers romans de Germain', in J. Lévi-Valensi and A. Fenet (eds) *Le Roman et l'Europe* (Paris: PUF, 1997), pp. 341–52.

Solesmes, M., *Entre désir et renoncement* (dialogue avec Julia Kristeva, Sylvie Germain *et al.*), (Paris: Dervy, 1999).

Wolfreys, Julian, 'Affirmative memories, resistant projections: Sylvie Germain's *La Pleurante des rues de Prague*', in *The Rhetoric of Affirmative Resistance: Dissonant Identities from Carroll to Derrida* (New York: St Martin's; Houndsmill, Macmillan, 1997), pp. 155–93.

Ferrudja Kessas

WORKS

Beur's story (Paris: L'Harmattan, 1990).

SELECTED SECONDARY CRITICISM

Hargreaves, Alec G., 'History, gender and ethnicity in writing by women authors of Maghrebian origin in France', *L'Esprit Créateur*, 33(2) (1993), 23–34.

Ireland, Susan, 'Writing at the crossroads: cultural conflict in the work of beur women writers', *French Review*, 68(6) (1995), 1022–34.

Sybille Lacan

WORKS

Un père: puzzle (Paris: Folio, 1994).

Points de suspension (Paris: Gallimard, 2000).

SELECTED SECONDARY CRITICISM

Anon., 'La statue du commandeur', *Le Monde Radio-Télévision* (24 July 1995), p. 30.

Baroche, Christiane, 'Review of *Un père: puzzle*', *Magazine Littéraire* (1 March 1997), p. 95.

Delvaux, Martine, 'Who's who? *Un père* de Sibylle Lacan', in Lucie Lequin and Catherine Mavrikakis (eds), *La Francophonie sans frontière* (Paris: L'Harmattan, 2001), pp. 225–35.

Louise L. Lambrichs

WORKS

Le Cercle des sorcières (Paris: La Différence, 1988).

La Dyslexie en question (Paris: Robert Laffont, 1989).

Journal d'Hannah (Paris: La Différence, 1993).

La Verité médicale (Paris: Robert Laffont, 1993).

L'aimer avant qu'il naisse, with Jean-Pierre Relier (Paris: Robert Laffont, 1993).

L'Art de faire autrement des enfants comme tout le monde, with Réné Frydman (Paris: Robert Laffont, 1994).

Le Livre de Pierre (Paris: La Différence, 1995).

Le Jeu du roman (Paris: La Différence, 1995).

A ton image (Paris: L'Olivier/Seuil, 1998).

Les Revoltés de Villefranche, with Mirko Grmek (Paris: Seuil, 1998).

Les Fractures de l'âme, with Fabrice Dutot (Paris: Robert Laffont, 1999).

Aloïs ou la nuit devant nous (Paris: Olivier/Seuil, 2002).

ENGLISH TRANSLATION

Hannah's Diary (Journal d'Hannah), trans. Siân Reynolds (New York: Quartet Books, 1999).

Soraya Nini

WORKS

Ils disent que je suis une beurette (Paris: Fixot 1993).

Hip-hop, illustrations by Farid Boudjellal (Nice: Z'éditions, 1996).

Samia (2000), dir. Philippe Faucon (film script by Phillipe Faucon and Soraya Nini).

SELECTED SECONDARY CRITICISM

Holmes, Diana, *French Women's Writing 1848–1994* (London: Athlone, 1996).

McConnel, Daphne, 'Whose identity crisis is it anyway? Questions of cultural and national identity in two novels by second-generation Maghrebians in France', *LittéRéalité*, 12(1) (2000), 39–49.

McIlvanney, Siobhán, 'Female identity in process in Soraya Nini's *Ils disent que je suis une beurette*', *Modern & Contemporary France*, 6 (1998), 505–17.

—— 'Radicalising convention: feminist readings of literature and language in Soraya Nini's *Ils disent que je suis une beurette*', in Brigitte Rollet and Emily Salines (eds), 'Gender and identities in France', *Working Papers on Contemporary France*, 4 (University of Portsmouth, 1999), 63–71.

Vassberg, Liliane M., 'Immigration maghrébine en France: l'intégration des femmes', *French Review*, 70(5) (1997), 710–20.

Marie Redonnet

WORKS

Le Mort & Cie (Paris: POL, 1985).

Doublures (Paris: POL, 1986).

Splendid Hôtel (Paris: Minuit, 1986).

Forever Valley (Paris: Minuit, 1987).

Rose Mélie Rose (Paris: Minuit, 1987).

'Redonne après Maldonne', *L'Infini*, 19 (1987), 160–3.

Tir & Lir (Paris: Minuit, 1988).

'Redonnet, Marie (1948–)', in Jérôme Garcin (ed.), *Le Dictionnaire: littérature française contemporaine* (Paris: François Bourin, 1988), pp. 358–9.

Mobie-Diq (Paris: Minuit, 1989).

Silsie (Paris: Gallimard, 1990).

'Portraiture 1', *Les Lettres Françaises* (1990), 12–13.

'Réponses pour une question brouillée', *Quai Voltaire*, 2 (1991), 45–8.

'Zori', *Txt*, 26/27 (1991), 33–6.

'Le dernier grand maudit', *Quai Voltaire*, 1 (1991), 33–45.

Seaside (Paris: Minuit, 1992).

Candy story (Paris: POL, 1992).

'Une Petite Arche miraculeuse', *L'Infini*, 38 (1992), 80–7.

Nevermore (Paris: POL, 1994).

Le Cirque Pandor suivi de *Fort Gambo* (Paris: POL, 1994).

'The story of the triptych', in *Rose Mellie Rose*, trans. Jordan Stump (Lincoln: University of Nebraska Press, 1994), pp. 111–20.

Villa Rosa (Charenton: Flohic, 1996).

'Seulement un trou avec n'importe quoi autour', *Europe*, 74(808–9) (1996), 48–55.

'A quoi pensez-vous?', *Libération* (31 December 1999), p. 86.

L'Accord de paix (Paris: Grasset, 2000).

Jean Genet, le poète travesti (Paris: Grasset, 2000).

ENGLISH TRANSLATIONS

Forever Valley, trans. Jordan Stump (Lincoln: University of Nebraska Press, 1994).

Hôtel Splendid, trans. Jordan Stump (Lincoln: University of Nebraska Press, 1994).

Rose Mellie Rose, trans. Jordan Stump (Lincoln: University of Nebraska Press, (1994).

Candy Story, trans. Alexandra Quinn (Lincoln: University of Nebraska Press, 1995).

Nevermore, trans. Jordan Stump (Lincoln: University of Nebraska Press, 1996).

INTERVIEWS

Hassoun, Pascale and Chantal Maillet, 'Entretien avec Marie Redonnet', in *Patio/Psychanalyse 10: l'autre sexe* (Paris: L'Eclat, 1988), pp. 135–43.

Stump, Jordan, 'Interview with Marie Redonnet', in Marie Redonnet, *Forever Valley*, trans. Jordan Stump (Lincoln: University of Nebraska Press, 1994), pp. 103–13.

SELECTED SECONDARY CRITICISM

Bosshard, Marianne, 'Marie Redonnet et Chantal Chawaf: divergences et convergences dans deux écritures engagées', in Michael Bishop (ed.), *Thirty Voices in the Feminine* (Amsterdam and Atlanta, GA: Rodopi, 1996), pp. 174–81.

Cottenet-Hage, Madeleine, 'Redonnet, Marie', in Christiane P. Makward and Madeleine Cottenet-Hage, *Dictionnaire littéraire des femmes de langue française: de Marie de France à Marie Ndiaye* (Paris: Karthala, 1996), pp. 494–6.

Darrieussecq, Marie, 'Marie Redonnet et l'écriture de la mémoire', in Dominique Viart (ed.), *Ecritures contemporaines 1: mémoires du récit* (Paris and Caen: Lettres Modernes Minard, 1998), pp. 177–94.

Fallaize, Elizabeth, 'Filling in the blank canvas: memory, inheritance and identity in Marie Redonnet's *Rose Mélie Rose*', *Forum for Modern Language Studies*, 28 (1992), 320–34.

—— 'Marie Redonnet' in *French Women's Writing: Recent Fiction* (Basingstoke: Macmillan, 1993), pp. 160–75.

Gaudet, Jeannette, 'Marie Redonnet: *Splendid Hôtel*', in *Writing Otherwise: Atlan, Duras, Giraudon, Redonnet and Wittig* (Amsterdam and Atlanta, GA: Rodopi, 1999), pp. 126–61.

Gingrass-Conley, Katharine, 'Check-out time at the *Splendid Hôtel*: Marie Redonnet's new mythological space', *Neophilologus*, 77 (1993), 51–9.

Golopentia, Sanda, 'Ni destin, ni vocation: *Silsie* de Marie Redonnet', in Michael Bishop (ed.), *Thirty Voices in the Feminine* (Amsterdam and Atlanta, GA: Rodopi, 1996), pp. 87–101.

Lebrun, Jean-Claude and Claude Prévost, 'Profil: Marie Redonnet', in *Nouveaux Territoires Romanesques* (Paris: Messidor/Sociales, 1990), pp. 193–8.

Leclerc, Yvan, 'Autour de Minuit', *Dalhousie French Studies*, 17 (1989), 63–74.

Mazza-Anthony, Elizabeth, 'Border crossings in Marie Redonnet's *Splendid (Seaside) Hôtel*', *Studies in Twentieth-Century Literature*, 20 (1996), 491–504.

Motte, Warren, 'Redonnet's symmetries', *French Forum*, 19(2) (1994), 215–28.

Picard, Anne-Marie, 'Dans le paysage, une figure. . . presque féminine: le triptyque de Marie Redonnet', *Australian Journal of French Studies*, 31(2) (1994), 228–40.

—— 'Arrêts sur images: identité et altérité dans *Le Désert mauve* de Nicole Brossard et *Rose Mélie Rose* de Marie Redonnet', *Dalhousie French Studies*, 32 (1995), 101–12.

Rye, Gill, 'Time for change: re(con)figuring maternity in contemporary French literature (Baroche, Cixous, Constant, Redonnet)', *Paragraph*, 21(3) (1998), 354–75.

Schoots, Fieke, 'L'écriture minimaliste', in Michèle Ammouche-Kremers and Henk

Hillenaar (eds), *Jeunes auteurs de Minuit* (Amsterdam and Atlanta, GA: Rodopi, 1994), pp. 127–44.

—— *Passer en douce à la douane: l'écriture minimaliste de Minuit: Deville, Echenoz, Redonnet et Toussaint* (Amsterdam and Atlanta, GA: Rodopi, 1997).

Starre, Evert van der, 'Marie Redonnet', in Michèle Ammouche-Kremers and Henk Hillenaar (eds), *Jeunes auteurs de Minuit* (Amsterdam and Atlanta, GA: Rodopi, 1994), pp. 53–67.

Stump, Jordan, 'Translator's introduction', in Marie Redonnet, *Hôtel Splendid*, trans. Jordan Stump (Lincoln: University of Nebraska Press, 1994), pp. v–ix.

—— 'Separation and permeability in Marie Redonnet's triptych', *French Forum*, 20(1) (1995), 105–19.

—— 'L'eau qui efface, l'eau qui anime: du triptych de Marie Redonnet', in Yolande Helm (ed.), *L'Eau: source d'une écriture dans les littératures féminines franco-phones* (New York: Peter Lang, 1995), pp. 103–11.

—— 'At the intersection of self and other: Marie Redonnet's *Splendid Hôtel*, *Forever Valley* and *Rose Mélie Rose*', in Michael Bishop (ed.), *Thirty Voices in the Feminine* (Amsterdam and Atlanta, GA: Rodopi, 1996), pp. 267–73.

Went-Daoust, Yvette, 'Ecrire le conte de fées: l'œuvre de Marie Redonnet', *Neophilologus*, 77 (1993), 387–94.

Leïla Sebbar

For regularly updated bibliographical and other information, including references to Sebbar's extensive journalistic writings, please refer to www.limag.com. Items marked * may be found at: http://clicnet.swarthmore.edu.

WORKS

'Sur sa culotte en toile de matelas', *Sorcières*, 9 (1977).

On tue les petites filles: essai (Paris: Stock, 1978).

'Si je parle la langue de ma mère', *Les Temps Modernes*, 379 (February 1978).

Le Pédophile et la maman (Paris: Stock, 1980).

Fatima ou les Algériennes au square (Paris: Stock, 1981).

Des femmes dans la maison: anatomie de la vie domestique, (collection of photographs) with Dominique Doan, Luce Penot, Dominique Pujebet (Paris: Nathan, 1981).

Shérazade, 17 ans, brune, frisée, les yeux verts (Paris: Stock, 1982; reprinted 1984, 1995).

Le Chinois vert d'Afrique (Paris: Stock, 1984).

Parle mon fils, parle à ta mère (Paris: Stock, 1984).

Les Carnets de Shérazade (Paris: Stock, 1985).

Lettres parisiennes: autopsie de l'exil, correspondence with Nancy Huston (Paris: Barrault, 1985; J'ai lu, 1999).

'Travail de ménagère, travail d'écrivaine', in *Présence de Femmes: gestes acquis, gestes conquis*, ENAG, 4 (winter 1986), 45–8.*

'Ismaël dans la jungle des villes', illustr. Tito, *Je bouquine*, 29 (1986), 5–59.

J. H. cherche âme sœur (Paris: Stock, 1987).

'L'explosion', in Bernard Magnier (ed.), *Paris-Dakar et autres nouvelles* (Paris: Souffles, 1987).

Génération métisse, photographs by Amadou Gaye, texts by Leïla Sebbar and Eric Favereau, preface by Yannick Noah (Paris: Syros-Alternatives, 1988).

'Si je ne parle pas la langue de mon père', in Adine Sagalyn (ed.), *Voies de pères, voix de filles* (Paris: Maren Sell, 1988).

'Le ravin de la femme sauvage', *Nouvelles Nouvelles*, 15 (summer 1989), 42–52; also in Christine Ferniot (ed.), *Les Meilleures Nouvelles de l'année 89–90* (Paris: Syros-Alternatives, 1990); also in Denise Brahimi (ed.), *Un siècle de nouvelles franco-maghrébines: recueil de textes* (Paris: Minerve, 1992), pp. 177–88.

La Négresse à l'enfant (Paris: Syros Alternatives, 1990).

'Palmes' (1990).*

Femmes des Hauts-Plateaux, Algérie 1960, photographs by Marc Garanger, text by Leïla Sebbar (Paris: La Boîte à Documents, 1990).

Le Fou de Shérazade (Paris: Stock, 1991).

'Le bal' (1991);* also in *Esprit/ Les Cahiers de l'Orient*, 36–37 (1995), 299–306.

Lorient-Québec: l'esclave blanche de Nantes (Quebec: Hurtubise HMH, 1991; Montreal: Gamma, 1996).

'La photographie', in Daniel Zimmermann (ed.), *Trente ans après, nouvelles de la guerre d'Algérie* (Paris: Le Monde Editions/Nouvelles Nouvelles, 1992), pp. 106–12.

Marseille, Marseilles, photographs by Yves Jeanmougin, text by Leïla Sebbar, Nabile Farès and Moncef Ghachem (Marseille: Parenthèses, 1992).

Le Silence des rives (Paris: Stock, 1993).

'Lamentation', in Anouar Abdallah (ed.) *Pour Rushdie: cent intellectuels arabes et musulmans pour la liberté d'expression* (Colibri: La Découverte/Carrefour des littératures, 1993), pp. 270–1.

'Le jasmin' (1993).*

Une enfance d'ailleurs: 17 écrivains racontent, ed. with Nancy Huston, including Leïla Sebbar's 'La moustiquaire' (Paris: Belfond, 1993), pp. 241–53.

'Enquête sur l'exotisme VII: réponses de Leïla Sebbar', *Les Carnets de l'Exotisme*, (1993), 121–2.

'La jeune fille au gilet rouge dans Babel' (1994).*

Chère Taslima Nasreen. . . (Paris: Stock, 1994).

Mémoire de Kabylie: scènes de la vie traditionnelle 1937–1939, ed. with and photographs by Germaine Laoust-Chantreaux, preface by Camille Lacoste-Dujardin, including text by Leïla Sebbar, 'Etrangère, ma sœur' (Aix-en-Provence: Edisud, 1994), pp. 7–9.*

'Shérazade, la syllabe perdue', 'Les Mille et Une Nuits dans les imaginaires croisés', *Cahiers d'Etudes Maghrébines*, 6–7 (1994), 101–2.

Les Yeux de ma mère (play), France-Culture, 1994; (Copenhagen/Gotenburg: Kaleidoscope Corona, 2000).

'Lettre à un groupe d'étudiants en français de l'université de Swarthmore (PA, USA) au sujet de la nouvelle "Le bal"' (12 December 1995).*

La Jeune Fille au balcon (Paris: Seuil, 1996; reprinted 1998).

Le Baiser (Paris: Hachette, 1997; reprinted 1999).

J'étais enfant en Algérie: juin 1962 (Paris: Sorbier, 1997).

Une enfance algérienne (collection of previously unpublished texts edited by Sebbar), including Sebbar's 'On tue les instituteurs' (Paris: Gallimard, 1997; Folio 1999), pp. 189–98.*

'Les femmes: le monde', contribution to debate, *Europe*, 821 (1997), 58–60.

Val-Nord: fragments de banlieue, stories by Leïla Sebbar, photographs by Gilles Larvor (Paris: Syros, 1998).

'La Seine était rouge', *Le Maghreb Littéraire*, 2(3)(1998), 95–8.

'Père et fils', 'Mère et fils', in *2000 ans d'Algérie* (Paris: Séguier, 1998), pp. 159–62.

Soldats (Paris: Seuil, 1999).

'La jeune fille aux Pataugas' (1999).*

La Seine était rouge (Paris: Thierry Magnier, 1999).

'Les mères du peuple de mon père dans la langue de ma mère', including English translation by Dawn M. Cornelio, *Sites*, 3(2) (1999), 389–96.

'Papier d'orange', in *Ecrivains/Sans-Papiers* (Paris: Bérénice-MRAP, 2000), pp. 201–4.

'Le peintre et son modèle', *La Revue des Deux Mondes* (December 2000), pp. 59–63.

'De l'autre côté de la mer, c'est loin', *Revue de Femmes en Méditerranée*, 1–2 (March 2000), 102–5.

Une enfance outre-mer, ed. Leïla Sebbar, including Sebbar's 'Les jeunes filles de la colonie' (Paris: Le Seuil, Point Virgule, 2001), pp. 185–97.

ENGLISH TRANSLATIONS

Sherazade, Missing: Aged 17, Dark Curly Hair, Green Eyes (*Shérazade, 17 ans, brune, frisée, les yeux verts*), trans. Dorothy Blair (London: Quartet Books, 1991; reprinted 1999).

My Mother's Eyes (*Les Yeux de ma mère*), trans. Stephen J. Vogel, in Françoise Kourilsky (ed.), *Playwrights of Exile, An International Anthology* (New York: Ubu Repertory Theater Publications, 1997), pp. 222–61.

Silence on the Shores (*Le Silence des rives*), trans. and introd. Mildred Mortimer, (Lincoln and London: University of Nebraska Press, 2000).

Algerian Childhood (*Une enfance algérienne*), trans. Marjolijn de Jager (Saint Paul, Minnesota: Ruminator Books, 2001).

INTERVIEWS

Notre Librairie, 111 (1992), pp. 55–7, with Tahar Bekri.

Pourquoi, 272 (March 1992), with Jean Eymery.

Cahiers d'Etudes Maghrébines, 8 (1995), 239–44, with Barbara Arnhold.

Nouvelle Donne, 13 (April 1997), 4–7, with Evelyne Bellanfat.

SELECTED SECONDARY CRITICISM

Abu-Haidar, Farida, 'The female persona in Algerian fiction', in Laïla Ibnlfassi and Nicki Hitchcott (eds), *African Francophone Writing: A Critical Introduction* (Oxford and Washington: Berg, 1996), pp. 69–87.

Achour, Christiane, 'Leïla Sebbar: l'île, espace d'exclusion ou de croisement?', in Christiane Achour (ed.), *Diwan d'inquiétude et d'espoir. La littérature féminine algérienne de langue française: anthologie critique* (Algiers: ENAG, 1991), pp. 174–97.

Brahimi, Denise, 'Shérazade d'après "Shérazade, 17 ans, brune, frisée, les yeux verts" de Leïla Sebbar', in Denise Brahimi, *Maghrébines: portraits litteraires* (Paris: L'Harmattan-Awal, 1995), pp. 165–74.

Chaulet-Achour, Christiane, 'Des livres, des femmes, l'Algérie', *Bulletin of Francophone Africa*, 5 (spring 1994), 73–81.

Chikhi, Beïda, 'Shérazade de Leïla Sebbar', in Henri Mitterand (ed.), *Dictionnaire des œuvres du XXe siècle: littératures française et francophone* (Paris: Dictionnaires Le Robert, 1995), p. 448.

Dejeux, Jean, 'Leïla Sebbar, "La négresse à l'enfant: recueil de nouvelles"', *Hommes et Migrations*, 1134 (July 1990), 70–1.

—— 'Leïla Sebbar, *Le Fou de Shérazade*', *Hommes et Migrations*, 1140, (February 1991), 60.

Djaout, Tahar, 'Une écriture au "beur" noir', *Itinéraires et Contacts de Cultures*, 14 (1991), 156–8.

Douin, Jean-Luc, 'Au pays de la peur', *Le Monde des Livres* (16 April 1999), p. I.

Hargreaves, Alec G., 'Writers of Maghrebian immigrant origin in France: French, Francophone, Maghrebian or Beur?', in Laïla Ibnlfassi and Nicki Hitchcott (eds), *African Francophone Writing: A Critical Introduction* (Oxford and Washington: Berg, 1996).

Hugon, Monique, 'Leïla Sebbar ou l'exil productif', *Notre Librairie*, 84 (1986), 32–7.

Laronde, Michel, 'Leïla Sebbar et le roman "croisé": histoire, mémoire, identité', *CELFAN Review*, 7(1–2) (1988), 6–12.

—— 'Métissage du texte beur', *Plurial*, 4 (1993), 101.

—— (ed.) *Autour de Leïla Sebbar* (Toronto: La Source, 2002), forthcoming.

Majumdar, Margaret A., 'A travers le miroir: le regard de l'Autre sur l'Autre', *Bulletin of Francophone Africa*, 5 (spring 1994), 12–27.

Merini, Rafika, *Two Major Francophone Women Writers: Assia Djebar and Leïla*

Sebbar: A Thematic Study of their Works (New York and Oxford: Peter Lang, 2000).

Mortimer, Mildred, 'Language and space in the fiction of Assia Djebar and Leïla Sebbar', *Research in African Literatures*, 19(3) (1988), 301–11.

—— *Journeys through the French African Novel* (London: James Currey, 1991).

—— 'On the road: Leïla Sebbar's fugitive heroines', *Research in African Literatures*, 23(2) (1992), 195–201.

—— 'Mapping new territory: a study of physical displacement in Leïla Sebbar's *Shérazade*', *Journal of Maghrebi Studies*, 1(1/2) (1993), 58–62.

—— 'Coming home: exile and memory in Sebbar's "Le Silence des rives"', *Research in African Literatures*, 30(3) (1999), 125–34.

Orlando, Valérie, 'A la recherche du "devenir-femme" dans le Troisième Espace de culture: "Shérazade: 17 ans, brune, frisée, les yeux verts" de Leïla Sebbar', *Women in French Studies*, 2 (1994), 19–31.

—— *Nomadic Voices of Exile: Feminine Identity in Francophone Literature of the Maghreb* (Athens, OH: Ohio University Press, 1999).

Segarra, Marta, *Leur pesant de poudre: romancières francophones du Maghreb* (Paris: L'Harmattan, 1997).

Simon, Catherine, 'Une enfance algérienne', *Le Monde des Livres* (23 May 1997), p. III.

Abraham, Nicolas and Maria Torok, *L'Ecorce et le noyau* (Paris: Flammarion, 1987); *The Shell and the Kernel: Renewals of Psychoanalysis*, vol. 1, trans. Nicholas T. Rand (Chicago: University of Chicago Press, 1994).

Adamson, Ginette and Eunice Myers (eds), *Continental, Latin-American and Francophone Women Writers* (Lanham and New York: University Press of America, 1987 (vols. I and II); 1997 (vols. III and IV)).

Atack, Margaret and Phil Powrie (eds), *Contemporary French Fiction by Women: Feminist Perspectives* (Manchester and New York: Manchester University Press, 1990).

Bacholle, Michele, *Un passé contraignant: double bind et transculturation* (Amsterdam and Atlanta: Rodopi, 2000).

Badinter, Elisabeth, *XY: de l'identité masculine* (Paris: Odile Jacob, 1992).

Barthes, Roland, *S/Z* (Paris: Seuil, 1970).

——'La mort de l'auteur', in *Essais critiques IV: le bruissement de la langue* (Paris: Seuil, 1973), pp. 61–7; 'The death of the author', in Roland Barthes, *Image, Music, Text*, ed. and trans. Stephen Heath (London: Fontana, 1984), pp. 142–8.

—— *Roland Barthes by Roland Barthes*, trans. Richard Howard (London: Macmillan, 1977).

—— *La Chambre claire* (Paris: Cahiers du cinéma/Gallimard/Seuil, 1980).

Baruch, Elaine Hoffman and Lucienne Juliette Serrano, *She Speaks/He Listens: Women on the French Analyst's Couch* (New York and London: Routledge, 1996).

Bataille, Georges, *Eroticism*, trans. Mary Dalwood (London and New York: Marion Boyars, 1987).

Battersby, Christine, *The Phenomenal Woman: Feminist Metaphysics and the Patterns of Identity* (Cambridge: Polity Press, 1998).

Baudrillard, Jean and Marc Guillaume, *Figures de l'altérité* (Paris: Descartes, 1994).

Beauvoir, Simone de, *Le Deuxième Sexe* 2 vols (Paris: Gallimard, 1949; repr. 1976); *The Second Sex*, trans. and ed. H. M. Parshley (London: Picador, 1988 [1953]).

Bénayoun-Szmidt, Yvette and Najib Redouane, *Parcours féminin dans la littérature marocaine d'expression française* (Toronto: La Source, 2000).

Benjamin, Jessica, *The Bonds of Love: Psychoanalysis, Feminism, and the Problem of Domination* (London: Virago, 1990).

Bhabha, Homi K., *The Location of Culture* (London and New York: Routledge, 1994).

Bishop, Michael (ed.), *Thirty Voices in the Feminine* (Amsterdam and Atlanta, GA: Rodopi, 1996).

Bordo, Susan, *Unbearable Weight: Feminism, Western Culture and the Body* (Berkeley and Los Angeles: University of California Press, 1995).

Braidotti, Rosi, *Nomadic Subjects: Embodiment and Sexual Difference in Contemporary Feminist Theory* (New York: Columbia University Press, 1994).

Brinker-Gabler, Gisela and Sidonie Smith (eds), *Writing New Identities: Gender, Nation and Immigration in Contemporary Europe* (Minneapolis: University of Minnesota Press, 1997).

Bronfen, Elisabeth, *Over Her Dead Body: Death, Femininity and the Aesthetic* (Manchester: Manchester University Press, 1992).

Brook, Barbara, *Feminist Perspectives on the Body* (London and New York: Longman, 1999).

Brown, Lyn Mikel and Carol Gilligan, *Meeting at the Crossroads: Women's Psychology and Girls' Development* (Cambridge, MA and London: Harvard University Press, 1992).

Butler, Judith, *Gender Trouble: Feminism and the Subversion of Identity* (London: Routledge, 1990).

——*Bodies that Matter: On the Discursive Limits of Sex* (New York and London: Routledge, 1993).

Caruth, Cathy (ed.), *Trauma: Explorations in Memory* (Baltimore and London: Johns Hopkins University Press, 1995).

Castarède, Marie-France (ed.), *La Voix et ses sortilèges* (Paris: Les Belles Lettres, 1987).

Caws, Mary Ann *et al.* (eds), *Ecritures de femmes: nouvelles cartographies* (New Haven and London: Yale University Press, 1996).

Célestin, Roger and Eliane DalMolin (eds), 'Autobiography', special issues, *Sites*, (Part 1) 1(2) (autumn 1997) and (Part 2) 2(1) (spring 1998).

——(eds), 'Writing in French in the '90s: novelists and poets', special issues, *Sites*, (Part 1) 2(2) (autumn 1998), (Part 2) 3(1) (spring 1999) and (Part 3) 3(2) (autumn 1999).

Chevalier, Jean and Alain Gheerbrant (eds), *Dictionnaire des symboles* (Paris: Robert Laffont/Jupiter, 1982).

Chodorow, Nancy, *Femininities, Masculinities, Sexualities: Freud and Beyond* (London: Free Association Books, 1994).

Cixous, Hélène, 'Le sexe ou la tête?', *Les Cahiers du GRIF*, 13 (October 1976), 5–15; 'Castration or decapitation?', trans. Annette Kuhn, *Signs*, 7(1) (autumn 1981), 41–55.

——'*Coming to Writing' and Other Essays*, introd. Susan Rubin Suleiman, ed. Deborah Jenson, trans. Sarah Cornell, Deborah Jenson *et al.* (Cambridge, MA and London; Harvard University Press, 1991).

——*Readings: The Poetics of Blanchot Joyce, Kafka, Kleist, Lispector, and Tsvetayeva*, ed., trans. and introd. Verena Andermatt Conley (New York and London: Harvester Wheatsheaf, 1992).

Cixous, Hélène and Catherine Clément, *La Jeune Née* (Paris: 10/18 UGE, 1975); *The Newly Born Woman*, trans. Betsy Wing (Manchester: Manchester University Press, 1986).

Cixous, Hélène and Mireille Calle-Gruber, *Photos de racines* (Paris: Des femmes, 1994).

Cornwell, Neil, *The Literary Fantastic* (New York and London: Harvester Wheatsheaf, 1990).

Cottenet-Hage, Madeleine and Jean-Philippe Imbert (eds), *Parallèles* (Quebec: L'Instant même, 1996).

Curti, Lidia, *Female Stories, Female Bodies: Narrative, Identity and Representation* (London: Macmillan, 1998).

Dagognet, François, *La Peau découverte* (Le Plessis-Robinson: Laboratoire Delagrange–Synthélabo, collection 'les Empêcheurs de penser en rond', 1993).

Darrieussecq, Marie, 'L'autofiction, un genre pas sérieux', *Poétique*, 107 (Paris, 1996), 369–80.

Davis, Colin and Elizabeth Fallaize, *French Fiction in the Mitterand Years: Memory, Narrative, Desire* (Oxford: Oxford University Press, 2000).

Deleuze, Gilles and Félix Guattari, *Kafka: pour une littérature mineure* (Paris: Minuit, 1975); *Kafka: Toward a Minor Literature*, trans. Dana Polan (Minneapolis and London: University of Minnesota Press, 1986).

DeSalvo, Louise, *Writing as a Way of Healing: How Telling Our Stories Transforms our Lives* (London: The Women's Press, 1999).

Dobson, Julia and Gill Rye (eds) 'Revisiting the scene of writing: new readings of Cixous', special issue, *Paragraph*, 23(3) (November 2000).

Douglas, Mary, *Purity and Danger: An Analysis of Concept of Pollution and Taboo* (London: Routledge and Kegan Paul, 1986).

Eakin, Paul John, *Fictions in Autobiography: Studies in the Art of Self-Invention* (Princeton: Princeton University Press, 1985).

Fallaize, Elizabeth, *French Women's Writing: Recent Fiction* (Basingstoke: Macmillan, 1993).

Felman, Shoshana, *What Does a Woman Want? Reading and Sexual Difference* (Baltimore: Johns Hopkins University Press, 1993).

Felman, Shoshana and Dori Laub, *Testimony: Crises of Witnessing in Literature, Psychoanalysis, and History* (New York and London: Routledge, 1992).

Foster, Hal, *The Return of the Real: The Avant-Garde at the End of the Century* (Cambridge, MA: MIT, 1996).

Foucault, Michel, *The History of Sexuality 1: An Introduction*, trans. Robert Hurley (London: Penguin, 1990).

—— 'Qu'est-ce qu'un auteur?', in *Dits et écrits, vol. 1, 1954–1988* (Paris: Gallimard, 1994), pp. 789–821; 'What is an author?', in James D. Faubion (ed.) *Aesthetics, Method and Epistemology: Michel Foucault*, vol. 2, trans. Robert Hurley and others (London: Allen Lane, 1998), pp. 205–22.

Freedman, Jane and Carrie Tarr (eds), *Women, Immigration and Identities in France* (Oxford and New York: Berg, 2000).

Freud, Sigmund, *The Interpretation of Dreams* (1900), Penguin Freud Library, vol. 4 (London: Penguin, 1976).

—— *On Metapsychology: The Theory of Psychoanalysis*, Pelican Freud Library, vol. 11, (Harmondsworth: Penguin, 1984).

Fuss, Diana, *Essentially Speaking* (London: Routledge, 1989).

Gadamer, Hans-Georg, *Truth and Method*, trans. J. Weinsheimer and D. G. Marshall (London: Sheed and Ward, 1975).

Gaudet, Jeannette, *Writing Otherwise: Atlan, Duras, Giraudon, Redonnet, and Wittig* (Amsterdam and Atlanta: Rodopi, 1999).

Genette, Gérard, *Figures III* (Paris: Seuil, 1972).

Green, Mary Jean Matthews (ed.), *Postcolonial Subjects, Francophone Women Writers* (Minneapolis and London: University of Minnesota Press, 1996).

Greer, Germaine, *The Whole Woman* (London: Doubleday, 1999).

Griffiths, Morwenna, *Feminisms and the Self: The Web of Identity* (London and New York: Routledge, 1995).

Guberman, Ross Mitchell (ed.), *Julia Kristeva Interviews* (New York: Columbia University Press, 1996).

Hargreaves, Alec G., *Voices from the North African Immigrant Community in France: Immigration and Identity in Beur Fiction* (Oxford: Berg, 1991).

—— 'Figuring out their place: post-colonial writers of Algerian origin in France', *Forum for Modern Language Studies*, 29(4) (1993), 335-45.

Hayes, Elizabeth T. (ed.), *Images of Persephone: Feminist Readings in Western Literature* (Florida: Florida University Press, 1994).

Henke, Suzette, *Shattered Subjects: Trauma and Testimony in Women's Life-Writing* (New York: St Martin's Press, 1998).

Héritier, Françoise, *Masculin/Féminin: la pensée de la différence* (Paris: Odile Jacob, 1996).

Herrmann, Claudine, *Les Voleuses de langue* (Paris: Des femmes, 1976).

Hirsch, Marianne, *The Mother–Daughter Plot: Narrative, Psychoanalysis, Feminism* (Bloomington and Indianapolis: Indiana University Press, 1989).

Hitchcott, Nicki, *Women Writers in Francophone Africa* (Oxford: Berg, 2000).

Holmes, Diana, *French Women's Writing 1848–1994* (London: Athlone, 1996).

Horner, Avril and Angela Keane (eds) *Body Matters: Feminism, Textuality, Corporeality* (Manchester and New York: Manchester University Press, 2000).

Hughes, Alex, *Heterographies: Sexual Difference in French Autobiography* (Oxford and New York: Berg, 1999).

Hughes, Alex and Kate Ince (eds), *French Erotic Fiction: Women's Desiring Writing 1880–1990* (Oxford: Berg, 1996).

Hutton, Margaret-Anne (ed.), 'French fiction in the 1990s', special issue, *Nottingham French Studies* (spring 2002).

Huughe, Laurence, *Ecrits sous le voile: romancières algériennes francophones, écriture et identité* (Paris: Publisud, 2001).

Ibnlfassi, Laïla and Nicki Hitchcott (eds), *African Francophone Writing: A Critical Introduction* (Oxford and Washington, DC: Berg, 1996).

Irigaray, Luce, *Ce sexe qui n'en est pas un* (Paris: Minuit, 1977); *This Sex Which is Not One*, trans. Catherine Porter with Carolyn Burke (Ithaca, NY: Cornell University Press, 1985).

——*Le Corps-à-corps avec la mère* (Montreal: Editions de la pleine lune, 1981); 'Body against body: in relation to the mother', trans. Gillian C. Gill, in Luce Irigaray, *Sexes and Genealogies* (New York: Columbia University Press, 1993), pp. 7–21.

——*Ethique de la différence sexuelle* (Paris: Minuit, 1984); *An Ethics of Sexual Difference*, trans. Carolyn Burke and Gillian C. Gill (London: Athlone Press, 1993).

——*Je, tu, nous: pour une culture de la différence* (Paris: Grasset, 1990); *Je, tu, nous: Toward a Culture of Difference*, trans. Alison Martin (New York and London: Routledge, 1993).

——'Au-delà de tout jugement, tu es', *Sémiotiques*, 10 (June 1996); 'Beyond all judgement, you are', trans. Michael Worton, *Journal of the Institute of Romance Studies*, 7 (1999), 1–10.

——*Entre Orient et Occident* (Paris: Grasset, 1999).

Jackson, Rosemary, *Fantasy: The Literature of Subversion* (London: Methuen, 1981).

Jackson, Stevi, *Heterosexuality in Question* (London: Sage, 1999).

Juranville, Anne, *La Femme et la mélancolie* (Paris: Presses Universitaires de France, 1993).

Katrak, Ketu H., 'Decolonizing culture: toward a theory for postcolonial women's texts', *Modern Fiction Studies*, 35(1)(1989), 157–79.

Klein, Melanie, *Love, Guilt and Reparation and Other Works 1921–1945* (London: Virago, 1988).

Kristeva, Julia, *Pouvoirs de l'horreur: essai sur l'abjection* (Paris: Seuil, 1980); *Powers of Horror: An Essay on Abjection*, trans. Leon S. Roudiez (New York: Columbia University Press, 1982).

——*Soleil noir: dépression et mélancolie* (Paris: Gallimard/Folio, 1987); *Black Sun: Depression and Melancholia*, trans. Leon S. Roudiez (New York: Columbia University Press, 1989).

——'Entretien avec Julia Kristeva: L'avant-garde aujourd'hui', *Avant Garde*, 4 (1990), 158–75.

——*Contre la dépression nationale* (Paris: Textuel, 1998).

——*Le Génie féminin: la vie, la folie, les mots, I Hannah Arendt* (Paris: Fayard, 1999), *II Melanie Klein* (Paris: Fayard, 2000) and *III Colette* (Paris: Fayard, 2002).

Kuhn, Annette, *Family Secrets: Acts of Memory and Imagination* (London: Verso, 1995).

Kundera, Milan, *Identity* (London: Faber & Faber, 1999).

Lacan, Jacques, 'The mirror stage as formative of the function of the I', in *Ecrits: A Selection*, trans. Alan Sheridan (London: Tavistock, 1977).

Lansky, Melvin R. (ed.), *Essential Papers on Dreams* (New York: New York University Press, 1992).

Laronde, Michel, *Autour du roman beur: immigration et identité* (Paris: L'Harmattan, 1993).

Lejeune, Philippe, *Je est un autre: l'autobiographie, de la littérature aux médias* (Paris: Seuil, 1980).

LeMoncheck, Linda, *Loose Women, Lecherous Men: A Feminist Philosophy of Sex* (New York and Oxford: Oxford University Press, 1997).

Lury, Celia, *Prosthetic Culture: Photography, Memory and Identity* (London: Routledge, 1998).

Mainil, Jean (ed.), 'French erotic fiction: ideologies of desire', special issue, *Nottingham French Studies*, 37(1) (spring 1998).

Marcus, Laura (ed.), *Sigmund Freud's The Interpretation of Dreams: New Interdisciplinary Essays* (Manchester: Manchester University Press, 1999).

Mathieu, Nicole-Claude, *L'Arraisonnement des femmes: essais en anthropologie des sexes* (Paris: Editions de l'école des hautes études en sciences sociales, 1985).

McGinn, Colin, *Ethics, Evil, and Fiction* (Oxford: Oxford University Press, 1997).

Michel, Christian, 'Le réel dort aussi: un panorama du jeune roman français', *Esprit*, 225 (1996), 43–67.

Millett, Kate, *Sexual Politics* (London: Hart-Davis, 1971).

Moi, Toril (ed.), *The Kristeva Reader* (Oxford: Basil Blackwell, 1986).

——*Sexual/Textual Politics: Feminist Literary Theory* (London and New York: Routledge, 1991).

——*Simone de Beauvoir: The Making of an Intellectual Woman* (Oxford and Cambridge, MA: Blackwell, 1994).

Morgan, Janice and Colette T. Hall (eds), *Redefining Autobiography in Twentieth-Century Women's Fiction* (New York and London: Garland Publishing, 1991).

Motte, Warren, *Small Worlds: Minimalism in Contemporary French Literature* (Lincoln: University of Nebraska Press, 1999).

Nussbaum, Martha, *Love's Knowledge: Essays on Philosophy and Literature* (New York and Oxford: Oxford University Press, 1990).

Phillips, Anita, *A Defence of Masochism* (London: Faber & Faber, 1998).

Rich, Adrienne 'Compulsory heterosexuality and lesbian existence', *Signs*, 5 (1980), 631–60.

Riffaterre, Michael, *Fictional Truth* (Baltimore and London: Johns Hopkins University Press, 1990).

Rosaldo, Renato, 'Ideology, place, and people without culture', *Cultural Anthropology*, 3 (1988), 77–87.

Rosello, Mireille, *Infiltrating Culture: Power and Identity in Contemporary Women's Writing* (Manchester and New York: Manchester University Press, 1996).

Roudinesco, Elisabeth, *Jacques Lacan. Esquisse d'une vie: histoire d'un système de pensée* (Paris: Fayard, 1993).

Russell, Diana E. H. (ed.) *Making Violence Sexy: Feminist Views on Pornography* (Buckingham: Open University Press, 1993).

Rye, Gill, 'Women's writing', in Abigail Gregory and Ursula Tidd (eds) *Women in Contemporary France* (Oxford and New York: Berg, 2000), pp. 133–51.

——*Reading for Change: Interactions between Text and Identity in Contemporary French Women's Writing (Baroche, Cixous, Constant)*, Modern French Identities Series 9 (Bern: Peter Lang, 2001).

——(ed.), 'Contemporary women's writing in French', special issue, *Journal of Romance Studies*, 2(1) (spring 2002).

——'New women's writing in France', *Modern and Contemporary France*, 10(2) (May 2002), pp. 165–75.

Sartre, Jean-Paul, *Situations I* (Paris: Gallimard, 1947).

Scott, Malcolm, *The Struggle for the Soul of the French Novel* (Basingstoke: Macmillan, 1989).

Segal, Hanna, *Dream, Phantasy and Art* (London and New York: Routledge, 1991).

Segal, Lynne, *Straight Sex: The Politics of Pleasure* (London: Virago, 1994).

Seidler, Victor J., *Rediscovering Masculinity: Reason, Language and Sexuality* (London and New York: Routledge, 1989).

Sellers, Susan, *Language and Sexual Difference: Feminist Writing in France* (Basingstoke: Macmillan, 1991).

——Susan Sellers, *Hélène Cixous: Authorship, Autobiography and Love* (Cambridge: Polity Press, 1996).

Serres, Michel, *Variations sur le corps* (Paris: Le Pommier, 1999).

Sheringham, Michael, *French Autobiography: Devices and Desires, Rousseau to Perec* (Oxford: Clarendon Press, 1993).

Shiach, Morag, *Hélène Cixous: A Politics of Writing* (London: Routledge, 1991).

Sontag, Susan, *On Photography* (New York: Farrar, Straus and Giroux, 1973).

Sorrell, Martin (ed.), *Elles: A Bilingual Anthology of Modern Poetry by Women* (Exeter: University of Exeter Press, 1995).

Stanley, Liz, *The Auto/biographical I: The Theory and Practice of Feminist Auto/biography* (Manchester: Manchester University Press, 1992).

Steedman, Carolyn, *Landscape for a Good Woman* (London: Virago, 1986).

Stephens, Sonya (ed.), *A History of Women's Writing in France* (Cambridge: Cambridge University Press, 2000).

Suleiman, Susan Rubin, *Subversive Intent: Gender, Politics, and the Avant-Garde* (Cambridge, MA and London: Harvard University Press, 1990).

Thomas, Lynn, *Annie Ernaux: An Introduction to the Writer and her Audience* (Oxford: Berg, 1999).

Todorov, Tzvetan, *Introduction à la littérature fantastique* (Paris: Seuil, 1970).

Vance, Carole (ed.), *Pleasure and Danger: Exploring Female Sexuality* (London: Pandora Press, 1989).

Viart, Dominique (ed.), *Ecritures contemporaines 1: mémoires du récit*, (Paris and Caen: Lettres Modernes Minard, 1998).

Weeks, Jeffrey, *Sexuality and its Discontents: Meanings, Myths and Modern Sexualities* (London: Routledge and Kegan Paul, 1985).

Whitford, Margaret, *Luce Irigaray: Philosophy in the Feminine* (London: Routledge, 1991).

Wilcox, Helen *et al.* (eds), *The Body and the Text: Hélène Cixous, Reading and Teaching* (London: Harvester Wheatsheaf, 1990).

Worton, Michael, 'Thinking through photography, remembering to love the past', in Monique Streiff-Moretti, Mireille Revol Cappelletti and Odile Martinez (eds), *Il senso del nonsenso: scritti in memoria di Lynn Salkin Sbiroli* (Naples: Edizioni Scientifiche Italiane, 1994), pp. 733–53.

—— 'Looking for kicks: promiscuity and violence in contemporary French fiction', *Nottingham French Studies*, 37(1) (special issue, 'French erotic fiction: ideologies of desire', ed. Jean Mainil) (spring 1998), 89–105.

—— *Typical Men* (catalogue of the exhibition 'Typical Men: Recent Photography of the Male Body by Men') (Nottingham: Djanogly Art Gallery, 2001).

Worton, Michael and Judith Still (eds), *Intertextuality: Theories and Practices* (Manchester: Manchester University Press, 1990).

—— (eds), *Textuality and Sexuality: Reading Theories and Practices* (Manchester: Manchester University Press, 1993).

INDEX

Literary works can be found under authors' names. 'n.' after a page reference indicates the number of a note on that page. Page numbers in **bold** refer to main entries.